Deniza D. Martin
Collection

BEYOND STONEHENGE

OTHER BOOKS BY GERALD S. HAWKINS

SPLENDOR IN THE SKY

THE MOON TONIGHT

STONEHENGE DECODED
  (*with John B. White*)

THE LIFE OF A STAR
  (*with Fred Moore*)

METEORS, COMETS AND METEORITES

THE SUN AND ITS PLANETS

EARTH AND SPACE SCIENCE
  (*with C. W. Wolfe, H. Skornik, L. J. Battan and R. H. Fleming*)

BEYOND

GERALD S. HAWKINS

STONEHENGE

HARPER & ROW, PUBLISHERS

NEW YORK, EVANSTON, SAN FRANCISCO, LONDON

STANDARD BOOK NUMBER: 06–011786–9

LIBRARY OF CONGRESS CATALOG CARD NUMBER: 72–79671

Designed by Dorothy Schmiderer

To Dorothy Zoe

CONTENTS

PREFACE

Stonehenge is a landmark in time and space. To go beyond is to explore into the mind of man at his earliest beginning. The story has taken me to exciting places—Lake Titicaca, the "roof of the world," the great pharaoh temples on the banks of the Nile, the moors and brays of Scotland.

As an astronomer I have been able to add factual comments on the archaeological legacy of the Northern Hemisphere continents. I am greatly indebted to international scholars and specialists in that wide spectrum of disciplines that converge on the heritage of *Homo modernus*. I have appreciated conversations and correspondence with Sir Fred Hoyle, Professors Grahame Clark, Glyn Daniel, Arthur Beer, and G. H. S. Bushnell of Cambridge University; Professors Fred L. Whipple, Halam Movius, Owen Gingerich, and Dr. Hugh Hencken of Harvard University; Dr. Thor Heyerdahl, Professor R. J. C. Atkinson of the University of South Wales, and staff members of the Smithsonian Astrophysical Observatory and the British Broadcasting Corporation.

My wife Dorothy has become part of the book as a member of the expeditions, ceramic expert, and editor-in-residence. Tony Morrison, photographer and tropical wildlife expert, has joined cheerily in expeditions and speculations. I have appreciated discussions with Alexander Marshack, Professor Alexander Thom of Oxford University, Harry L. Bricker, Jr., Harrisburg, Pa., officials of the Geophysical Institute of Peru and the Peruvian Air Force, and officials and colleagues in Egypt.

GERALD S. HAWKINS

Norwich, England

xi

FOREWORD

It is altogether fitting that the work described in this book was carried out by an astronomer affiliated with the Smithsonian Astrophysical Observatory.

The Smithsonian Institution was founded in 1846 with the express purpose of realizing James Smithson's bequest "for the increase and diffusion of knowledge among men." The founding, a happy circumstance for Anglo–U.S. relations, began with the melting down of 99,962 British gold sovereigns in the Philadelphia mint. Since that time the Institution has been at the forefront of international cooperation in the sciences and the arts.

Discovery of the American geometrical mounds and earthworks was reported in the very first volume of the *Smithsonian Contributions to Knowledge.*

Samuel P. Langley, third secretary of the Smithsonian Institution and founder of its Astrophysical Observatory, recognized Stonehenge as the forerunner of the great national observatories like Greenwich and Washington.

Succeeding secretaries have maintained this awareness of the place of man in his greater environment. The Astrophysical Observatory currently spreads the diffusion of knowledge far and deep, from meteoritic particles to cosmic dust, from the moon to the sun and stars, forward into the cosmological future and backward into the roots of the past.

BEYOND STONEHENGE

1 PHONE CALL

It was a hot morning in June. The sun streamed through the window, and the air conditioning was flagging. The neon bulb on my office intercom flashed. The secretary spoke in an unnatural tone, alerting me to something out of the ordinary.

"President of C.B.S. News on the line."

"Thanks. Put him through."

"We're going to prove your theory, Professor."

"What theory?"

"About Stonehenge being a computer—that temple locked to the sun—man reaching for the universe. . . ."

I had my own thoughts as New York spoke. The plan, it seemed, was to film the sun rising over the heel stone in glorious summer color. But one photograph does not prove a theory. Not a theory about the mind of prehistoric man.

A scientist has special requirements for a proof, much testing, probing, discussion, before it is stamped Q.E.D.

The voice on the line was there, demanding a response.

"How?" I said.

"We'll film the sunrise through the archway on Midsummer's Day, and then get that moon eclipse, the one predicted by the Aubrey holes."

A fair summary of the theory for a busy head of a hectic television news service. My mind raced. I searched for a background to the call. I guessed he was calling because of an article fresh out in *Harper's* magazine. The article described how, if my calculations were correct, the archways and stones pointed to the rising and setting of the sun and moon at critical dates of the year, and June 21, coming up next week, was one of these. The article said that Stonehenge would be functioning quietly and unnoticed as it had for the past four thousand years, a lonely monument to the scientific ability of prehistoric man. And if one

PLATE 1. *A prehistoric stage-set to mark the sunrise vista.*

2

followed my theory about counting moon cycles, then the stone-age computer signaled the danger of an eclipse right now, this month, in high summer. Eclipses have been held in awe by man through the ages—that sudden darkness at noon as the moon blots out the sun, the blood-red glow of the moon in the earth's shadow whispering ''fearful change.''

Over the phone we discussed the irony of using the hardware of modern technology to probe into the thinking of early man, centuries before Christ. What to early man was the vital earth-sky environment now passes unnoticed in the ''technological 20th.'' Each dawn he saw the sun rise at its appointed place on the skyline, a different spot each day, and he noted and marked the important positions where it reached the northerly extreme in summer and the deep south point in winter. He marked the midway point, heralding the first day of spring and fall. It was an ecological ritual.

The moon did much the same, rising and setting at a different place on the skyline each day. (Astronomically the day is the full 24 hours, diurnal. The moon at the full rises at the time of sunset, and then is later by 48 minutes on the average each night after that.) The place where the moon came up was picked out, and the farthest north–south positions were marked for the moon by monolithic slabs.

The sun repeats itself each year, as simple, regular, and understandable as Apollo's chariot swinging around the zodiac. But the moon does not. Diana is fickle. The northerly extreme of one year is beaten by a few diameters in the next. If there was a moon marker for one particular year it needed to be displaced a few feet in the year following. Then it would retrace its steps. After a little less than nineteen years the post, or stone, would be back again at the starting place. For people looking for rhythms and repetitions in a primitive environment it was a satisfying end to the time of watching, observing and discussing.*

* Not only did the moon swing from extreme north to extreme south in 2 weeks compared to the sun's 6 months, but it edged farther north and south each year, repeating its pattern of rising and setting after 18.61 years, a little less than 19. It would be close enough for the Stonehengers to take the eighteenth or nineteenth year, whichever was nearer, depending on how the moon cycle fell; but it would be slightly out of line then, because 18.61 is the exact number. After three cycles, three of these 18- or 19-year swings, the moon would be rising over the original marker to a very good approximation. A moment's figuring shows

3

Admittedly this is a speculation, but a British researcher has identified more than thirty holes in the Stonehenge avenue that fit this pattern of moon watching year by year.

I had the advantages of astrophysics and a modern observatory. There was no need of standing to watch moonrises, recording and committing to memory the events over a lifetime. These events could be computed, a hundred years in fewer than so many seconds, with the azimuths and other angles printed out in consecutive order in the high-speed print-out of a digital electronic computer. By comparison this seemed a lazy substitute for the "intense interest taken in the moon's movements," as Alexander Thom put it, that led "acute minds to seek a deeper understanding." The most to be extracted from the computer was the advantage of time compression and the basic numbers associated with the problem. It could be no substitute for the heritage of ritual and thought process that went along with this life-absorbing early environment work.

"Professor, we want to put the computer on the screen and get you to explain how the machine works way back in history. . . ."

A historical novelist had only moments before called at my office with the same request. Jay Williams was in search of material for his new novel, *Uniad*. He sat, humanist in the scientist's den, bugging the conversation with a transistorized tape recorder under his gray tweed jacket. He also was intrigued by the penetration of the minds of a vanished culture through the medium of an electronic computer. The plot of the novel was to show how the minds of people, the masses, could be manipulated, controlled, by a math machine.

We had sat and talked over our common interests. Behind him I could see through the wide aluminum-framed window over fresh summer

---

how if the moon's cycle is taken as $18\frac{2}{3}$, then three cycles will take exactly 56 years.

At Stonehenge there were 56 special holes, now visible as white chalk spots, equally spaced in a near-perfect circle. Did the Stonehengers settle for 56 as the number that governed the swing of the moon? It is a very good fit, much better than either 18 or 19. The next best number is 93, but there is no circle with this number. Did they observe through a life span with a period of 56 years as the time frame, or was the number derived from the subperiods 18, 19, in some way?

leaves down into the girl-peppered tennis courts of Radcliffe College. To the side was the gray concrete-block wall of the office, my bookcase, and a desk side table. It was quiet and conducive to thought. My visitor remarked how the cement offices opening from the long corridor were like a monastery of the Old World—sandstone cloistered, with granite-bonded cells. But that atmosphere was dispelled by the desk calculator, the Dictaphone, and the taken-for-granted telephone—technical items beyond the reach of a medieval monk.

Jay's concern was the invasion of privacy. He was worried about the impact of modern technology on human lives. A computer stores personal facts in a dehumanizing process—magnetized cores, holes in the ubiquitous punched card. A touch of a button or the use of a master program card releases this information *en bloc*. Confidentiality is lost. Control of access is difficult. As giant computers are connected together across the country by telephone line, control is more necessary and yet more difficult. Fail-safe procedures become as complicated as the prevention of the accidental firing of a nuclear warheaded missile. Program cards come in, and humanism goes out. (Ever tried to get an error put right in a computerized bill?)

He shifted his gaze from the tennis courts to the walls of my office. He wanted to see for himself the workings of a late-type digital computer—was it beauty or beast?

In the beginning, I explained, it was the old-fashioned pencil and scratchpad and eraser. Then IBM 650 appeared, a machine that could be addressed only by writing binary "zeros" and "ones." It worked slowly by present-day standards. But it saved pencil drudgery, and it never made numerical slips. By stages machines were speeded up. By stages the language used to communicate with the machine was changed, became more intricate and rule-ridden. My generation of scientists preferred to develop the equations, the data, and then hand the package to a specialist programmer whose job was to write it out for the machine in that system of rules and language required by the machine at that time.

We went down the corridor into another office to see the first step in dealing with the beast (?). I introduced him to the program-interface component—human, fragrant, female. Jay was impressed. Later he wrote in his novel: "It wasn't that she was beautiful by any means, but the very sunlight appeared to sink amorously into her and glow upon her skin and in her brilliant eyes . . . She was smiling radiantly . . . walked with a fine, swinging erect grace that made everyone else look stoop-shouldered.''

The office contained piles of paper, stacks of cards, coffee cups, ground-down cigarette stubs in square glass ashtrays. There was beauty but nothing electronic, no hardware. We walked across the vinyl-tile corridor to another small room where punched program cards chattered into hoppers.

''Where's the machine?'' said Jay.

''Half a mile away, in another building. These cards are read and transmitted by phone lines. I'll drive you over.''

To the sky-blue hall of the computer building, through cinderblock corridors, through aluminum-framed swing doors, over more vinyl, it was the same question: ''Where's the machine?''

''You're in it,'' I said.

The novelist stared. It was a large room. Cards clattered; banks of tape transports zipped in spurts. In the center a male operator watched two green picture tubes, constantly pressing the keys in front of him. He was strained, intent. Jay's bug picked up snatches of conversation. He wrote more words in his mind:

She pushed the doors open and he followed her into an immense room which seemed to be full of typewriters, on metal stands. Cool daylight from fluorescent lamps in the ceiling filled the place, and glanced back from steel trim and grey-painted metal. There were metal cases, in the upper parts of which disks of electronic tape spun jerkily; other, longer cases painted pale-blue lurked in the distance. Near the door, a man sat at a console where lights flickered, and on a circular screen rows of numbers appeared and disappeared with dazzling rapidity. Not far from him, a second man fed bundles of cards like the one Pippa had shown Paul into the trays of a squat machine which flipped them into its innards, digested them, and spat them out again in stacks. A man and two women wandered like farmers among the rows of typewriters . . . the room was filled with a racket of clicking, buzzing, humming, chattering . . . Pippa bent close to Paul, raising her voice over the noise. . . .*

This digital computer was working on a dozen problems simultaneously. The progress of each job showed in cryptic sentences on the

* From *Uniad*.

6

screen. The operator controlled the amount of attention given to a particular job, and changed the priorities by punching the keyboard.

I asked for the astro-archaeology program to be run as a demonstration. In routine operation the data would be sent from the main building over the line in the morning, processed according to priorities, and returned, completed, in the afternoon. Jay stood at the control center, momentarily looking like his hero in *The Siege*. Within seconds the program was signaled "completed" on the green tubes. Before we could walk over to catch the print-out at the side of the room, it was buried under a pile of folded paper.

Madison Avenue was winding up the conversations in the phone. I was jolted by the urgency of the voice.

FIG. 1.

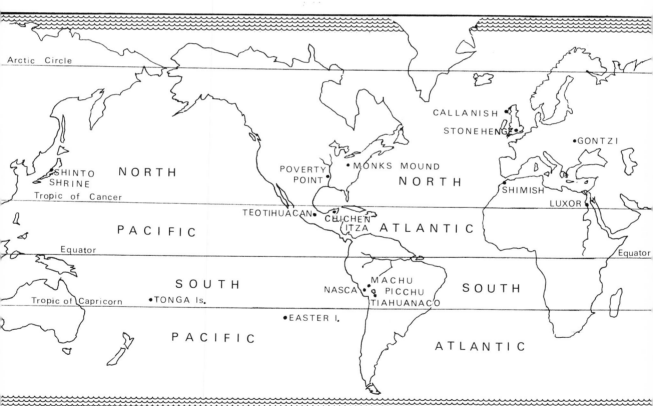

"Professor, you're going to go to Stonehenge with our camera crew."

"Well, I would be happy to cooperate at some convenient time—"

"Tonight! The instructions are with your air ticket at Logan Airport."

"But—"

"Thank you, Professor!"

2   STONEHENGE

It was to be a sunrise semester, by astrojet, 600 miles per hour into the dawn.

I met the TV producer-director in the prestressed concrete overpass tube that carries passengers to TWA planes at Kennedy. I recognized him by his aggressive crew cut, Madison Avenue suit, and dark sunglasses. Success was his business. "One bad show and you're out."

He needed to be filled in beyond my magazine article. We had 5½ hours from New York, less the time out for form filling, movie, and flight-routine meals.

"Give," he said.

Stonehenge I was a 350-foot-diameter, exactly, circular ditch; there was a gap at the northeast; two chalk banks, one outside, the other inside the ditch; post holes; a ring of 56 pits, and some large erected stones.*

The ditch was a quarry, not a designed trench; oblong pits of varying length and depth were hewn out of the chalk, and the dividing walls broken through to complete the ditch. Soon after it was dug, the ditch began to fill up with rubble and soil by the process of natural erosion. This is proved by the mishmash of objects in the fill—broken tools of the workmen, deer-antler picks, ox-bone shovels, pottery shards, and meat bones.

Present-day students have worked on the chalk with antler picks and bone shovels. It is not easy. The chalk of the cretaceous escarpment has to be pried out in lumps by jabbing in the tip of the antler, then the loose rubble raked into a pile, shoveled into a basket with the flat shoulder blade of an ox, and carried to a designated spot. A man, or girl, can move a cubic yard of this chalk in a nine-hour day, sometimes more.

---

* Plans are reproduced in the Appendix. A keyed, numbered plan appears on p. 284. Site photographs are with the text.

9

PLATE 2. (top left) *The first aerial picture of Stonehenge (1904), captive balloon.*

PLATE 3. (bottom left) *Vertical balloon photograph (1904).*

PLATE 4. (above) *Limbered balloon winch wagon with balloon.*

11

The Stonehengers dug about 3,500 cubic yards to make the banks—ten man-years of work.* The outer bank was 8 feet wide and 2 or 3 feet high; the inner one twenty feet wide and 6 feet high. The rubble stacks at a fairly steep angle. Viewed from the center it would be a glaring white wall, presumably flat on top to make an artificial horizon.

It would fit the astronomical theory if the chalk wall were higher nearer the heel stone, but whether or not this was so cannot now be determined. The bank long ago succumbed to erosion. All that remains is a low rise of a foot or so under the green turf.

The ditch-bank circle enclosed an area comparable to Homer's ancient city of Troy. Incidentally, Heinrich Schliemann's pick-and-shovel gang moved 325,000 cubic yards of soil in three years when he was ruthlessly digging for Priam's gold.

The heel stone was set 90 feet outside the entrance gap at the northeast. It is more than 20 feet long from base to tip and weighs 35 tons; the Stonehengers moved it 20 miles from Marlborough Downs—not an *extra*extraordinary feat for this megalithic (large-stone) culture. It is sandstone, but unlike most of the others it is not smoothed by tooling. "Heel" may be connected with the so-called friar's heel mark on the stone, or from the Welsh word *haul* (pronounced "hayil"), meaning "sun."

Stones may have stood at the entrance gap. Archaeologists have excavated two large holes there (D and E), and some "undigested notes" by Inigo Jones, architect to James I, suggest that four stones were standing in the early seventeenth century.

The slaughter stone, No. 95, might have been one of them, either in

---

* Richard Atkinson, University of South Wales, disagrees with this estimate; his estimate is about 50 percent smaller. All estimates in this book are approximate, and, of course, open to dispute.

Sixteen miles north of Stonehenge the prehistoric diggers made the largest earth-pyramid in Europe, Silbury Hill. It covers 5½ acres and stands 130 feet high—more than half a million tons of chalk hewn and hand-carried. Willingly? I do not see these projects carried out by slave, or semislave, labor as were the pyramids of Egypt or the fortifications of Peru. The Secondary Neolithic culture of southern England lived in scattered hamlets, and there were no trappings of centralized power such as a palace or habitable temple complex. Physical slavery seems out of the question. But mental slavery—rigid following of a religious belief, slavery to an idea—is a different matter. It is a subject for speculation later in this book.

PLATE 5. *The village of Avebury built within the megalithic circles. An oblique aerial view showing the ancient mound of Silbury Hill, top right, and the stone-lined avenue leading from Avebury.*

13

hole E or now lying flat to cover its own pit. Local guides used to hold their circle of tourists entranced by pointing out the channels (natural and well smoothed by rain water and the shoes of visitors since the stone toppled) as where "the warm blood of Druid victims ran." Did not Caesar write in the *Gallic Wars* how Druids used "figures of an immense size, whose limbs, woven out of twigs, they fill with living men and set on fire, and the men perish in a sheet of flame"? Those wicker cages for human sacrifice! True, he did, but Stonehenge was a ruin when Caesar invaded, and the Druids of whom he writes were Celtic and one thousand years later than Stonehenge.

Stonehenge I is the earliest, crudest structure, yet it contains the perfect circle of the Aubrey holes, 285 feet in diameter, divided into 56 equal segments, astronomically sophisticated. For a nonliterate people, two millennia before Euclid, this was no small feat of practical geometry. Also it showed a comprehension of the value of the numeric. Nonliterate peoples tend to give up counting when they run out of fingers and toes—any number larger than 10 is counted as "many." Yet the Stonehengers purposefully divided the circle into 56 parts.

The holes were just visible to John Aubrey in the seventeenth century. Now they are not. There is nothing to be seen on the flat turf. Holes 33 to 54 have never been excavated. They were found by bosing* (a process of sounding the ground with a sledgehammer and listening for soft spots). In a winter of deep frost, the holes under the turf show as individual raised domes.

The British government has withheld permission to dig since the excavations of Lt. Colonel William Hawley in the 1920's, and rightly so. Each decade new techniques are added to science, and secrets under the turf can wait. Since Hawley we have radiocarbon dating of charcoal, thermoluminescence dating of pottery, and a highly developed discipline of cataloging and describing artifacts inch by cubic inch. In the future we will have ultrasonic, electrical, and other nondestructive tests that will reveal the undersurface without resort to digging. An excavation

---

* Not to be confused with dowsing, the art of divining flowing water by the pull of a hand-held twig. In 1971, British army officers tested a group of dowsers who were acknowledged by the trade as experts. Result: their performance was no better than guesswork. Their success at finding gold and buried treasure was equally poor.

can be made once only. The archaeologist destroys his own evidence. (An expert once threw an empty cigarette packet down a hole while I watched, and then refilled the hole with the shells and debris. It was at Ipswich, Massachusetts, a midden of the coastal Indians circa A.D. 500, with quartz arrowheads, rope-marked pottery, and bird bones. The packet was a notice to future archaeologists: "Warning, the archaeological horizons are disturbed.")

Each Aubrey hole was straight-sided, circular, flat-bottomed, and from 2 to 4 feet in depth. Up to 6 feet in diameter, the centers were never more than 21 inches off the mathematical perimeter. The holes were dug out with antler and ox-bone shovel and then filled up again with chalk rubble, two man-days of labor for each hole, digging it out and ramming it back.

"What did they do that for?" said the producer.

The stewardess, who came from Iowa, collected the martini glasses. The dinner tray was put in front of us with the stratosphere-cold cutlery and the oven-hot dish. We had two seats in a three-seat block, and the spare seat was filled up with photos, papers, and a large, unfolded plan of the site.

"I don't know. It is difficult to guess the 'why.' Hawley said the holes had stones which were taken out again. He found charred bones—human—so cremation was going on. He found bone pins—for the hair, I guess—and stone chips as if they were planting stone 'seeds.' What puzzled everybody was a carved chalk ball found in hole 21. My theory, you know, says the holes were a computer, or counting device. The years were counted off by moving a stone or something around the circle from hole to hole each year. Maybe this chalk ball was the marker. If it was buried there was no danger of its being moved by mistake. A buried icon, image of the sun."

Stonehenge II followed I on the archaeological scheme of things with the avenue; the ring-ditch around the heel stone, and (maybe) the four station stones making the large rectangle 91–94, and holes at B and C. At this phase, between 2000 and 1800 B.C., the bluestones were brought to the site from Prescelly Mountain, Wales—at least 82 stones and a distance of 250 miles.

It can be argued that although the station stones came later than the

15

PLATE 6. *The northeastern extension of the Stonehenge avenue revealed by crop markings. The buried ditches turn to the right toward the river Avon.*

16

ditch,* it was not *much* later, and the rectangle may really be part of the structure of Stonehenge I instead of II or III.

Either way, these four positions fit the astronomy. They mark the winter and summer sun, parallel to the heel stone line from the center, but they also mark the moon, *and* through all turning points of the 56-year moon cycle!

A person standing at 91 saw the winter moon reach its most northerly extreme when it set over 94. Year by year the moon fell back, setting a few degrees nearer to 93. After nine winters it was over 93. Then it reversed until after 19 years (18.61, to be precise) it was setting once again on the long side of the rectangle, 94–91. The corresponding pattern of summer moon*rise* was viewed by looking east from 93.

What has become of stones 92 and 94? The same question can be raised about other stones such as B, C, and D. Hawley found pressure marks at the bottom of some of these holes, proving that a stone had stood there. And what of the stones gone from other megalithic sites, the rings at Avebury and West Kennet? Historians tell how the stones at Avebury were deliberately destroyed by heating with fire, cracking with cold water, and smashing with sledgehammers. The megaliths were regarded as evil. A hundred years ago it was fashionable to rent a hammer at West Amesbury to chip off a souvenir at Stonehenge. Then again, medieval farmers and villagers used these sites as quarries. (Stonehenge is now protected by scores of tiny underground "geophones" laid like a minefield around the site. These pick up the vibrations of footsteps at night, "even of a dog.")

The avenue reaches out toward the midsummer sunrise. A leveled highway, four lanes wide, is paralleled by a ditch and bank on either side. It shows clearly on aerial photographs, and the course has been traced to the village of West Amesbury, almost to the river Avon. The bluestones were dragged along this sacred way from the Avon on the

---

* The circular ditch around 92, if it was intended to be circular, is distorted where it meets the inner bank, and so 92 is presumably later than the ditch-bank of Stonehenge I. Two station stones now remain at 91 and 93. The other corners are empty. 91 is uncut, rough, like the heel stone, and 93 is partly tooled. The other sandstones, the sarsens and trilithons which came with Stonehenge III, are tooled. So the station stones could be approximately contemporaneous with the heel stone, or later with the sarsens.

17

last stage of the long haul. The avenue was impressive then, an indelible white roadway following an easy contour over the plain.

The entrance gap was too narrow for this avenue. It was widened 25 feet by dumping chalk rubble into the eastern portion of the ditch. My estimate of the work effort spent on the avenue is 18,000 man-days. This does not include the narrow ditch dug around the already standing heel stone, or any clearing of vegetation.

Two thousand years before Hadrian's Wall the barbarians had a proven capability equal to the Romans. The avenue is dead straight where it has to be straight, level-surfaced and wide. The Roman roads were designed for marching armies and chariots: conquest, trade, and control. Neolithic Britons did not have the wheel. Perhaps, like Central American Indians, they knew of it but had no use for it. Certainly they left no evidence of any type of vehicle. If some urgent necessity had demanded it, such as conquest, the avenue might well have continued up to Scotland. The Stonehengers certainly had the engineering ability.

Bulldozers and graders recently pushed a new motorway across the hill to the north of Stonehenge. The blades uncovered ancient rings of pits, stone holes, and post holes. Rescue archaeologists quickly made notes before the roadwork continued.

The old road to Bath which skirts the heel stone was made by hand labor in a way similar to that of the avenue. At first sight it is straight, but a careful look shows a few feet of deviation at the stone. This was a most fortunate occurrence. There could be no test of sunrise theories if the stone had been leveled and the hole buried under the road.

The bluestones are of five kinds, not really blue—dolerite, rhyolite, olive-green volcanic ash, Cosheston sandstone, and calcareous ash. The one thing these stones have in common, apart from a gray-green color when wet, is the Prescelly Mountains on the Pembroke peninsula. Since this is the nearest location to Stonehenge where all five types of rock are found, it is assumed to be the origin of the stones.

At stage II, judging by the holes, the bluestones were meant to be set in a double ring of 38 spokes. The 38 can be regarded as two semi-circles of 19, the full circle being punctuated by a large stone (now only a hole) diametrically opposite the entrance. According to the astronomical theory, this ring was a further counting device to keep a

PLATE 7. *Rescue archaeology. Professionals and volunteer students make a hasty study of prehistoric post holes before a motorway cuts across Salisbury Plain.*

19

PLATE 8. *Stonehenge from the west. Note the tenon knob on the top of the west pillar of the great trilithon.*

PLATE 9. *Stonehenge III from the heel stone.*

tally of the moon cycles, 19 and 19 making a total of 38. But this was not an improvement over the 56 of the Aubrey circle; 37 was a better fit (2 × 18.61 = 37.22). Was this a megalithic goof? This is no more than speculation, unwarranted in the minds of some scholars because the answers are beyond our ken. Whatever the intent of the builders, the bluestone double ring was never completed. There were no holes dug in the western quadrant.

Stonehenge III is what we see today—bluestone horseshoe; bluestone circle; sarsen circle of thirty archways; Y and Z holes and the trilithons. . . .

"What's that?"

The stewardess adjusted the movie screen; the galley was piled with used trays; passengers stood in the aisle, leaning against the seats, talking about the Tower of London, the Folies-Bergère, the price of Irish whisky. The cabin was lit softly with a reading light here and there.

"Trilithon comes from the Greek," I said. " 'Three stones.' Massive blocks were shaped, dressed, and set up in a hole in the chalk with twenty feet protruding above ground. Stone 56, the largest hand-worked monolith in England, must weigh 50 tons. The upright was shaped at the top in the form of a small knob, a tenon, which fitted into a hemispherical cup in the lintel crosspiece."

"O.K., O.K. Two up and one across."

"Yes, but not an archway to walk through. Far too narrow. A slot for looking through."

I showed him a photo in the Parisian magazine *Match*. A nude Stonehenge goddess was squeezing hard but could not quite get through the slot.

There were 5 trilithons set in a U. The great trilithon at the end stood 24½ feet high with lintel; the next 21½ feet and those at the mouth of the U were 20 feet. Three are complete, and two are fallen. The trilithons were ringed around by the sarsen (perhaps meaning heathen stone) circle. These 30 uprights were joined at the top by flat lintels, held in place by mortise and tenon joints.

The sarsen uprights are placed with the inner surface touching a circle of diameter 97 feet 4 inches, average error less than 4 inches. The

21

space between the uprights was uniform, except that space between stones 1 and 30, which was wider to mark the sunrise at midsummer as seen from the center. One can marvel at the ability to fit huge blocks together as if they were wood; mortise and tenon is expected of a cabinetmaker, not stonemasons working with nothing more than round stone mauls, bashing and chipping. And the notion of freestanding lintels boggles the mind; there was nothing like it in prehistoric Europe. The Lion Gate at Mycenae was centuries later, the Maya and Tiahuanaco stonework later still. *Henge,* according to the best guess, stands for hanging in the air, as in the Gardens of Babylon. Henry of Huntingdon, an early English chronicler, said the name describes stones which "hang as it were in the air." If the builders wished to impress the emerging civilization of the Continent with a prize-winning "first" in architecture, this was a sure way to do it.

The critical sunrises, moonrises, sunsets, and moonsets are framed by the archways of the sarsen circle as seen through the trilithons. Midwinter sunset appears through the great trilithon, 55–56. The next trilithon, 53–54, marks the extremes of the full moon when it rises at midsummer, in that lunation closest to June 21. The observer saw two gaps in the sarsen ring through this trilithon: the northerly gap, 8–9, gives the same direction, and hence the same view, as the line 91–93 in the earlier station stone rectangle; 9–10 repeats 92–93. The companion trilithon, 57–58, marks the extremes of the full moon when it sets at midwinter. 51–52 points through the sarsen gap to winter sunrise; 59–60 points to summer sunset.

These were remarkable properties for the ancient structure. They were found by a computer calculation based on maps and charts. It was my contention that the astro-lines were deliberate, intended, because the same phenomenon of sun and moon is marked in rectangular Stonehenge I and curved Stonehenge III. Once is suggestive; twice is confirmative.

The producer sat back, tapped a pencil on his teeth. He began to think about checking other alignments besides the famous heel stone. He wanted to film the sun and moon through the trilithons, summer and winter, bring the whole thing to life after 3,500 years.

After the trilithons, there was a last burst of construction, going on as late as 1500 or 1400 B.C. Then, it seems, Stonehenge fell into disuse,

PLATE 10. *The winter sun shines feebly through the pillars of the sarsen circle.*

put out of action by a change of climate from a Mediterranean brilliance to the conditions of present-day England.

The bluestones were placed in the center as an oval, then taken down and set in the irregular bluestone circle, part of which remains today between the sarsens and trilithons. Nineteen bluestones were erected in a horseshoe within the trilithons. These are smoothly polished and show the finest tooling of any stones at the site.

R. J. C. Atkinson of the University of South Wales has speculated that the bluestones were intended to go in the Y and Z holes at this stage. Whatever the intention, nothing went in. The 29 Z and 30 Y holes were dug and left empty and open for the soil to blow in. Evidence of the spade shows a light wind-blown filling, with a chip of a bluestone at the bottom of some of the holes. Was this chip a token of a stone? A fragment planted so that it would grow? Actually Stonehenge chips were found scattered under the turf for a wide area. Was it a ritual scattering? The stones had important and possibly occult value to the builders, as evidenced by their transportation from as far away as Wales and their use and reuse in the buildings; were these stones smashed to unrecognizably small fragments by the Stonehengers themselves? Clearly we can't lay the blame entirely on nineteenth-century hammers—the chips are found at the deep, Stonehenge-period horizons.

Rings of holes and circles of stone. In support of my theory, these numbers fit the moon cycles: 19 is the first approximation to 18.61, and 30 is the nearest whole number to the moon month, which averages 29.53 days. Originally I suggested that a stone was moved around the sarsen circle, one archway each day. The stone was in step with the moon. Start at full moon, once around the circle, and the moon is back to full. Because of the difference between 30 and 29.53 an adjustment would be needed after a few months; the stone would have to be dropped back one archway.

But not so with the Y and Z holes. By use of the Y holes for one month (30 days) and the Z holes in the next month (29 days) the moon marker would keep in step for several years.

"Who built it?"

No single group, no unique, identifiable mastermind. Construction and alterations were taking place at Stonehenge for longer than five centuries—about 25 generations. Several cultures were involved, each identified by characteristic artifacts—pottery, tools, jewelry—by their customs as indicated by the manner of burial, and by skeletal remains, whether brachycephalic (broad head) or dolichocephalic (long head).

An archaeologist speaks of a "cultural lens." People connected by one set of ideas live and die, leaving artifacts in the soil over a wide area. These are covered over by the debris of the next culture and so forth.

If the culture is nonliterate, all that remains is a scattering of objects over the area of habitation, a lens, at a certain depth in the soil, between the layers of the preceding and following cultures.

Stonehenge I was built by the Secondary Neolithic culture, II by the Beaker culture, and III by Wessex man. (Here, as in other discussions, I refer to *Homo sapiens* without prejudice to the sexes. Man is used as a word for mankind; it carries with it equal rights for male and female, unless the evidence in context is otherwise. Stone Age man (male) wore necklaces and ornaments. Stone Age man (female) did likewise, and may have shared or controlled the leadership. The role of the sexes is an open question.)

The Stone Age covers an enormous time span in prehistory. Stone implements are found in England buried under the mud and rock deposited by the ice. Early man was roaming and hunting there 500,000 years ago, before the ice. When the ice sheet covered Scotland and reached halfway down England, hunters crossed the land bridge from continental Europe in search of game. In summer, according to the archaeological evidence, herds of reindeer, mammoths and woolly rhinoceros lured men up to the wall of ice. In winter the population of southern England fell to a low of less than 250.

Cro-Magnon man, flat-faced, upright, is regarded as the forerunner of modern man, *Homo sapiens* (man the wise). His bones date back to 30,000 B.C. and are found throughout Europe. Aurignacian man (named for a region in France whose caves contain numerous artifacts) was of this stock. He made small flint tools, burins, and bone implements and ornaments, a few of which have been found south of the ice line in England. Then followed the Gravettians, Solutreans, and Magdalenians. The roving Gravettians had a cultural lens that spread from south Russia to Spain.

Soon after 10,000 B.C. the land bridge was breached and the North Sea

PLATE 11. *Ancient burial mounds on the Downs southeast of Stonehenge high-lighted by the winter sun. On the left near the modern crossroads a long barrow, center at the edge of the woods a bell barrow, and beyond are disk barrows.*

joined with the English Channel. Symbolically, it was now a matter of immigration rather than the directionless pursuit of game. Practically, the men and families took the step, made the sea journey, and stayed in the new land. The Tardenoisians dug shelters for winter habitation and roamed the hills in summer, hunting with dogs brought over from France. The shore-loving Azilians settled on the coast. Theirs was a fishing culture, and the members rarely hunted inland. The Maglemosian culture, Middle Stone Age (Mesolithic), was busy making stone and bone tools for carpenters and hunters. It seems they had a busy trade.

The Neolithic age was Cro-Magnon's brave new world. He controlled his environment. He cleared forest and scrub, planted seeds, and harvested; he bred quality cattle and corraled the animals; he built circular earthwork enclosures on hilltops. He developed the art of moving huge stones.

Neolithic people with their methods and ideas arrived in England about 3000 B.C. They worked for a thousand years clearing forests, building hamlets and mounds. Toward the end of this era, the culture is classified archaeologically as Secondary Neolithic. This was the climax of the Stone Age in Britain, just before the Bronze Age, and Stonehenge I is Secondary Neolithic.

It is difficult for us to reconstruct these cultures in any detail. They are known merely by a scholarly label and judged in a modern time frame.

Flanders and Swann, two sophisticated humorists, had a comment on this in their Broadway show. The chief architect of Stonehenge is being harassed by a man-in-the-street who objects to the structure. It spoils the landscape and disturbs the environment: Don't you know this is the last breeding place for mammoths hereabouts? When he is snubbed by the architect he fights back: Don't think I'm neolithic, I'm Secondary Neolithic, you know! And what's more I own two polished axheads and a bone implement of undetermined use!

Harper's magazine explored the idea of digging up the New York tumulus. Many fragments of devitrified glass were found bearing the inscription *Coke*. This culture extended to the Chicago tumulus and even farther. One of the future diggers said the *Coke*-culture lens was worldwide. He had dug everywhere and was now melting samples of ice in the Antarctic to get *Coke* artifacts to prove his theory!

The builders of Stonehenge II were known as the Beaker culture. They got their name from beaker-shaped drinking cups. Pottery fragments are found at the Stonehenge II layer. Not much more is known about them than that. Persons of high standing in this culture were buried individually in circular mounds, called tumuli or barrows. Males had one shape of tumulus, females another. Bodies were buried, knee to chin, close to the surface in an urn with earthly valuables, gold, amber, and jet ornaments. These little green hillocks, so numerous on Salisbury Plain, are now protected by law. In bygone days it was a popular sport of the idle rich to dig for treasure, particularly Bronze Age treasure.

Stonehenge III was Early Bronze Age. The spade uncovers the Wessex people, the culture that designed, built, and used the stony structure of Stonehenge. Secondary Neolithic, Beaker, Wessex—these cultures combined created a masterpiece of all time, a monument to the labors of body and mind over a full five centuries.

Poet Michael Drayton wrote:*

> Ill did those mighty men to trust thee with their story:
> That hast forgot their names who reared thee for their glory.

Those men are anonymous. Their thoughts are thin in the air. We can attempt to read into the prehistoric mind with astronomical detective work. The spade again gives some meager facts about their living and dying, and their community life.

The Wessex population was industrious and highly organized. There were miners, field cultivators, and traders. Almost certainly there was a strong sociopolitical organization because the culture supported a wealthy class of rulers. The burial mounds of the great lords show a sample of that wealth—an amber disk bound with gold; jet necklaces from Scotland; bronze, gold, and amber amulets; amber from the Baltic; gold inlaid boxes; blue faïence beads from Egypt; ceremonial bronze weapons.

And Wessex industry and organization were great enough to plan and execute Stonehenge—that eighth wonder of the ancient world, an archi-

* Drayton (1563–1631), ''Polyolbion.''

28

tectural gem, awesome, haunting, strangely beautiful; a stupendous feat of engineering, precise, incomprehensible to succeeding generations; observatory, computer, embodiment of celestial knowledge from centuries before.

"How did they do it, Professor?"

The cabin was hushed, passengers asleep under orange-colored blankets. Low lighting inside, dark outside. The hostesses chatted in the kitchen behind us. We were over the coast of Wales, nosing down the long, invisible glide path to London Airport.

"Do you mean 'construct it' or 'design it'?"

"Make it."

The 4- or 5-ton bluestone blocks were carried, slid, and lowered down the Prescelly Mountains to the natural harbor of Milford Haven, and then conveyed by boat or raft along the Bristol Channel, up the Severn estuary to the river Avon. Eighty-two monoliths, at least, were transported along this route. The stones were sought out by the Beaker people, perhaps in the way the argonauts searched widely for the Golden Fleece. Suitable rocks were nearer at hand, yet some intense necessity drove them to Prescelly.

Is there any truth in Geoffrey of Monmouth's twelfth-century story of magic? Legends cannot be taken as hard scientific evidence. According to Geoffrey,* Merlin said to King Ambrosius, (sometimes identified as the father of King Arthur, though others would have Uther Pendragon as Arthur's father, and still others make Uther his uncle):

Send for the Dance of Giants that is in Killarus, a mountain in Ireland. For a structure of stone is there that none of this age could raise save his wit were strong enough to carry his art. For the stones be big, nor is there stone anywhere of more virtue, and, so they be set round this plot in a circle, even as they be now set up there, here shall they stand forever. . . . in these stones is a mystery, and a healing virtue against many ailments. Giants of old did carry them from the furthest ends of Africa. . . . not a stone is there that lacketh in virtue of witchcraft.

Geoffrey then continues with an entertaining account of a battle to gain the stones, and the transportation by sea. Hawsers and ropes

* *Histories of the Kings of Britain*, translated by Sebastian Evans. (London: Dent, 1904).

PLATE 12. *"Phantom forms of antediluvian giants . . ." (Sir Walter Scott).*

failed to move the stones, "never a whit the forwarder," but wizard Merlin "put together his own engines" and succeeded.

Legend or not, the stones must have come part of the way by sea. Wooden fragments do not survive in the damp British climate, and there is nothing left of the boats of 2000 B.C. But immigration across the Channel (there are Beaker artifacts in England and on the Continent, and Stuart Piggott, an Edinburgh University archaeologist, also finds connections between the Wessex culture and French Brittany) is evidence enough for seagoing experience.

The alternative suggestion, that the five types of bluestone rock were found separately and nearer Stonehenge, is not convincing. A chunk of bluestone dolerite was unearthed in a long barrow near the river Wylye. It must have had magical significance to be included in the burial. Perhaps it broke off during the transportation. Persuasive evidence, say the experts, to pinpoint the route as up the Bristol Avon, 15 miles overland to the river Wylye, up the Salisbury Avon, and then the last haul from Amesbury via the sunrise causeway avenue to the chosen site.

Sea and river travel was arduous and risky; overland dragging was a feat of strength. With no wheel, each stone was hauled by a team of workers over temporary roadbeds, eased along on stone-adze-shaped wooden rollers.

The sarsen blocks, which did not come from Wales, were a larger and worse problem: 50 tons dead weight, sullen and seemingly immovable, half-buried in the Marlborough Downs. The response of the engineers would surely be to call for "more rollers" and "more men." A rough-shaped boulder like the heel stone would need a flat-bottomed cradle on which to slide.

The hauling has been reenacted in present times. It takes 16 men for each ton weight—provided the slopes are gentle, not more than a 1-foot rise in 15. So on this basis a sarsen block required 800 men to do the hauling, and many more to clear the way and carry rollers from the back to the front of the forward-moving stone. With 75 stones (30 uprights, 30 lintels, 15 stones in the 5 trilithons) to go, there was much blood and toil, tears and sweat.

Geologist Patrick Hill, of Carleton University, Canada, has picked out the "path of minimum effort." The quarry was on the Downs south of the river Kennet, the path 3 miles downhill to the Vale of Pewsey, across the valley, then by water along the shallow Avon. Atkinson favored a route first proposed by John Wood in 1747: the source was the Gray Weather rocks north of the river Kennet; the path went through Avebury, that second important Beaker monument, where the stones were sanctified on the way, in Merlin fashion, with virtues of healing and witchcraft.

When the sandstone blocks arrived at Stonehenge they were tooled and dressed, though a crude, preliminary shaping must have taken place at the point of origin on the Downs. Rough chunks were sliced off by the hot-cold-bash method, that method used by the villagers of Avebury to crack the stones in medieval times.

"Fine" tooling was a further, slow process. A maul, a natural boulder of 50 pounds, was held with both hands, legs astride, over the monolith. Bash! and a puff of rock powder came away. After a few hours a groove was pounded into the surface. Then another. The ridges between the grooves were flattened, and a smooth surface produced by rubbing stone against stone. This tooling, hardly noticed on a 10-minute tour of the monument, took an estimated 60,000 man-days of work.

The monoliths were set base in hole, and hauled vertical by ropes and poles. The snug-fitting lintels were raised up on wooden towers according to one speculation, or maybe hauled up on temporary earthen ramps, Egyptian style, according to another, and were dropped into place on top of the uprights. Total estimated workload for the entire project—1,497,680 man-days.

This was truly dedicated labor, the effort of a community held together spiritually by a common eros. Some driving force was within the individual, an inspiration to achieve what hitherto was impossible, to build what Henry James once described as a creation standing "as lonely in history as it does on the great plain."

"Why did they do it?"

A vital, difficult question, one seeking out those navigation marks of C. W. Ceram which connect man's future with his five thousand years of heritage. Astronomy has given a partial answer. The sun-god was one of their motives, the famous Ra of ancient Egypt, the Kon-Tiki of Peru. Throughout a full five centuries the Stonehengers—Secondary Neolithic, then Beaker people, then Wessex—were watching the sun and moon, the mystery of the environment, following the periodicities, and predicting that awe-filled danger time of eclipses. The foundations are laid out with this astronomical-mathematical pattern, though in all probability the intricate scientific basis was not known to the average worker whose sweat was used in the construction. Only a priest-cult would know the full workings. But impressive though the sun and moon are, these physical objects alone could not produce the compelling stimulus.

Before the astronomical discoveries, the Stonehenge motive was thought to be religious. Not Druidism; that theology was Celtic and came later. Not incipient Christianity; not Judaism, though one or two authors have argued for this connection. A religion with a lost creed.

Another possible motive was spiritual, a concern for life after death. That was the otherworldly driving force that built the pyramids and the mausoleum at Halicarnassus, two of the seven wonders of the world. Cremations were found in and near the Aubrey holes. Stonehenge is at the center of a wide field of important burial tumuli, 350 within 2½ miles. It could well have been a focal point of departed souls.

Environmental awareness, religion, life and death—what was the synthesis, the cultural integration of these themes?

The astrojet was now over Salisbury Plain. It had taken 10 minutes to travel the bluestone distance from Prescelly, a journey which must have taken as many years by raft and roller.

History provides exact dates, the year, month, day. Prehistory does not. Willard F. Libby, Nobel Prize winner, developed a method for dating organic materials—the radiocarbon clock. Carbon 14 is one of the natural pollutants in the atmosphere produced by cosmic rays. It is absorbed by plants, eaten by animals and humans, and becomes part of the cultural debris. The proportion of C_{14} in a bone or tree trunk decreases year by year, and the amount of C_{14} relative to normal carbon, C_{12}, gives the age. After about 70,000 years the radioisotope has decreased below the threshold of detection and the clock has run down.

A charcoal fragment from Aubrey hole 32 was measured. The date, on a revised half-life value, was 2000 B.C. ±275. Items from other holes have given dates of 2100 and 2200 B.C. On this approximate clock, Stonehenge began at the close of the third millennium before Christ. As for Stonehenge II and III, a deer antler from the ramp down to the base of one of the trilithons gave a date of about 1700 B.C.

These dates agree with the time scale of the Neolithic, Beaker, and Wessex cultures as determined in other regions of the cultural lens. The faïence beads from pharaohic Egypt in the Wessex grave and the bronze found at late Beaker levels also fit the time picture. We can take the first construction as beginning around 2200 B.C., the climax of activity as 1700 B.C., and the disuse and abandonment of the site as occurring by 1400 B.C.

Recently Colin Renfrew of Sheffield University has put forward a revision of all Stonehenge dates, making them 500 years older than the presently accepted chronology. The correction, he claims, is necessary because of variations in the C_{14} content of the atmosphere since 3000 B.C. This would push Stonehenge back as early as or earlier than the Gizeh Pyramids. The computer-found alignments are sensibly unaffected, however, because the change in the angle of tilt of the earth's axis, obliquity, over the years is so small. If Stonehenge functioned as an observatory so many thousands of years ago, it will function so today.

Despite its roughness, radiocarbon dating is an improvement over the well-intentioned guesswork of chroniclers. The age of Stonehenge tended to increase with each generation of writers, with each guess. Twelfth-century Geoffrey gave it a date of A.D. 400, Inigo Jones (1620) said it was Roman, seventeenth-century Aubrey, 500 B.C., and Norman Lockyer in the present century said 1850 B.C. It is as though the writers stopped short at the great age of Stonehenge, there was an acceptance gap, and the mind was able to approach the truth only by graduated steps. The hard, radiocarbon fact is an age of at least 4,100 years.

Stonehenge was begun in the same millennium as the Great Pyramid of Gizeh, a few centuries before Hammurabi set down his legal code and Abraham dwelt in Canaan. It was a flourishing center 2,000 years before the Mayan glory of Central America, and was wrapped in desolate mystery as Moses led the Exodus.

The astrojet touched down on schedule at Heathrow. It was a cold, green dawn. We went breakfastless to C.B.S. headquarters in the city to rendezvous with the camera team. With a three-car convoy we headed immediately for Salisbury and the famous plain. Assignment Stonehenge.

"Get that sunrise!"

3 SUNRISE

We came to Salisbury.

This cathedral city, capital of Wiltshire, was founded by disgruntled priests of Old Sarum who, feuding with the soldiers of the garrison in 1217, took the noble path of discretion—out and southward to the river Avon. The earliest streets were laid out to the four points of the compass, and the area is known today as the Chequers.

The television team chose the hotel opposite the Red Lion Inn as the base. Stonehenge had fallen under the hammer at the Red Lion. Traditionally the public auction was held there, and the parcel of land containing the old stones had changed hands at least six times in the nineteenth century, being valued more for its sheep grazing than for its prehistory. One truculent owner threatened in the London *Times* to topple the stones and ship them to the United States. The last time Stonehenge was auctioned it was for a price of about £6,000 to Mr. C. Chubb, later Sir Cecil, who presented it to the Crown in 1918. Later the land for a mile around the site was purchased by public subscription and presented to the National Trust.

Stonehenge is the No. 2 tourist attraction in Britain. (No. 1 is the Tower of London.) The first year it went public it had 30,000 visitors; by 1935 there were 60,000, and currently the number exceeds 700,000. The annual takings in admission fees exceed with a healthy margin the final hammer price at the public auction. Salisbury is filled each summer by visitors in transit to Stonehenge from continental Europe, America, the Orient, and India. Yet there is no signpost leading to the prehistoric wonder. The city fathers, according to the landlord of the Red Lion Inn, think that tourists come to see the city, not the stones.

The hotel manager watched as tripods, TV cameras, sound equipment, and lamps blocked the entrance foyer. Boxes of film and reels of cable tripped the hotel guests. The manager was over thirty, but trustworthy, with a sunless pallor, a polite English manner, too busy ever to have visited Stonehenge, though he told sightseers that it was

35

36

FIG. 2. *17th-century view of Stonehenge from Inigo Jones.*

37

"six miles north and turn left at Amesbury." He diplomatically apologized to the other guests for the disruption and arranged a special sunrise schedule for the TV crew—breakfast 2:30 A.M.; afternoon tea 10:00 A.M. Perhaps he had served the modern-day Druids. They would have a similar schedule. Each year on June 21, or that day nearest the summer solstice, the white-cloaked and hooded, tennis-sneakered Druids hold their own dawn ritual. They tap the heel stone and chant "Arise, O sun." Druid equipment would be equally disruptive in the entrance foyer—oak tree branches, long trumpet, incense and harp. (Wicker sacrifice cages?)

The crew shuttled the foggy six miles between hotel and site. Like cosmic pawns their working and actions were locked to the ever-turning celestial sphere. Sunrise and moonset; sunset and moonrise.

Waiting through the dawn at Stonehenge was an eerie experience. The crows that nested in the crevices were silent; the stones were softly unreal. They stood over us, delicately silhouetted against the purple velvet sky, waiting as if sentinels to frame the dawning sun. Thomas Hardy had Tess of the d'Urbervilles stand here before she was taken away to her fate. "The whole enormous landscape bore that impress of reserve, taciturnity, and hesitation which is usual just before day. The eastward pillars and their architraves stood up blackly against the light, and the great flame-shaped Sun-stone beyond them; and the stone of sacrifice midway."

John Evelyn wrote in his diary (July 22, 1654): ". . . Stonehenge, indeed a stupendous monument, appearing at a distance like a castle. . . ." The other famous diarist, Samuel Pepys, found the stones "as prodigious as any tales I ever heard."

For me it was not a first visit. Having grown up in England, I knew of the structure at an early age. Later I passed by the site regularly on my way to and from the Larkhill missile base. This was in the era of development and testing of ground-to-air missiles. Happily the test vehicles were not armed and were fired north over Salisbury Plain, away from Stonehenge. My diary was not as complete as Evelyn's, nor as eloquent as Pepys', but I did make visits to the stones whenever the opportunity arose.

On June 12, 1961, my wife and I had filmed the sunrise from the center of the circles. It was 11 days before the solstice, and the sun's disk stood one diameter to the east of the heel stone. The next day it would be a fraction closer, and the next, and by June 21 the disk by estimation would stand well and truly over the stone. That film (alas, lost in the mail between Radio Diffusion Française TV and the Smithsonian Astrophysical Observatory) had been a useful check on the plan-based calculations. A film on the solstice day would be confirmatory.

The TV crew looked gross in this place. Microphone cables wove between the stones; purpose, to catch the dawn chorus of the birds. Two tripods stood on the altar stone; purpose, to film the golden orb in wide angle and telephoto. A colored searchlight stood near the ditch, on loan from a circus down the road; purpose unknown. Its beam shone into the predawn darkness, high on the lintels, low over the dew-laden grass. This searchlight brought to the director-producer a hair-tearing problem. Cows. They congregated in the beam and moved over the pasture with the light; big brown eyes stared at one more strange event in this strangest of places.

A soundman had doubts: Would the sun come up in the archway as predicted? (He did not trust the computing machine that had kept him up all night.) Would it come up ever? (He was cold; summer in England can be chilly.)

Apprehensively I looked to the heel stone with high-power binoculars. Birds were stirring in the distance on Larkhill. A shred of purple-tinged mist hung over the avenue. Would it obscure the first flash of sunrise? On rare occasions the rim of the sun can shine a pale green for a few seconds. But this trick of refraction is with clear air over an open sea horizon. I knew there would be no green flash this morning, inland over rolling hills. Now there was a shaded line of burnt sienna along the brow of the hill. Aurora, rosy goddess of the dawn, arose. Gold and ruby spread through the high cirrus, then lower through the ground mist. There it was. Magnified, crimson, startling in the rapidity of its movement through the trees.

The script synchronized with the motion. "The sun *does* rise over the heel stone . . . folklore is now fact . . . a door to the past has been opened. . . ."

Those were powerful words. I was gratified to see the folklore verified. Many have stood at Stonehenge waiting for this solstice sunrise, but only a few have seen it.* Weather conditions in England do not often permit the full process of sunrise to be seen from first flash to full orb.

The position measured from the film agreed with previous calculations to within a tenth of a degree. This was the day before Midsummer's Day, and the interval of 24 hours would place the sun slightly higher, but by an amount not noticeable to the unaided eye.

True, the camera had proved the alignment of the heel stone toward the sun. With this line confirmed, the dozens of other computed sun-moon lines must fall into place. Stonehenge did work as an observatory; the circles could function as an eclipse computing device. But this didn't prove the theory. It showed that it was possible, very possible. But there was an acceptance gap to be bridged. There would be scholastic arguments and counterarguments, challenges, rival theories. A mathematical step is proved without debate from its axioms, but a theory touching the social sciences is never Q.E.D.

As a Sunday press book critic said of another theory, it would be "riding to the hounds of culture . . . down the dales of acceptance . . . then bay at the heels of the Philistines." The Stonehenge theory needed acceptance, and there was the ambush of criticism ahead.

The camera crew was to continue for more data and material. They climbed Mount Prescelly to the place where dolerite rock meets rhyolite, a rugged ascent with cameras and tripods, unbelievably difficult with 5-ton monoliths. They set up again at midwinter when the sun was in the great trilithon and the moon usurped the sun's position over the heel stone. The alignments worked well.

* At Stonehenge, the critical dawn has come to be defined as that sunrise which occurs on the day of the astronomical solstice, which in turn is that instant when the center of the disk of the sun reaches its highest declination, numerically equal to the obliquity of the earth's axis (currently $23°.5$). Because of the leap year irregularity—the calendar year not being exactly equal in length to the true tropical year—the sunrise day can fall on June 20, 21, or 22. In Stonehenge times the critical sunrise was probably that dawn nearest in time to the solstice instant, remembering that that instant can fall in the late evening, G.M.T. In some diaries the day of midsummer is sometimes marked as June 24. This is the old, ecclesiastic, and legal date, fixed in the early centuries A.D. It was the solstice when originally set up, but calendar errors have subsequently made it incorrect. The errors in the length of the calendar year were substantially corrected in the "New Style" calendar of Pope Gregory XIII, but he did not at that time bring the legal and ecclesiastic dates into line with events in the sky.

41

At daybreak I returned to Salisbury to absorb the whirl of events. I walked the quiet streets, past the antique stores, through the stone portico, down to the river Avon. The magnificent Gothic cathedral stood reflected in the water. The oldest clock in Britain, pre-pendulum, pre-Galileo, registered the early hour. Sunlight caught the tip of the spire, tallest in England, 404 feet high, an inspiration to man through the centuries. The cathedral was a favorite subject of landscape artist John Constable; one such masterpiece hangs in the National Gallery, London, another in the Frick Collection, New York. The cathedral, described as "medieval man reaching up to heaven," is claimed by architects to be the finest example of monumental Gothic in the British Isles.

The cathedral axis is aligned due east. The high altar marks the sunrise position as averaged through the seasons of the year. This orientation was the rule in Christian churches; it was astronomical, not geographical; toward the sun, not toward Jerusalem. Sun alignment "has its origin," states the *New Catholic Encyclopedia,* "in the cosmic orientation of Greco-Roman temples." It has eschatological significance—pertaining to heaven, death, judgment. The concept is pre-Christian, and sun-pointing is a custom that dates back into the dim, pagan past.

Salisbury cathedral is parallel to the equinox line, F-93, at Stonehenge, to the base of the pyramids at Gizeh, and to the axis of the temple in the paws of the Sphinx. That temple of the Egyptian desert, built more years before Christ than Salisbury is after, is dedicated to Ra-Hor-Akhty, the sun's disk rising on the eastern horizon, god and symbol of life. Pseudo-Germanus of Constantinople gave this theme a retread three millennia after the pyramids and three centuries before the decoding of the hieroglyphic sun-god prayers: "Christ is our sun, and from the East he will restore the paradise we lost." The very word "orientation" stems from the Latin *orior,* to rise. Pope Gregory added an antipagan correction: "Worship the son of God, not the god of the sun," he said.

I reflected how the present is connected to the past by a tenuous, often invisible, thread. A custom is continued, reinforced, as cultures are joined across the chasms of space and time.

The pointed arch, the definitive shape in Gothic architecture, is inherited from Teutonic structures. Filarete, a medieval architect,

42

states that the Gothic arch is the shape of two upright saplings tied together at the top as in a neolithic wooden hut. The cathedral congregation, facing the east window, is a reenactment of a Teutonic tribe facing the barbaric sun-god Balder through the door of the hut.

Boston Stump, the tower of Boston's main church (Lincolnshire, not Massachusetts), is a landmark of the East. Lanterns used to be hung at the top to guide ships at sea and travelers crossing the swampy fens. (Was this the source of Paul Revere's idea?) It is an edifice to the time-god. It has a numerical, cabalistic, architecture—365 spiral steps, 7 windows, 12 bells. The life of medieval man was time-factored. The relentless passing of the days, months, and years was a divine mystery, flowing with God.

The Avon was clear, smooth, and quick-running. There was an island in the river, the chosen site for the New Sarum Society's Stonehenge Museum, a display-research complex planned for the late seventies. I walked along the sandy pathways by the river, over little bridges to the meadow. Trout swam at the bottom, head to stream, fast enough to stay in one place. A willow tree stirred in the early morning air. The old country town was ready to follow the pulse of circadian rhythm, a pulse synchronized with the sun. In the days of Thomas Hardy, the horse-drawn wagons would flow in at dawn with fresh produce. The market-place thronged with people about their work. The bustle reached a crescendo at noon, subsiding in the P.M. cheer of the taverns, and then wagoners pulsed out into the countryside again.

Salisbury has several fine bookstores, antique and dusty. There is no telling what will show up on the shelves or in the leather-bound piles on the floor. Novels, pamphlets, poems, old manuscripts. These are the places for hunting out Stonehenge books. As a rule of thumb, any Stonehenge book is rare. Hundreds of titles are listed, but each work seems to have been a strictly limited edition; many are private printings. No one library, not even the Library of Congress or the British Museum, has a full set.

The earliest known perspective drawing of Stonehenge is a manuscript by one L. D. H., 1574. The general features are recognizable, the viewpoint being to the northwest, looking southeast. The pillar of the great trilithon, stone 56, leans the wrong way, and stone 16 is shown displaced from the sarsen circle.

FIG. 3. (above) *Earliest known perspective of Stonehenge from a Dutch manuscript, 1574, drawn in ink with watercolor tints.*

FIG. 4. (right) *A print from Camden's* Britannia, *1586.*

The next drawing, in William Camden's *Britannia,* 1586, is distorted and almost unrecognizable. It shows men digging for bones, and a bump on L.D.H.'s original drawing becomes a nonexistent castle. Antiquarian Colt Hoare said Camden "makes so palpable a mistake in the number of the circles that I question if he ever visited them himself." Perhaps Camden got an artist to copy Paper's drawing (it had come out 12 years before, and Camden's picture is from the same perspective viewpoint). The additional stones to the left and outside of the sarsen circle could be the heel and slaughter stone. Camden thought the stones might be "artificially made of pure sand; and by some glewy and unctious matter, knit and incorporate together. . . ."

John Aubrey's important manuscript of the 1660's exists as a single handwritten copy in the Bodleian Library, Oxford. Never published *in toto,* the manuscript would be a headache for an editor. The writing is

44

A The Stones call'd Corsstones, 12 Tonn Weight 24 foot high, 7 broad, and 16 round
B The Stones call'd Coronetts, of 6 or 7 Tonns
C The place where   Mens bones are dug up

I. Kip Sculp

45

illegible in places; the pages are reused and scrappy. His book *Brief Lives* was left unpublished in similar disarray. For this book Anthony à Wood hurled his most unkind epithet at Aubrey: "roving and magotie-headed"! Yet *Brief Lives* is potential film-script material with a full and earthy *Tom Jones* flavor. The unpublished Stonehenge manuscript led Hawley to the "Aubrey holes." Puzzling over the scribble on Aubrey's plan of the monument, he deciphered the writing to be "cavities." There were no cavities or depressions to be seen in the 1920's, but Hawley dug as though following the instructions on an old map of buried treasure.

Architect Inigo Jones wrote an account of Stonehenge for James I. The king read the manuscript, but his subjects did not. Thirty years

FIG. 5. *Dr. Charleton's perspective, 1663.*

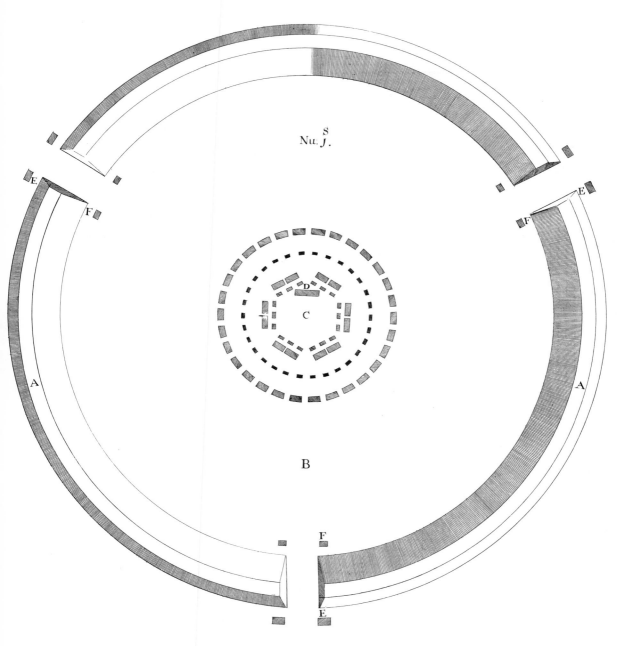

FIG. 6. *Earliest known plan prepared for King James I by Inigo Jones, drawn circa 1625, published 1655.*

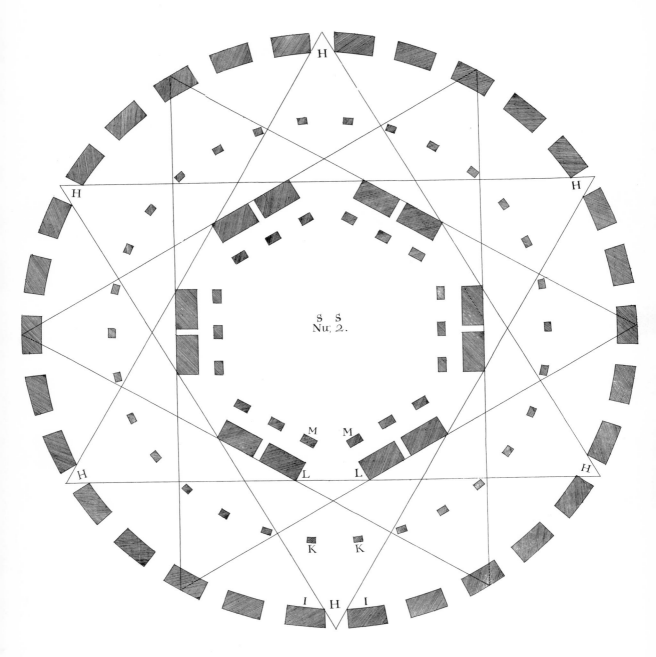

FIG. 7. *Stonehenge restored, according to Inigo Jones. He incorrectly surmised a hexagonal figure based on a twelve-pointed star.*

later John Webb, the son-in-law of Jones, inherited the "few undigested notes," which were embellished and published in 1655. Very few copies were distributed because of the Plague, and the remaining stock was destroyed in the Fire of London, 1666. This was the first book-length publication on the monument, with speculations freely added as to the builders (Romans, clearly, because ancient Britons were "savage and barbarous people") and the purpose ("a temple dedicated to the sky god, Coelus"). The volume was reprinted in 1725 by D. Browne, Jr., at the Black Swan without Temple Bar. The reprint is a valuable rarity, the original nearly priceless.

The drawings of Stonehenge by architect Jones are lacking in architectural precision. The great trilithon, leaning dangerously, is recognizable, and also the sunrise archway which stood erect as today, but the plans of the monument in general are inaccurate and incomplete: three avenue-entrances are shown, set 120° apart, instead of one (Jones probably confused the mound at 92 and the stone at 93 with entrances); stone 91 is not shown; the axis passes between two trilithons, whereas it should pass through the slot 55–56; six trilithons instead of five; a hexagon of 18 bluestones, instead of a horseshoe.

Inigo further confused the issue by showing Stonehenge restored as a precise (but imaginary) Greco-Roman structure, with the extra trilithon to close off the horseshoe. Subsequent writers followed his example with "restored" plans, all different.

Did other stones stand in the avenue in the seventeenth century, and if so, where? And was there a monolith beyond the ditch opposite the heel stone to mark the midwinter sunset?

How much more could we learn by exact measurement and surveying? I thought of the western half of Stonehenge intentionally left undug beneath the turf. Special photography from the air revealed hidden features in Babylonia, Etruria, and Yucatan—ditches, tombs, pits, buried foundations. Infrared film picked out items of different composition, rock and soil, by means of thermal contrast and slight variations in reflected sunlight. Holes dug and refilled ages before showed as darkened patches in the vegetation.

An air survey of Stonehenge would give the exact height above a fixed reference datum of each stone, precise to inches. Stereo-measurements would give ground contours at 1-foot intervals. That gentle unevenness of the ground, important in the sighting of a stone against the skyline, could be determined. New alignments could be computed. Undiscovered features would yield to the infrared probe.

The last plan was drawn in the 1920's, and before that, Petrie's in the 1880's. Now modern precision was available. Photogrammetry was speedy, accurate, decisive.

We must explore from the air.

4   A NEW MAP

Stonehenge was perfection.

The balanced archways are in the center of a circle within the circles of the outer banking and Aubrey ring. This classical concentric plan shows best from the air. The builders never saw this pattern, the full grandeur of their work, except in the inward eye. The geometry can be appreciated only from a point vertically above the structure or in a scaled plan. But no plan existed, unless there were wooden models, marks in the sand, or in baked clay. Then the pattern could be seen. But this is conjectural.

The serpent at Brush Creek, Ohio, 1,348 feet long from fangs to tail, must be seen from the air, yet it was made by earthbound North American Indians. The immense pre-Columbian desert drawings in Peru (described later in this book) are unrecognizable on the ground. The Giant of Pevensey was cut into white chalk in prehistoric times. According to legend the long nude male figure had powers of fertility. Villagers maintained the masculine outline by digging the turf as it grew over the chalk. Not so for that figure cut into the chalk at Cerne Abbas, Dorset. If this eye-popping nude male were scaled down to size, the erect phallus would be more than a foot long. The Victorian villagers colored it green. Now the National Trust keeps the figure, phallus and all, chalk white and in good order. The best view is obtained from overhead in a light aircraft.

Pevensey, Peru, the design at Stonehenge—these were not made to be seen in their artistic entirety by people restricted to walking on the ground. Is there a connecting idea, a global common cultural urge?

In our era the Sahara has been used as a giant canvas. The artist took a bulldozer and drove wide geometric furrows across the sand. Why did he do it? He obtained his kick by viewing the handiwork in a hired helicopter.

The circular ring is magic. It signifies eternity, without beginning or end. The wizard drew a circle of white chalk for his spell. Bernardin de

FIG. 8. *Enormous earthwork serpent at Brush Creek, Ohio.*

Saint-Pierre, for whom nature was "magnificent and mysterious," had his ethereal twins Paul and Virginia live "in the exact center of a basin formed by a ring of rocks." The Junkers in Kleist's *Michael Kohlhaas* feared "they would never get out of the magic circle in which they found themselves charmed." In Homer's *Odyssey* "assemblies of elders sit on stones in circles."

Mathematically the circle is that shape that encloses maximum area for a fixed length of boundary; that figure where the radius exactly marks off six chords; it is the curve of the apex of a right triangle; the perimeter of six touching equilateral triangles; all sectors of the perimeter of the circle have equal curvature.

In classical times the circle was perfection—ethereal, celestial. Aristotle, the ancient Greek authority, leaves no doubt about this in his writings. Base material (earthy, fleshy) falls in a straight line toward the center of the universe (the earth), but celestial material moves in eternal circles around the earth. No effort, no energy, is required. The

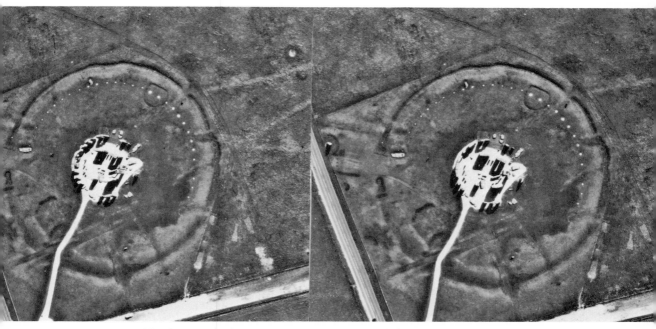

PLATE 14. *A stereo pair as used in the new plan of Stonehenge.*

magic of the circle guaranteed the rising of the sun each day, traveling in its celestial orbit. It guaranteed the immutability of the stars in their courses.

How much magic hovered over that white circle on Salisbury Plain? Some, to be sure. A scientist myopically looks at numbers—periodicities of the sun, moon, and eclipses—hard facts, nothing more. But a vast ritualistic superstructure can be built on these numbers and geometries—magic, hypnotic to the mind, occult beliefs powerful enough to inspire the builders to go to the absolute limit of their physical capabilities.

The photogrammetric air survey of Stonehenge added new perspective to the ancient site. It brought a precision of measurement that would have been admired by those Stone Age/Bronze Age engineers. It uncovered new hard facts to be mixed with the legend. It set off fresh speculation.

The survey was carried out by Hunting Surveys, England. My liaison

53

with the photogrammetric engineers was Mr. C. R. Herschel, descendant of Sir William Herschel, the musician-astronomer who discovered Uranus and was immortalized by Keats: "Then felt I like some watcher of the skies/When a new planet swims into his ken." William Herschel passed by Stonehenge when he was summoned to Windsor Castle by George III to be appointed Royal Astronomer. Later, with royal financing, he was to build the then largest telescope in the world, slung in a wooden pyramid and turned on a circular brick trackway by men at a windlass. Astronomer Herschel looked heavenward to Coelus, his descendant earthward to Dis.

Stereoscopic air pictures are taken with a single-lens camera, not the twin-lens type used in home photography. A special minimum-distortion lens pokes out from the belly of an airplane. The plane flies level and straight, and exposures are made in sequence, automatically. A special photogrammetric shutter is used to nullify the movement of the airplane.

Back at the laboratory, two pictures, red and green, are projected. The operator looks through special glasses. A miniature Stonehenge sits there in the machine, three-dimensional, vividly real. A small white spot moves in the machine, controlled by hand dials. It can be moved along the ground; up, up to perch on top of a stone; down, down into the shallow of a ditch. The machine reads height of stone or height of ground above datum. The method is accurate, absolute, unambiguous, mechanically final. The details are safely left with the engineer.

When I saw the first photogrammetic plan I was puzzled. The number of stones was wrong. There was an extra stone mapped in the bluestone horseshoe.

I raised the question with Mr. Herschel. The engineers put the film back in the infallible machine and redid the measurements.

Apologies!

The object was not a stone. It was human.

The error was excusable and quite understandable. There was a gentleman, a sightseer (bald-headed), who happened to stand in a gap in the line of bluestones at the instant of the click-click of the passing plane. His shadow was like that of a stone; his head top looked like polished dolerite. *Vertical object, height 5 ft 10 ins,* recorded the machine.

"The stones yet remaining are not to be numbered," wrote the ancient chroniclers. And Renaissance poet Sir Philip Sidney, the "perfect gentleman," wrote in his "Wonders of England":

> Near Wilton sweet, huge heaps of stone are found,
> But so confused, that neither any eye
> Can count them Just, nor Reason Reason try. . . .

The druidic William Stukeley boldly challenged this: "All added together make just 140 stones. . . . Behold the solution of the mighty problem, the magical spell is broke, which has so long perplexed the vulgar! they think 'tis an ominous thing to count the true number of stones, and whoever does so, shall certainly die after it."

King's architect Jones dismissed the myth: "Though it scarcely merits an answer, yet to satisfy those which in this point may be curious, let them but observe the order of the circles as they now appear, and not pass from one to the other confusedly (noting nevertheless where they begin) and they'll find the just number easy to be taken." But Jones confused broken stones with a fallen archway. His counting differed from Camden's, which differed from Aubrey's and that of Charles II, who allegedly skipped lightly around the ring while his mistress waited impatiently in the coach. "Behold," carped Dr. Walter Charleton, "the discrepancies of men's judgments, even in things easily determinable by the senses! and how hard it is to discern truth with other eyes!"

Hard also with photogrammetric sky-eyes.

The Stonehenge taboo has no greater effectiveness than the mummy's curse. That death curse was invented by frustrated newsmen while Howard Carter slowly dug in the Valley of the Kings. But does it carry some meaning from the past? That question is for the legend experts to decide. "Archaeology is incapable of dealing with myth," wrote digger Sir Cyril Fox, and equally so for mathematical science. Was there some threat over the rings and horseshoe; did the numbers 19, 30, 29, and 56 hold valuable knowledge not to be divulged? Knowledge was jealously guarded in classical times. Thales of Miletus was rewarded, so the accounts go, for telling the king how many times the diameter of the sun could be divided into the circle of the zodiac.*

* 720, or 360 divided by the sun's diameter in degrees, ½.

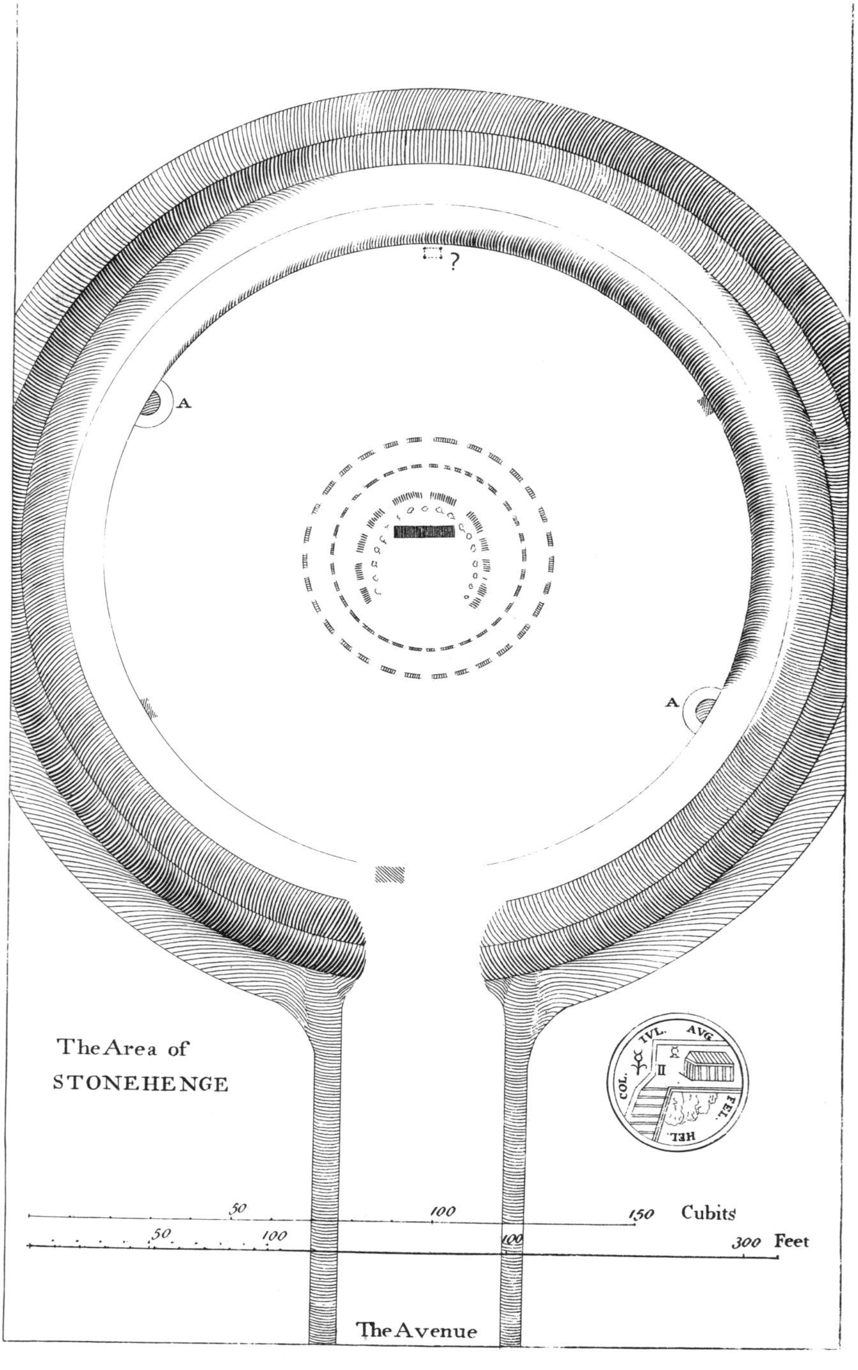

?

A

A

The Area of
STONEHENGE

50   100   150   Cubits

50   100   100   300   Feet

The Avenue

The legendizer and historian Diodorus of Sicily wrote in the first century B.C.:

The moon as viewed from this Island [Hyperborea, Britain?] appears to be but a little distance from the earth and to have on it prominences like those of the earth which are visible to the eye. They say that the god [moon?] visits the Island every 19 years. . . . There is also on the Island both a magnificent sacred precinct of Apollo (sun-god) and a notable temple [Stonehenge?] . . . and the supervisors are called Boreadae, and succession to these positions is always kept in the family.

If Diodorus did mean Stonehenge in this secondhand legend, and some authors (Lewis Gidley, John Wood) think that he did, and if the Boreadae connived to keep the numerology a secret, they succeeded. Charles II did not count aright, Inigo Jones added an extra trilithon, and the photogrammetric camera was fooled.

The new map is reproduced in the Appendix of this book and in Plate 15. It shows contours at 1-foot intervals. For the first time in the history of the monument the bumps and dips of the terrain are precisely recorded.

Previous authors gave 288 feet as the diameter of the Aubrey ring; measured from the new plan it is 285 feet. The sarsen circle diameter is 99 feet 1 inch, measured at the center of the stones, and 97 feet 4 inches at the inner face.

The slope of the ground was surprising—a casual visitor sees a flat 2 acres. A more careful look shows a slight slope downward to the heel stone, the "gentle declivity" of Henry Browne. Actually the land drops from 339 feet above mean sea level at the southwest rim to 332 feet at the beginning of the avenue. This is a drop-off of 7 feet, a slope of 1 in 55, more than 1 degree.

It caused difficulty for the Stonehengers on two counts. First, a slope in the ground means extra work in hauling the stones. Second, a tilted surface is not good for pointing to distant phenomena on the horizon.

The first problem had a practical Stone Age engineering solution: put more men on the ropes. The second problem had a choice of solutions.

FIG. 9. (left) *William Stukeley's plan, 1740, showing the suspected stone at the perimeter opposite the avenue entrance.*

Silbury Hill, comparable in volume to the second pyramid at Gizeh, testifies to neolithic earth-moving capabilities. The area within the circular Stonehenge ditch could have been leveled. The Stonehengers could have built up a wedge-shaped mesa, about 6 feet high at the entrance gap. Approximately 10,000 cubic yards of fill would be required for this, no more than three times the volume dug from the ditch. Or the chalk bank could be made higher at the northeast side so that the top of the wall made a level, wraparound rim. Or the monolithic marker stones could be made of compensating height.

The Stonehengers did not grade the area. They *may* have chosen a graded, level-topped bank, as has already been mentioned. The now badly eroded bank does drop a small 5 feet against the 7-foot fall across the site. The height of the wall could have been "adjusted" to make a flat horizon.

They did compensate in the height of the stones. This can be ascertained from the new contoured plan. The tip of the heel stone is 344.6 feet above sea level, 15.4 feet above ground level. The difference in height of the exposed section over that of a man makes up for the slope of the ground.

By choosing to level the stone tops, and not the ground, the builders avoided much earth moving. And the choice led to a spectacular sunrise marker. If the heel stone was an easy-to-place stump, Henry James could not have written about the "great flame-shaped Sun stone" standing "blackly against the light." That view through the eastward pillars and their architraves would lose its drama. The choice, the decision not to grade, intentional or otherwise, accentuated the earth-sky harmony.

Another outlying stone, 93, lines up with the skyline for a man standing at 91. The latter has now fallen over outward from the circle. It stood 9 feet high when first set up. The extra height of 91 compensated for the fall in the ground.

Continuing the hunch—that the monoliths were arranged with tops flush, or nearly so, with the horizon—the stone missing from the 6-foot hole in the mound at 92 was 16 feet 6 inches long, and stood 10 feet 6 inches above the turf when viewed from 93. The monolith in 94 was 8 feet above the ground (we cannot deduce the total length because the

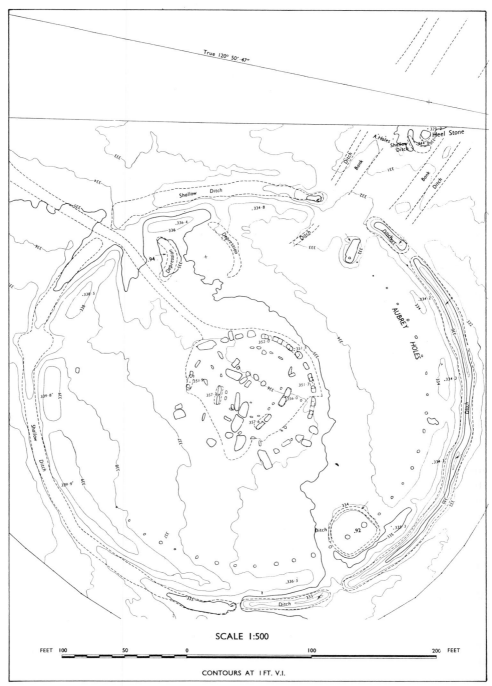

SCALE 1:500

FEET 100 50 0   100   200 FEET

CONTOURS AT I FT. V.I.

PLATE 15. *Contoured plan of Stonehenge.*

59

hole is as yet unexcavated). The moon posts in the "A" holes must have been a good 14 feet high, those in the entrance 12 feet.

These elementary Holmesian deductions are unprovable because the stones and posts are gone, but it would make sense astronomically to aim the monoliths, by vertical adjustment, level with the horizon like the sights of a gun.

Critics have split megalithic hairs over the so-called errors of alignment. For a physical scientist, when all the data is in and analyzed, an error is an error is an error. If a distant 30-ton boulder is out of line by a few feet, by one or two solar diameters (720 of which are required to fill the circumference of the horizon), then, in my opinion, it is not fruitful to speculate on the how or the why of the error. (Imagine the reaction of the rank-and-file worker if the chief architect wanted sideways adjustments after the back-breaking megaliths had been lowered into the slippery chalk holes!)

Critics claim that the errors are disproof of the astronomical theory. Stonehenge man was capable, in theory, of placing a stone, with the accuracy of the naked eye, 0.05 degrees. Because he did not, and because these errors are unexplained, the sun-moon theory must be wrong— *quod NON erat demonstrandum.*

The new map gave a chance for a second look at the errors. "Errors," not "building mistakes," for only a portion of the machine-computed discrepancies are megalithic. There is an unknown contribution from other sources—small unavoidable displacement of those stones that were reerected, such as the archway 57–58, down 1797, up again 1958; slight earth movements; tilting; the difficulty of locating below-the-turf holes; and lastly, my own unavoidable fraction-of-an-inch error in reading "XY" positions from the chart.

Atkinson commended the then Ministry of Public Building and Works for its part in the reconstruction, and rightly so. Every care was taken to seat the 40-ton oblong boulders in the old impressions in the chalk at the bottom of the holes. But no person would claim the stones to be back in place *exactly.* In the same way I took every precaution in the measurement of the chart. An error of one-hundredth of an inch (this is the limit of accuracy of the mapping) gives an uncertainty of $\pm 0.2°$ in azimuthal bearing, ± 0.1 in the vertical, for the solar and lunar orb.

Small differences compound together to give the final, machine-computed error. This is printed out as the difference between the position of the sun or moon, 1800 B.C., and the direction of pointing of the archways as given by the chart. A vertical error of +0.5° means "the lower limb of the disk of the sun was one-half a degree above the skyline at that place to where the archway pointed."

Map and map-reading errors could be avoided by photographing the sun and moon as these show through the archways. But this does not work for the missing stones with holes beneath the turf. Nor would I take my chance with British weather in observations over a 56-year cycle.

The new chart was made under National Geographic Society sponsorship with the best available air reconnaissance techniques, double-checked (for petrified tourists, etc.), and measured to the limits of accuracy. The alignments and final errors are given below.

ASTRONOMICAL ALIGNMENTS AT STONEHENGE DETERMINED PHOTOGRAMMETRICALLY

Stone	Seen from	Azimuth	Astro-object		Horizon	Error
Heel	Center	51.13	Sunrise	+23.9	0.63	+0.37
91	92	49.76	Sunrise	+23.9	0.63	−0.44
Heel	30–1	51.48	Sunrise	+23.9	0.63	+0.60
94	93	50.63	Sunrise	+23.9	0.63	+0.10
Heel	55–56	51.38	Sunrise	+23.9	0.63	+0.53
23–24	59–60	307.27	Sunset	+23.9	0.37	+1.69
92	91	299.76	Sunset	−23.9	0.53	−0.40
93	94	230.63	Sunset	−23.9	0.53	−0.94
6–7	51–52	131.77	Sunrise	−23.9	0.30	+0.79
15–16	55–56	230.19	Sunset	−23.9	0.53	−0.66
A1	Center	43.65	Moonrise	+29.1	0.60	+0.98
93	92	320.19	Moonset	+29.1	0.37	−0.85
57–58	53–54	320.75	Moonset	+29.1	0.37	−1.14
59–60	51–52	318.72	Moonset	+29.1	0.37	−0.07
94	91	319.83	Moonset	+29.1	0.37	−0.66
21–22	57–58	316.56	Moonset	+29.1	0.37	+1.12
92	93	140.19	Moonrise	−29.1	0.35	−1.41
53–54	57–58	140.75	Moonrise	−29.1	0.35	−1.13
9–10	53–54	142.01	Moonrise	−29.1	0.35	−0.50
91	94	139.83	Moonrise	−29.1	0.35	−1.60
93	91	297.29	Moonset	+18.8	0.37	+1.38
20–21	57–58	292.79	Moonset	+18.8	0.37	+4.73
93	57–58	299.35	Moonset	+18.8	0.37	−0.09
8–9	53–54	122.75	Moonrise	−18.8	0.33	+0.19

We compared the new data with the old. We found interesting changes. The new errors were smaller, the root-mean-square dropped from 1.3° in the preliminary 1963 values to 0.9°. This was as it should be: part of the error component was eliminated. We were getting closer, marginally closer, to the basic values. 91–93 showed a large error in both old and new measurements and has therefore been removed from the set. In December 1972, at a conference on the "Place of Astronomy in the Ancient World" at the Royal Society, London, I discussed this diagonal and suggested that the viewing point for 91 might have been some marker in the early central structure that has been obliterated by later building.

Not all of the alignments could be measured from the new stereo plan because the features were buried and did not show. For these alignments the preliminary* and less accurate values must suffice.

We investigated the heel stone in particular detail. We had the ground contours, height of stone top above datum, altitude of distant skyline (with and without trees), and, of more value beyond numbers, a modern sunrise picture. The mathematics is in the Appendix, but, for the second of C. P. Snow's "two cultures," the problem can be put in words: Levelness is

$$\textit{Height of stone} \quad \text{EQUALS} \quad \textit{Height of man} \text{ (toes to eyeballs)} \quad \text{PLUS} \quad \textit{drop-off in terrain.}$$

A man with eyes 5 feet 6 inches above the ground sees 8 inches of the heel stone protrude above the skyline today. This assumes no trees—the line of the base ground is visible between the isolated trees.

The sun, when in line with the heel and archway, does not stand today exactly tangent, like a cartwheel on the road. The lower edge is −0.1 below the hill.†

* See Gerald S. Hawkins, *Stonehenge Decoded* (New York: Doubleday, 1965), for the preliminary data.

† This is an on-the-spot observation. The new map reading in the table on page 61 gives +0.60° for 1800 B.C. (+0.1° for A.D. 1970)—an example of unavoidable chart measuring errors. For the particular case of heel stone and archway we rely, of course, on the actual ground-based photography of sunrise.

The approximate age estimate of the heel stone is 1800 B.C., and the sun was 0.5° higher than now because of the slight change in the angle of tilt (obliquity) of the earth's axis. This would place the lower limb of the sun 0.4° above the stone, or 20 inches higher than the tip. But if the stone was upright in 1800 B.C., then the tip was 20 inches higher, and the bottom of the disk was a scant 0.1° below; if the priest-observer stood in archwayless Stonehenge I, the stone would be displaced to the right because the center of the Aubrey ring is to the left of the center of the sarsens and the error would be +0.09°—sensibly zero; if . . .

But I do not care to push the "ifs" as far as this. The Gertrude Stein triple tautology holds good. An error contains many unknowns within its margin. Did the high priest sit on a throne to watch the sunrise? If he did, his eye level would be 15 inches lower. Or did he stand in splendid pomp on an altar stone? And how correct is 5 feet 6 inches for his toe-to-eye height; was he brachycephalic or dolichocephalic? Interesting questions—answers unknown.

Sufficient to know that the sunrise looks very much the same now as it did then. The leaning of the heel stone happens to make up for the small movement of the earth's axis in the intervening years. It is a composite vista—black architraves, heel stone, and brilliant sun's disk. When the sun crowns the stone the tip is lost in the yellow, watery glare. A small offset, if there is one, or was one, is of no consequence. "Stonehenge man stood here then, tense, expectant, waiting for a god that brought warmth and fertility and life . . . ," as Charles Collingwood said on C.B.S. News.

Sunrise is different the world over. Only in the tropics and on the road to Mandalay does the sun come up like thunder, i.e., vertically. North of latitude 66½° it doesn't come up at all on December 21; at the geographic pole it makes a slow, never-setting spiral around the sky from the spring equinox to autumn.

Stonehenge is at latitude 51.2° north; here the sun at midsummer takes off from the horizon in a low sloping path. Four minutes elapse between "first flash" and "breaking clear." During this interval the disk has moved sideways by two whole diameters. The Stonehengers had several points to mark if they chose—bright rim, disk bisected, or tangent. They chose the sun when it was tangent, fully risen. The sun moved slowly eastward, climbed as it rose until the full orb stood momentarily over the heel stone.

First flash of sunrise showed a little to the west, dead center in the avenue at the time of construction. The avenue pointed to this first moment of sunrise, accurate to minutes of arc. Stones B and C would mark this instant if they were at eye-level height when erected. These stones are, of course, now missing, toppled perhaps like the slaughter stone. That monolith is a mystery. It was tipped over deliberately, purposefully. A pit was dug ahead of time and the stone pushed in it. (The depression shows up in the contours of the map, dropping from 333 to 332 and lower.) Maybe it stood in hole E, marking an equinox moonrise as seen from 94. Maybe it stood on its northern end as an auxiliary to the heel stone as viewed from the center.

The new map gave fresh insights into Stonehenge I and II, but what of the central structure, Stonehenge proper? The builders of III treated the sloping land in a masterful fashion. The archwayed circle is 100 feet in diameter, and the ground drops off by 2 feet from southwest to northeast, a considerable problem. The stereo-contours show this, running approximately parallel with the sarsen circle fitting inside contours 337 and 335.

This may not have been the exact height of the turf at the time of construction. There are two opposing actions at work. Erosion lowers the surface as rain dissolves the chalk where it meets the subsoil. Deposition raises the surface as the spongy, grass humus thickens with the seasons. Wind-blown dust accumulates, and debris is dropped and decays. Everything from Roman coins to broken flash bulbs are found in the so-called Stonehenge layer. At the site I saw a bone fragment in a disturbed area. Human remains? A Druid sacrifice? Not so; a colleague at Harvard who looked at the specimen said no more than "meat bone!" Radiocarbon measurements put the date at A.D. 500, proving it was later debris unconnected with Stonehenge.

There is a rough indication of the original turf at the site. Some of the stones were tooled to this level and no farther, the finishing process being done when the stone was upright and in position. The new gravel surface, showing light in the aerial photographs, has been brought in to replace the grass and is within inches of the original level. The central contours are therefore as they were 38 centuries ago.

Despite the slope, the tops of the moon trilithons are identical heights above datum, 357.6. Presumably the sun trilithons were also a matching pair, though only one is standing now, measured as 356.0 at the top.

A few arches of the sarsen circle have escaped the ravages of time. Reading clockwise from the sunrise arch the heights run 351.7; 351.5; 352.0; 351.9. Actually the stones have slight irregularities on the upper surfaces, and the accuracy of the stereo-measurement was ±3 inches, so that within the margin of measurement the stones are exactly the same height above datum. The structure is level on a sloping surface.

Nearly 4,000 years after the event we take this sort of thing for granted. Engineering is left to the engineers, surveying to the surveyor.

Modern methods are time-proven, simple and direct. In building a structure, architects start with a level surface. Walls go up each the same height, and therefore the next floor is automatically level. Two up and one across—it all starts from a datum plane. Angles are measured with a theodolite; the telescope cross hairs are set to zero elevation and pointed to a man holding that long, upright, graduated stick. If the telescope height is, say, 5 feet 6 inches and the graduated stick reads the same, then the base of the theodolite and the bottom of the stick are at the same height above datum. The fundamental reference for the instrument is a tiny bubble floating in a drop of alcohol no bigger than a dime.

How did the Stonehengers build on a tilted surface? How would we do it?

Samuel Hill had a cement replica of Stonehenge III built in Washington State in honor of Klickitat County men who died in World War I. The engineers leveled the surface and erected blocks of equal height. That, of course, is the straightforward approach.

The Stone Age Wessex engineers had that capability. The 100-foot circle could have been dug lower at the southwest side and filled up at the northeast. Horizontality would be proved by the lack of flow of rainwater puddles. The sarsen blocks could be laid flat and checked off for length—tip the blocks upright, and the lintels will then be level by the principle of two up, one across. But the Stonehengers did not choose this method.

Another approach is "trial and error." Make a guess, try it for size; if too long, shorten it; if too short, start again with a new stone.

No doubt last-minute adjustments were made at the site, and on occasions the ancient British air might have been blue wode—but this was not the method chosen by the Stonehengers. Those engineers, emergent from the Stone Age, showed evidence of careful planning. Each stone was selected, shaped, dressed, and tailored to fit, making due allowance for the ground contours. It was not easy. The stones were randomly of different length. The moonrise trilithon goes into the chalk to a depth of 7 feet, whereas the matching moon-set trilithon goes down a scant 12 inches. The sarsen ring is a set of adjusted odd lengths. Somehow, by a technology unknown, the Stonehengers figured out beforehand the depth of hole required to match up (exactly, so far as the survey shows) with this collection of variables.

A builder would not tackle the problem today without steel yard tapes, plumb lines, spirit levels, telescopic sights, etc. He would need blueprints, clear and unambiguous, with plan and elevation, and subsets of drawings for each stone and hole with details thereof.

The Stonehengers had to accomplish their temple observatory without such luxuries.

Perhaps there was a Stone Age/Bronze Age equivalent for some of the above equipment. Item: steel yard tape. Professor Thom has found evidence for a standard unit of length. The "megalithic yard" is a common unit in the stone circles of England, Scotland, and Wales. Perhaps there was a standard yardstick of stout English oak or Scottish fir; perhaps it was divided into fractions for intricate work, megalithic inches. Item: plumb line. This is clearly a possibility. It was known in Egypt before Stonehenge, and word can travel as did the faïence mummy beads. Item: theodolite. A device was needed to measure the drop-off in the terrain before stone height plus hole depth was figured. Also the lintels needed to be checked for levelness after the archways were in place. The horizon could not be used as a reference because at Stonehenge it undulates. Item: spirit level, the time-honored way of defining a level surface; a liquid surface is perfectly flat when that liquid is still. Maybe the Stonehengers had the equivalent of a spirit level—a wooden channel, a hollowed log, water-filled, that bridged across the 100-foot circle.

Ingenuity solves a problem when fancy instruments fail. And there must have been a great deal of thoughtful planning and problem solving while construction was going on. The ingenious devices used in this unique project might be more surprising than Merlin's magic engines are, if by some time-machine journey that project could be viewed. Instruments of stone, wood, bone, and thread, inventions born of necessity. All that remains for present eyes is the enigmatic structure itself, hanging "as it were in the air."

We looked for new features from the air. The avenue, hardly visible on the ground, showed clearly. The silted ditch on either side was little more than 12 inches deep, but it was picked out by the photogrammetric machine. Sir Norman Lockyer and F. C. Penrose in 1901 traced the course for half a mile by placing stakes at the lowest point of the shallow trough. In summer high grass covers the evidence—James Bond agents resort to counting thistles to pick out the track. But the ground-based detective can be led astray. William Stukeley (1740) traced a fork in the avenue leading north toward Avebury, but there is only one causeway and it turns right about 600 yards from the monument, toward the village of Amesbury. Man-made structures obliterate the avenue at this point where, conjecturally, it meets the Avon.

The air survey confirmed the width and astronomical bearing of this causeway. Three dark spots showed in the air pictures, set in a row across the causeway in front of the heel stone. The grass was growing darker and more lush because of something beneath the turf. Invisible from the ground, these were three of the A holes excavated in the 1920's; the soil had not settled to its preexcavation state. The air survey gave an accurate fix on the position of these holes. The computer confirmed a moon alignment—A-1 marks the farthest extreme of the winter moonrise in its 19-year cycle. The others mark moonrise in those years before the extreme.

The eastern half of the perimeter ditch is shown to be 3 feet deeper than the western section. Contours drop from 334 to 329, a depth of 4 feet, at the northeast, but in the western sector the dip is no more than a foot. This difference results from archaeological digging and refilling.

The outer bank is contoured 6 inches high, the inner 15 inches. The ditch-bank of the avenue is less than 12 inches peak to trough.

We found a lush patch on the eastern perimeter between Aubrey holes 13 and 14. This was the position of a hole excavated in the twenties, classified as belonging to Stonehenge I or II, and labeled H. (Other refilled excavations—G, F, B, and C—did not show because the grass darkening had faded completely after 45 years of trampling feet.

Hole H had been reexcavated in the fifties and was still fresh.)

The computer confirmed a sun alignment. As seen from 93, H marked sunrise on the shortest day of the year, albeit with one of the largest errors at the site. Archaeologists differ as to whether this hole is a man-dug shallow pit or a natural depression made by tree roots and/or rain water soaking down and dissolving the chalk. Natural or unnatural, we must wait an authoritative opinion. Astronomically the evidence is toward the man-dug. The hole fits the sun-moon pattern; it was replaced by the sunrise archways 6–7, 51–52, with a reduced error ($+0°.79$). I expect to see a matching hole between 93 and 94 when the western perimeter is excavated. I expect to find evidence of markers beyond the perimeter of Stonehenge, nearer the skyline, where the added distance would facilitate the accurate setting of an alignment. In this regard, when the visitors' parking lot was extended in 1967 three large holes were found. At first the opinion was "tree holes." But at the bottom a ring of bark was found, 2 feet 6 inches in diameter—evidence of large, cut round posts. These posts, as shown in a pamphlet published by C. A. Newham, in 1972, line up precisely with the extreme northerly rising of the moon when viewed from the station stones.

Does the heel stone have a counterpart on the line from the great trilithon through Aubrey 28? It was not a requirement for Stonehenge III—the line to the winter sunset was framed by the double archways 15–16, 55–56—but an outlying stone would fit for Stonehenge I before the archways went up. Stukeley shows one in his plan (1740), and W. A. Judd claims to have found one in the late nineteenth century "still in the earth, about a foot under the surface."

We looked for telltale markings—darkening of the grass, a low mound, shading on the infrared film. There was nothing we could be certain of opposite to the heel. There were suspicious areas on the photographs, dark rings, patches, but not substantial enough for a positive identification. The southern heel stone, if it is there, must await the spade.

Vegetational marking can be misleading. The rings on the air reconnaissance of 1944 did not show twenty years later. These were "fairy rings," temporary markings, not telltale signs of buried things. Fairy rings, common in English meadows, look deceptively like the line of a circular tumulus. The fungus *Marasmius oreades* expands radially, and a large colony is the product of a century or more of growth. It changes position and does not depend on deep-soil variations.

Light parallel markings enter the site from the road to Bath and run close to the western edge of the sarsen circle. A short section was included on the final plan, labeled ''ditch'' and crossing contour 333 near the slaughter stone. History records a coach road in this position, shown on antique etchings. It is not prehistoric.

An intriguing feature was detected east of the old coach road on a line between 94 and the slaughter stone. Part of a circle, this was not superficial fungi. The ground was sunken; the darkening was caused by below-the-ground conditions.

What was it? Here the survey analysis could go no further.

The stereo-machine reported a circular ditchlike feature. The item, labeled ''depression'' and marked (+) at the center, is similar to the ceremonial ring cut around the heel stone and the station stone mounds. Could it be the outer rim of a bell-shaped tumulus? Unlikely, because the known burials at Stonehenge were laid unceremoniously in joined-up post holes. Could it be astronomical? The center of this partial ring does not fit the established sun-moon pattern.

The Daedalus eye could look no deeper. The spade or more refined methods of subsurface exploration would be needed for this and other hidden puzzles.

The air reconnaissance (''sortie'' as it was called by one ex-RAF pilot-engineer) was completed, all major objectives accomplished. The uncertainties in the previous measurements were eliminated, the exact contours of the surface determined, stone heights fixed above datum. Holes explored in archaeological digs nearly half a century earlier were relocated, and the depth of the ditches probed by stereo. A new feature, possibly a buried circular trench, was discovered and pinpointed on the chart. The new measurements, showing reduced alignment errors, would help to answer some of the criticism which was appearing in the literature sharply questioning Stone Age man as to how accurate and precise he intended to be.

I wrote up the results for the scientific journals. It was that private interval of grace that comes in all research projects, the time between the discovery and final appearance of the printed word. I mailed pre-publication copies of the chart to colleagues and continued with my other assignments—research on small lunar craters located in Mare Nubium and radio echoes from meteor particles in the upper atmosphere, lecturing on basic astronomy to the 200-student class at Boston University, committee meetings, administrative matters of the department and observatory.

Researchers sent plans of other sites with a request to "run it through the machine." The astro-archaeology program was turned to an Aztec temple, a neolithic encampment, an archway in the South Pacific, and an odd assortment of walls and foundations at Mystery Hill, New Hampshire.

A representative of the Tennessee Valley Authority wrote to me. A recreation area was in the planning stage. A lake was dammed off and as the water level rose a narrow isthmus would form with a rounded hill at the end. Could I design a Stonehenge-type monument for the site? The intention was to encourage campers to walk out at dawn to look at the sunrise, also moonrise, in the wraparound horizon. I was intrigued. Stonehenge, $51°.2$ north, required a rectangle of stones for the sun-moon lines. Farther north or south the figure becomes distorted to a pushed-over parallelogram. Only one other latitude, as far as I could determine, gave a distinctive shape, and that was $30°$, the latitude of the chosen TVA site.

I computed the shape, a neat hexagon, like a honeycomb cell. The design called for six stone uprights on a circular cleared area. The ground contour was a gentle cone, apex at the center, to give a runoff for rain water. Fifty-six Aubrey holes were called for around the perimeter, but these were not to be dug and refilled—the design called for brass plates inscribed with dates for eclipses and the moon-swing program as watched at Stonehenge.*

I waited during the interval for an opportunity to reply to the critics. I was heartened to see new ideas coming along, counterhypotheses being raised. Questions were acid, penetrating; the scholastic debate was at times heated as for testing gold in the fire. The astronomical model was able to supply answers; sometimes those answers led to a further discovery. A theory is dynamic, vital; it flourishes on the attempts to kill it.

---

* I do not know whether "Hexhenge" was completed or not. Massive trilithons at the center would be a tough engineering assignment. I do know that it reached the grading and leveling phase—by bulldozer, not bone shovel and bucket—and that concrete slabs were made to take the place of natural stone for the monoliths in the interest of trimming the budget.

5 THE CRITICS

"Damn it all, Hawkins, there must be others. Stonehenge can't be unique. It can't stand on its own. If it has this scientific basis, this astro-whatever-it-is, it has got to show up elsewhere in the culture."

The speaker was a researcher on prehistory, specialty Neolithic Europe. He spoke with authority over a sherry in the paneled common room of the University. He was right, of course.

There are no known cases in prehistory, or history for that matter, of an isolated advance, a burst of genius. Either it is the culmination of preliminary experiments that have gone before or it has its own repercussions, contemporaneously or later. Stonehenge as a ritual temple fitted in comfortably with the established ideas about European megalithic circles, though it was a cathedral among the temples, the most significant architecturally, the only one with trilithon and archwayed circle, and the ritual and liturgy were unknown.

The full answer to his challenge was yet to come, and forms the basis of a later chapter of this book. I could only respond at that time with Callanish, the so-called Scottish Stonehenge. This circle of stones set within a distorted cross on Lewis, the northernmost island of the Outer Hebrides, showed the alignments to the turning points of the sun and moon and astro-numerical properties. Callanish was just south of one of the astronomically significant latitudes, the Arctic Circle—of the moon. At the low point in the 18.61 year cycle the moon skirted along the southern horizon, as does the sun in December at the Arctic Circle, latitude 66°.5. I had figured out the data on paper, from maps and charts, and published my results. But the alignments were not as clean-cut as at Stonehenge, and Callanish by itself would not answer the broad criticism of lack of Stonehenge science elsewhere in the cultural lens.

Nor could one talk concretely of "science" at this stage. Yvonne Schwartz wrote: "One could as easily attribute to these early Britons a

71

magical understanding of the observational phenomena as a scientific one.''*

My theory was reviewed harshly: ''Tendentious, arrogant, slipshod and unconvincing,'' ''meretricious persuasion,'' ''literary gift-wrapping,'' ''Moonshine.''

A London tabloid newspaper announced with some relish: ''Stonehenge . . . is about to become the storm centre of one of the most intriguing scientific controversies for years. . . . *The barrage of criticism has already opened up.''* Clearly there was an acceptance gap.

As a scientist I welcome discourse and debate; this is the mechanism for absorbing a new idea, a possible advance, but I am humanistically sensitive to acrimony. When bitterness enters a discussion, logic exits. Fortunately the bulk of the criticism was constructive.

Before publishing the findings, I had, myself, like the devil's advocate, criticized my work. This is the self-testing process of a researcher. My first reaction, as a native-born Britisher, was ''it can't be possible; the weather was too bad.'' I was pleasantly surprised to find the devil's advocate wrong, and a better British climate in 2000 B.C. Nor did I like the size of the errors; one or two degrees was a mystifying displacement for men who bashed a mortise and tenon joint with an accuracy of inches. The fact that the lines were set generally *before* the turning point of the sun or moon puzzled me. I presumed it was due to missing a day of observation here and there. This effect would be less important for the sun than for the more quickly moving moon. Also I was surprised how I and my fellow astronomers, present and past, had missed the existence of the 56-year cycle. Perhaps it was because it was not regularly exact, jumping in steps of 9 or 10 years. But certainly, as an eclipse cycle, it was *the* cycle which kept in phase with the seasons of the year over a long period of time. (Two meteorologists were quick to spot that. They had been looking for rainfall correlation with eclipses, but they had found the classical saros cycle was not suitable; it slipped relentlessly by 11 days every 18 years, which soon gets out of phase with the seasons.)

Controversy is not new to Stonehenge, nor are satire and acrimony. The Jones-Charleton-Webb debate of the seventeenth century was vitri-

* *Science,* 148 (1965), p. 444.

FIG. 10. *Inigo Jones (1573–1652), architect general to James I and Charles I. "Brick and stone will decay, and time destroy the labors of the ablest architect; but the works of the learned will endure so long as reason and good sense shall have any being in the world." (Anonymous preface to Jones,* Stone-Heng.)

73

FIG. 11. *Walter Charleton, M.D., physician in ordinary to Charles II. "He was very eminent in his profession, and well skilled in the learned languages."* (*Anonymous preface to Jones,* Stone-Heng.)

olic. Said Walter Charleton: "Mr. Jones's Imagination had too powerful an influence over his reason, when he judged, upon such slender
evidences, that our Antiquity was anciently a Roman Temple. . . . He
[Jones] was forced to deprave the text [of Vitruvius]. . . . A course
highly disingenuous . . . scandalous . . . Shame and Discredit. . . ."
John Webb defended his late father-in-law, Inigo Jones, "from the
unworthy Calumnies of Dr. Charleton" in *A Vindication of Stone-Heng
Restored*. He attacked "this Doctor" who "writ against a man dead
. . . his Design, you see, hath been all along, solely, to perplex your
thoughts; foment Differences to disturb you, and raise doubts where
none can be justly made or found . . . shallow . . . frivolous . . .
vain. . . ." As for the ancient Danes whom Charleton had championed
as the builders of Stonehenge, their arts were, according to Webb,
"Necromancy, Sorcery, Perjury, Treachery, Cruelty and Tyranny:
their professions Adultery, rape, rapine, robbery, piracy and sacrilege;
their recreations homicide, filicide, fratricide, patricide, matricide and
regicide. . . ."

One of the barriers blocking acceptance of my findings was the in-
grained idea of a Stonehenge axis, a line about which all features of the
various structures were symmetrical. A. P. Trotter, as early as 1927,
wrote: "We may prolong the axis to the northeast, and find it hits
Copenhagen, or ten and a half miles to the southwest to the village in
which I live . . . and we may prolong controversies about it until we
fill a library." The notion of one single mathematically thin line creates
the idea of a single exact target for the structure, or at the most two, or
none at all if the "axis" is not aligned precisely to within some arbi-
trarily selected margin of error. But there is no such axis.

It is generally accepted that the line of the avenue makes an approximate central axis to Stonehenge II and III, but it is not absolutely
precise, nor does it fit Stonehenge I. The heel stone is about 6 feet to the
east of this line, and the entrance gap of Stonehenge I is 9 feet to the
west, hence the necessity of filling a section of the ditch when the avenue
was made. Nor do the centers of the various Stonehenges superpose.
The center of the Aubrey ring is a few feet displaced from the center of
the sarsen circle. These small deviations have been a source of confusion. It can be seen that to film the heel stone centrally between the
sarsen gap, 30–1, one has to place the camera lens about 12 inches to the

west of the middle of the sarsen circle so that the distant stone is centered in the slot. One axis-critic said: "Neither of the sunrise photographs cited above [plates 18, 19, *Stonehenge Decoded*] was, or could have been, taken either on the axis or from the center of the monument." Correct—but to pursue the argument is to split megalithic hairs.

Fred Wheeler summarized the situation: "Professor Hawkins' method adjourned the search for a unique axis, and used the directions defined by various pairs of stones and holes."*

The question of probability (mathematical) caused some difficulty. After a back-and-forth argument it became clear that one could not use statistical theory to calculate the probability of the set of stones pointing to the sun-moon positions by chance. As Sir Fred Hoyle, professor of astronomy and experimental philosophy, Cambridge University, remarked, it was more a question of hunches than mathematics:

Some workers have questioned whether, in an arrangement possessing so many positions, these alignments can be taken to be statistically significant. I have recently reworked all the alignments found by Hawkins. My opinion is the arrangement is not random. As Hawkins points out, some positions are especially relevant in relation to the geometrical regularities of Stonehenge, and it is these particular positions which show the main alignments.

Nor was there a need of proving a theory by probability when only one theory was up for consideration.

The question of probability (nonmathematical) was a human matter of considered opinion, credibility, acceptance. As Glyn Daniel, Professor and Fellow, St. John's College, Cambridge, said on C.B.S. TV: "It's quite possible that people who were nonliterate could have a kind of calculating machine of this kind; and so Stonehenge wasn't laid out in a haphazard way, and therefore there is a reason for those 56 points. Whether it is the reason that Professor Hawkins gives or not, we don't know; but it isn't chance."

The errors of alignment came in for more discussion. I published preliminary values for the air survey,† and final revised values.‡ The

* *New Scientist*, 31 (Aug. 4, 1966), 251.
† *Vistas in Astronomy*, Vol. 10 (New York: Pergamon, 1968), pp. 45–88. See Appendix of this book for reprint of article.
‡ *National Geographic Research Report*, 1965 Projects (Washington, D.C., 1971).

survey and measurement errors were reduced. Some authors considered them to be unacceptably large. But an error is an error—it will not go away; it has to be accepted.

The largest angular errors occurred in the trilithons, which led to the supposition that Stonehenge III was less accurate than I. Actually the alignments in terms of feet and inches are more accurate in III than I because of the compactness of the structure.

The values in the technical papers are bald, numerical, but beyond the bald figures lie the unpublished conjectures. In the mathematics there was no choice but to take the line to run between stone-hole centers, yet the observer could easily have stood to one side. The stone positions would be his base, his fixed reference, and he could note whether he had to stand x paces to the left or right. Then again, he might have been satisfied with the alignment as long as the orb was in the width of the archway slot. He built a symmetrical circle around the trilithons, and because the rising and setting points are not exactly opposite, he put up with a misfit where the moon, say, is hard over against the edge of a slot.

Sarsens 20–21, viewed through trilithon 57–58, give the worst error. The line is directed toward the midwinter moonset at declination $+19°$, but the displacement is $4°.7$ and the moon appears close up against stones 21 and 58. On reworking the slot with the new map data I noticed how the line from 57–58 to 93 was an exact fit within the accuracy of the survey. Were the trilithons used with the older station stones? Was there an intermediate stage of observation before the 30 stones were placed in position around the sarsen circle? Interestingly enough, the trilithon pairs are parallel to the long side of the rectangle, and the heel stone "works" for the sun when viewed through 55–56. And 93 is just visible, at a tight squeeze, through the two archways, 20–21, 57–58. Stone 93 marks the northern end of the slot, the exact position of the winter moon. It can be argued that this is fortuitous, made possible by irregular, natural breakage of the inner surface of the trilithon, but. . . .

Hoyle* made a bold hypothesis about the errors: they are deliberate—offsets made with a purpose, not accidental. This would tend to

* *Nature,* 211 (July, 1966), 454.

77

restore confidence in the building capabilities of the Stonehengers. He noticed how the "errors" were mostly one-way: the stone position was ahead of the turning point of the sun or moon on the horizon. By this device, the observer could determine the date of turning more accurately—if the sun passed the heel stone on June 18 (using our calendar for convenience) and was back again on June 24, then the solstice must have taken place on June 21.

Hoyle suggested the employment of four stones in the Aubrey ring computer, two moving counterclockwise for the sun and moon, and two clockwise for the nodes of the moon's orbit. The sun stone must be moved two holes every 13 days, the moon stone two holes each day with a correction every month. The four-stone method does not require 56, or any specific number of Aubrey holes, and Newham* considers this "one of the main weaknesses" of Hoyle's suggestion.

Later I speculated on the use of a single stone moved three holes each year. Robert C. Cowen, of the *Christian Science Monitor,* dubbed this the ein-stone method.

Speculation is anathema to the world of hard-fact archaeologists, but perhaps, as the editors of *Nature* said, "If the Ministry of Public Building and Works should keep the grass in order, is it not appropriate that distinguished astronomers should try to puzzle out what the placing of the stones may mean?"

The British journal *Antiquity* arranged a nondebate. Professor Hoyle commented on and extended the astronomical theory; six authorities were invited to present arguments for or against, and Jacquetta Hawkes commented on the six. As contributor No. 1, I confined myself to stating the case: Stonehenge (a) was a moon and sun observatory; (b) was a counting device for predicting horizon extremes of the moon, and for eclipses; (c) is a particular example of a widespread culture.

None of the five rejected the theory. No. 2, Richard Atkinson, wrote: "This is not to deny, of course, that they possessed a good deal of empirical knowledge of observational astronomy; for we must accept, I think, that the positions of at least the heel stone and the station stones, and indeed, the latitude of Stonehenge itself, are astronomically determined, even if we agree to differ or suspend judgment about the precise

* *Antiquity,* XLI (1967), 97.

significance of the alignments involved." No. 3, Alexander Thom, Oxford emeritus professor, wrote: ". . . I am prepared to accept that Stonehenge was a solar and lunar observatory."

The acceptance gap was closed, or closing. The lonely monument was recognized as more than a temple. It was a poem in stone, reaching from man to the revolving heavens. The full meaning, the reflection on man's evolution, of his place in the wider cosmic environment, was difficult to grasp. It bore on the stirring of civilization, on the mind and intellect of neolithic man.

Astro-archaeology set in motion a reevaluation of the builders of Stonehenge. At one pole they were classed as "howling barbarians," "practically savages," and at the other pole, geniuses. "A veritable Newton or Einstein must have been at work." Somewhere between these extremes a level of attainment was recognized comparable to that of ancient Egypt or Mesopotamia, though in quantitative, observational concern, the Stonehengers in 2000 B.C. possessed a higher intellect, a greater depth of understanding of cosmic order. But without writing or the survival of an oral tradition it is difficult to comprehend those men and their time. They were part of a delicate, nascent civilization.

As a schoolboy in England I listened to Winston Churchill's 1940 speech: ". . . if the British Empire and its Commonwealth last for a thousand years, men will say, 'This was their finest hour.' " The classroom had the usual world map on the wall with countries colored, mostly it seemed, in British red. We sat through air raids knee to chin in wartime earthen long barrows; we observed later, on clear days, the extreme azimuth of V-2 missile trails rising over the sea from occupied Holland, but for a schoolboy, the outcome of the war was confidently positive. The Empire, as described in the primary school, was all of British civilization, a permanent institution. Churchill's "if" was a classroom shock.

Looked at with historical perspective, civilizations do collapse. More have gone under than presently exist today. The Roman Empire came to a slow, painful end in the first three centuries A.D. Its decline and fall was analyzed in the seven full volumes of Edward Gibbon. The United States is a scant 200 years old; the American way of life may not yet have passed the test. Some of the scholarly reasons for the collapse of Rome are: (1) internal riots between the haves and the have-nots; (2) the high cost of political campaigns (to get elected a candidate had to mortgage his future; key voters were paid off by political appointments; public funds were diverted for bribes and nest-feathering); (3) overextended foreign commitments caused by the policy of Romanization; (4) unwilling soldiers drawn from an affluent society; (5) failure of creative leadership; (6) corruption of the Roman principles of virtue, purity, simplicity; (7) a high divorce rate.

American historian James Breasted was optimistic. He saw mankind engaged in a world conquest, spreading, upgrading civilization. It began in Egypt and went via Greece, Rome, and Europe to North America. The driving force was the unconquerable buoyancy of the human soul. "These things continue to reveal the age-long course along which the developing life of man has moved; and in following his conquest of civilization, we have been following a *rising trail*."*

This view reached an extreme in the single-track diffusion theory. Everything began in Egypt and/or the Fertile Crescent of Mesopotamia around 4000 B.C. and was carried to the corners of the globe by a light-brown heliolithic (sun and stone) race, "children of the sun." Nothing was invented twice. Nothing was thought of independently. The world owes it all—science, civilization, pyramids, poetry—to the valleys of the Nile, Tigris, and Euphrates. The natural law of progress was upward.

The other extreme is the multitrack theory, with isolated evolution. Different ethnic groups developed their culture, civilization, independently. No interaction.

Oswald Spengler, as a German schoolmaster in early retirement in Munich, shelved the question of progress. In a comprehensive study of European history he proposed organisms. A civilization is born, flourishes, and has a natural, limited-in-length life. The flourishing stage is marked by a burst of creativity, art, music, science. The end is signaled by affluence, banality, a uniform high standard of material comfort, but little else. His views shocked Europe, coming out as they did in Munich in 1918, at the moment of collapse of the old order. There is no possi-

---

* From *The Conquest of Civilization*.

bility of survival, he said; Western civilization is finished, dead as a withered flower.

Arnold Toynbee, English historian, had a similar overview. A civilization grows and progresses only as a response to outside challenges under the leadership of a creative minority. It collapses when the leadership fails to respond creatively. Toynbee, at the last writing, recognized 26 separate civilizations ranging from ancient Egypt to precommunistic China.

But what is meant by "civilization"? It is a loaded word. Samuel Johnson refused to include the word in his famous first (1772) dictionary, bluntly telling Boswell it was a limited commodity found only in a city, mainly central London. Clive Bell (*Civilization*, 1928) recognized a civilized person as the best kind of person, appealing to one's sense of propriety and good taste. The emperor of China dismissed the gift-bearing envoy of King George III, saying that in his civilized country there was no need of the importation of barbarian goods.

It is a humbling experience to recognize something outside one's own culture as civilized. Outside one's own neighborhood (Johnson), personality (Bell), or national boundary. We have to go beyond these barriers when talking of Stonehenge.

Civilization is intertwined with technology. Gordon Childe looks to the invention of writing as a necessary, civilizing step; Sven Nilsson expects to find coined money; Leslie White the harnessing of energy; Jacquetta Hawkes wine and barley beer; and Breasted requires agriculture and seagoing vessels. Without these attributes the various authors would classify a culture as uncivilized.

But civilizations cannot be pinned down to this or that requirement. Exceptions are the rule. Claude Lévi-Strauss isolatedly defines culture to begin when incest is legally and socially prohibited. Lévi-Strauss's definition puts Abraham's tribe in a compromising position, and eliminates the sister-marrying pharaohs of ancient Egypt and the Inca emperors of Peru.

Most authors agree on farming as a civilization prerequisite. We know that agriculture is not very visible through the Saran Wrap of the supermarket, but it is a main prop of American culture. Food growing sets up the economic base which gives the first essentials in a community's standard of living. Sociopolitical leaders were quick to recognize it as a readily taxable part of the gross national product. The earliest arithmetic was developed for the calculating of the percentage, 10, 20, and sometimes more than 50 percent, for the priests, an excess which was tapped off to support Toynbee's creative minority—which leads to another rule-of-thumb definition: No civilization without taxation!

But man for most of his existence has lived in a hunting ecology. With a small population to support, and with intelligent following of game herds, the hunting bands were not short of food. The culture had adequate food standards and, what's more, plenty of leisure time back at the base. It was a two- or three-day hunting work week. The early mound builders in central and eastern United States were a hunting culture. They showed a level of group organization which must surely pass under the heading of civilization. This, without agriculture.

A written language is another generally agreed prerequisite. H. G. Wells, author of 97 books and plays, stressed the need of the written word; before it was invented, communities in the Old World were "quasi-civilized." Because of the difficulties of the enigmatic Mayan script, and the secret knotted cords of the Inca, Wells put the New World squarely in the category of "primitive civilizations." Because we do it (and I myself am conscious of using the pen at this moment), we expect it of a civilization. Writing is a mind link. We cannot imagine communication of thoughts and ideas, preservation of laws and history, without it. Yet personal letters are giving way to the mailed tape cassette, and it is easier to telephone than to write.

Nonliterate cultures exist today, and have existed in the past. Anthropologists find a wealth of legend, social law, and conceptual thinking in present-day undisturbed tribes. A portion of our own Western heritage was passed across the preliterate gap when ballads, wise sayings, and ancient knowledge were set down at the time of the invention of writing. Greek philosophers regarded the written word as a vulgar exposure of the truth—better to keep it in the heart and mind.

The essential part of a civilization is perishable. It is finer than dust. Culture itself is fragile, easily destroyed, and this, our age, is the most destructive of periods. We find it hard to imagine a stable society. Our generation feeds on change. An archaeologist digging in the Les Eyzies caves of France was amazed at the uniformity. Layer after layer contained the same artifacts. Hundreds of generations of people lived, loved, and died in the manner of their forefathers. Yet that life pattern was precarious. It collapsed with some slight disturbance to the balance of the ecology.

I have seen a cultural pattern blown to the winds in a matter of years. The most marvelous climate of Spain is in a coastal strip at the foot of mountains west of Malaga. Before the airport, before the jets, it was difficult to reach this *costa del sol,* coast of the sun. The village I knew was secluded, a few rows of white cottages on the beach, near the boats which gave the food. The climate was taken for what it was—sunny, warm, no frost, one or two storms from the sea in the winter, and maybe a two-week rainy period. Bad weather was the exception. Fishing was regular and reliable as boats were pushed into the Mediterranean each evening. Fish could be traded for other produce, vegetables, cloth, wine. The storm was the worst trial of the year—one man slept away the bad days with heavy red wine; another wept at the sight of his beach-bound boat. It was a stable culture, not unhappy, rich in a heritage only dimly recognized. We knew the villagers and something of the customs. The singing, ubiquitous then, was a mixture of Moorish and Spanish, going back by hazy oral tradition to before the time when the last Arabs left. One song was sung as a Christian Christmas carol, with tambourine accompaniment and a strange, booming instrument made by stretching a drumskin over a hollowed palm tree stump, and played by stroking a wet bamboo stick attached to the drumhead. The words were now, after generations of transmission, difficult to interpret: "Oh, see how the fishes in the river drink./Drink and drink and return again to drink./ The fishes in the river, to see a god be born. . . ."

"Where is the river?" I said to a singer.

"A long way from here. Where the water is fresh. At Fuengirola."

That river was only 1½ kilometers from where we stood, so I did not ask the next question: "Which god?"

On a fiesta evening, as many as could squeezed into the best room of the cottage for singing and dancing. Children, beyond their bedtime, sat in night clothes high on the furniture to enjoy the entertainment.

There were local customs that would not appeal to women's lib. It was half-matriarchal, half-patriarchal, in organization. One woman confessed that she would like to wear a short skirt, or, pointing to my wife, *esta,* these shorts, but the village would burst into outrage, "it" would talk, her family would be shamed. On a very, very hot day, the grand-mothers bathed in the sea. This they did clothed, in their long black dresses and undergarments. It happened no more than once or twice a year. It was another festive occasion.

This was a miniculture with no leadership creatively to respond to an external Toynbee-type challenge. The jets came in with peseta, dollar, and pound sterling. There was a building boom; the village was trans-formed in two or three years. The vanguard of change was a motor scooter. The fisherman who lived opposite to our sabbatical-leave home explained to his friends how this machine took him many kilometers, much faster than a donkey, to a place where he was learning the build-ing trade. Much money. He sat on the quartz-cobbled lane while his wife cleaned the machine, and it was wheeled into its nighttime place of glory, the Granada-tiled best room. Then followed an explosive chain of scooters and more scooters, radio sets, TV, pressure of commercials, abandoned boats, a maritime promenade, and then demolition of the cottages to make a sea front of skyscraper hotels, and the newly trained builders and their families were relocated at the back of the town.

Not that this was bad. It was taken as progress. The population enjoyed an advance in material standards, a forward step circum-scribed marginally by the steep inflation that followed. Progress. But it does illustrate the fragile nature of a cultural pattern. Something was lost.

I am not a sociologist, but I have at times speculated on the preserva-tion of a culture, how it could be done, whether it is remotely feasible. Could "National Parks, Culture" be set up? Territorial areas set aside, protected, where visitors come to look at and appreciate the way of life within, as they look at the natural beauty of, say, Yosemite. Not the nineteenth-century Indian reservations. These were ghettos, too small and meager in resources to support the traditional culture, and created with a legacy of bitterness between settler and Indian. Not the Plym-outh Plantation or Williamsburg townships. These are excellently con-ceived and administered, but the recreation of the culture is done by playacting, not living. There is an element of serenity, contentment, and happiness in a culture before the impact of exposure takes place. People within it might be better off humanistically if the pattern was not disrupted. The Amish and Pennsylvania Dutch have preserved their cultural pattern despite material pressures. They have a cohesive core of religious and social values. To them the culture beyond their boundaries is a strange phenomenon. I recall stopping to speak with an Amish woman. She wore a long gray dress, work-flattened shoes, and a white cap. She walked through the August cornfield, pulled, and gave my wife a basket of white-tasseled cobs. When we offered to pay we were told: "God has indeed been bountiful to us this year's harvest, and it is only meet that we share his goodness."

Humanists try to untangle the technology from the civilization, the hardware from the software. Materially speaking, mankind appears less primitive with each stride into the future. We see progress from hand to hoe, horse plow to tractor; there is progress in the strict technicological sense in that museum-showcase set of artifacts which runs hand ax, spear, arrow, bullet, shell, bomb, nuclear missile. But what about the set of nonartifacts listed by James Robinson of Columbia University: religion, language, beliefs, morals, arts, manifestations of the human mind and reason? These also are measures of the man.

The cave paintings done when the European climate was as cold as Greenland are recognized as equal to the best art man can create. The work of Henry Moore, modern British sculptor, is derivative from Stone Age art. He acknowledges inspiration from one item 20,000 years old, "a lovely, tender carving of a girl's head no bigger than one's thumbnail." Picasso with his face-shaped vases echoes the lost art of Peru and Central America. Nonliterate Homer is still rated among the world's best poets.

I have looked at cave paintings firsthand. It was in the cave of La Pileta, "little holy font," near Ronda, the town perched on a precipice and used as a backdrop for Hemingway's stories of the Spanish Civil War. The cave was deep, several hundred yards into the limestone rock, and then a hundred feet down. The famous Abbé Breuil explored this cave alone with lantern and Tom Sawyer thread. Legendary Theseus went into the labyrinth of Knossos to kill the dread bull-monster of King Minos. He unrolled a ball of wool to help him find his way out. Beautiful Ariadne held the other end.

"These paintings are freshly done," I said to the man who had climbed up from the farm in the valley with his small white dog and rusty key to unlock the small iron-barred door. The black charcoal and

FIG. 12. *A mammoth drawn from life, cave Peche-Merle, France.*

red pigments stood crumbly on the wall as if pressed on recently with a stick. He was taken aback by my skepticism, but I was not the first to doubt the authenticity. Could a crayoned line, a handprint on the wall, stay fresh for 20,000 years? Here was instant contact with an artist who mused and worked beyond the ken of our own civilization. The first discovery of cave paintings was made 400 miles north of where I stood, at Altamira. The cave was laid bare when a dog chased a fox into the bush-covered opening. An amateur digger, Marcelino de Sautuola, was working in the black deposit at the entrance later, on a summer's day in 1879. His twelve-year-old daughter played in the cool shadows. Suddenly she ran out and pulled Don Marcelino into the soft-lighted rocky arch. "Bulls, papa, look at the bulls!" There they were on the ceiling, vivid colors, vibrant, living. But they were not bullring bulls; they were bison, extinct in western Europe for centuries. Archaeologists refused to believe. Paleolithic man, from the Old Stone Age, was not capable of this work. Specialists visited; the king of Spain visited; Sautuola stuck to his theory. Fantastic! Unbelievable! Forgeries! Sixteen years later more paintings were discovered at La Mouthe, in the French Dordogne. This entrance was sealed over by centuries of debris. A second cave. Once was ignorable; twice was a shock. The skeptics again examined the artwork and compared. A delegation of the Congress of the French Association of the Advancement of the Sciences arbitrated in the debate. The art was authenticated as Paleolithic. The acceptance gap was closed.

The artwork falls into periods and styles and can be classified by art historians in much the same way as museum oil paintings. There is an aesthetic unity spanning geography and time, with two broad schools, the realistic and the abstract. Cave painting is distinct, creative, and like the style, say, of the Impressionists or Dutch Masters, can be copied, imitated, but cannot be improved upon. The abstract patterns might well be used for modern textiles or murals. In the pictures there are mythical beasts—reindeer with webbed feet, bears with the head of a wolf, and masked sorcerers, spirit-men. The artists here were painting images from the mind, beyond the limit of reality. Cave art flourished in France, Spain, and Switzerland for thousands of years, a sustained, soulful outpouring of Cro-Magnon man. Suddenly, measured by the hands of the geo-homo clock, the artwork stopped. It was followed by degenerate ocher coloring of pebbles. Nothing more. Why did they do it? If this was truly creative, pure aesthetic pleasure, then man had made a hallmark of the higher intellect. It was inspired, a climax equaled but not surpassed by later generations, a clear signal of culture and civilization, the appreciation of art for art's sake. One school of thought supports this interpretation. Or must we look for a practical, utilitarian basis? Another school calls it "Quaternary magic," the quaternary being the last geological period, 600,000 years ago to the present. Some of the art is representative of the hunt and the breeding of animals. Bison are shown with spears and arrows; a clay-modeled bear was pierced with (spear?) holes. The model, and the attack on the model, gave magic power over the animal. In our civilization some people secretly wonder, when things go wrong, whether someone, somewhere, has a little model of them and is sticking pins in it! Another theory has the art inspired by a great but long-forgotten religion, Byzantine art being an analogy. I noticed in La Pileta that some of the painting was not placed for general viewing. There were abstracts and animal scenes in the large grottoes, but the masterpiece of the cave, an outline of a horse "in foal," was drawn on a smooth, curved wall in a crawl space to the side of the main passage. This can be interpreted either way. It could be the ultimate in "art for art's sake," like the sculptor I met in Gibraltar who filled his room with delicate busts and abstracts, yet never showed them. Or it could have been magic, deep and powerful, perpetrated in a secret niche.

I saw abstract designs that appealed to me as a scientist: short check marks in groups of five, six, or higher numbers. The group was connected across the top with another line, or crossed through in the modern manner of checking off things in groups of five. Were they counting something? There were serpentine rows of dots, red and black, then "stars" and "sun with rays." Were the marks calendric, astronomical? If the master artist possessed a mastery of numbers, that would be another shock. It would mean intellect beyond the minimal demands of hunting. A number is a crisp, factual indicator of higher thinking. These number marks are discussed in a later chapter.

For Stonehenge the key question was the intellect, or lack of it, of the builders—in essence, their creativity. Jacquetta Hawkes saw no comparison between the observatory-computer on the plain and the crude huts of Neolithic England. There were no signs of the appreciation of the arts in the dwellings, nothing comparable to the cave paintings or carved bone figurines. But Stonehenge in itself is an artistic creation, a supreme step in architecture. Like the Maya and ancient Egyptians, these people concentrated their artistry at the temple site, not in the ordinary dwellings.

The Stonehengers showed what Cambridge University's Grahame Clark called self-awareness. There was a compelling need to build from technical poverty a structure immense, beyond their material requirements.

For man to be cultured, civilized, he must be aware of time and its relentless flow. Then the past becomes a heritage to be transmitted in myth, legend, and saga; the present comes in focus as the living environment; the future is the great, unavoidable, hopefully controllable unknown. Awareness created anxiety, a need for knowledge, empirical, philosophical. None of this awareness shows artifactually in the soil, but it must have been well developed. For Clark, "It is open to discussion whether prehistoric man was an individual less ignorant than modern man, since advances in knowledge have been achieved by specialization, that is on narrow fronts." We know more and more about less and less. No single brain can now integrate the vast complexity. Between the specialties we have opened up perplexing fields of ignorance. Physicists still debate the fundamental nature of time: does it flow at a constant rate, is it reversible?

I was reading a magazine in a plane, a science fiction story. A man invented a backward-looking TV camera. It pointed along the negative time axis. His first stop in the past was 2000 B.C., Salisbury Plain. He watched the discussion, planning, construction. His TV time-probe unavoidably gave out an intense laser-beam flash. At each flash the group of priests turned, pointed, and figured the direction. Time was reversible at least in the mind of a science fictionist.

The jet, a VC 10, was London-bound. A British TV network had arranged a debate between various authorities on the subject matter of this chapter. Experts on archaeology, prehistory, anthropology. Critics, pro and con. Generalized and specialized arguments. Because of other commitments and pressure of research it was for me a fly-there-Saturday-fly-back-Sunday trip.

The producer was satisfied with the program. It had been recorded on video tape and was safely in the can, ready for its scheduled time slot sometime in the future. He went back over the details of the program and filled in a few gaps in the word picture. We were in the International Department Lounge at Heathrow Airport.

"I think this story is fascinating. It's beginning to fill in. Stonehenge . . . Callanish . . . those stone rows in France."

"Yes," I said, "it's a divergent subject, getting very complex, deep, interdisciplinary. We need more of this cooperation between the sciences. It was good to get the different views together.''

"Have you been to Peru?''

"No,'' I said.

"The desert markings there—very intriguing you know . . . old, nobody knows how old. Quite a mystery. Made by the Inca, or even earlier. Pre-Columbian culture, certainly.''

"I know they are called the Ancient Calendar of the Desert,'' I said, "and the pattern might be scientific, connected with the Maya. A lost civilization. It would be quite a task to measure all the hundreds of lines and calculate their pointing.''

"Someone has to look into it,'' said the producer.

"Whoever does will have to be thorough. Photographs from the air, maybe. Use ground-based survey marks. Do some archaeological probing, trace the clues. Those high deserts are risky. It would mean a full expedition—pack mules, Indian guides. International cooperation. . . .''

The Boston flight call interrupted my thinking-out-loud. The North Atlantic was a 3,250-mile journey. Dry, dusty Nasca was a seemingly impossible 3,700 miles farther to the south.

6   DESERT MYSTERY

An American in Lima has the dilemma of whether to stay at the Hotel Crillon or Bolivar. There is no Inca Hilton.

Lima's plazas, streets, and cathedral cornerstone were staked out in one day, January 18, 1535, by Francisco Pizarro, conqueror of Peru. He chose a barren spot below San Cristobal for his "City of the Kings." Streetcars now follow the line of Pizarro's stakes along the streets where overhanging Spanish colonial balconies jut out over the palm trees. The prison of the Inquisition is now the senate chamber.

Lima has an example of how legends can start. There was an Inca suspension bridge, famous in history, strung across a gorge of the river Apurímac, high in the Andes. Geographically the Apurímac River changes to the Ene, and then the Tambo River, before it reaches the coast. The bridge was allegedly built by emperor Inca Roca about A.D. 1350 on the Royal Road from Cuzco to the northern territories (not to Lima, as some chroniclers say, because Lima was not then founded). Inca roads were to foot and mule what Roman roads were to wheel and chariot—supply lines and communication arteries through the great empire, conquest spurs. The Peruvian engineering was superb. The suspension bridge was held by ropes as thick as a man's body. The cables were lashed around wooden beams at a tower on one side of the chasm, and fixed to the natural cliff on the other. The cables were renewed every two years, and permanent custodians, troll-like in the tower, maintained and guarded the bridge. It was safe, emperor-guaranteed, and approached through a long tunnel in the rock. The bridge was as enigmatic as it was spectacular. Thousands went over it—soldiers, priests, pack mules loaded with silver, book-writing chroniclers. Cieza de León estimated its length as 250 feet; Garcilaso de la Vega, 600; Sir Clements Markham estimated 90 feet and a height of 300 feet above the gorge, Lieutenant Lardner Gibbon of the U.S. Army said 324 precisely. The indisputable word of a measuring tape showed it to

91

be 148 feet long and 118 feet above the river. Such are the difficulties of eyeball estimates.

Thornton Wilder's classic *The Bridge of San Luis Rey* describes an osier suspension bridge with a ladder of thin slats swung across a deep gorge, and handrails of dried vines. It was the finest bridge in all Peru, and "visitors to the city of Lima were always led out to see it." When it broke, "on Friday noon, July the twentieth, 1714," five sprawling figures fell to their death. They were Doña María, the Marquesa de Montemayor, "the admiration of her city and a rising sun in the west," her orphan maid Pepita, Don Esteban, Uncle Pio, and a small boy, Jaime, the illegitimate son of Lima actress Camila, the Perichole. Brother Juniper saw the disaster just as he came around the shoulder of the hill at the brink of the gorge. A flitting thought passed through his mind: "Either we live by accident and die by accident, or we live by plan and die by plan."

The Missouri-born explorer Victor von Hagen, sponsored by the American Geographical Society, retraced the royal Inca road, the Highways of the Sun, and stood at a yawning, fearful gap, reached by a 250-foot, rock-hewn tunnel. Side windows had been punctured through the rock for ventilation. Here was the platform where the bridge had once hung. Here the noon wind rushed through the gorge and the osiers writhed violently like a snake; here the twanging noise filled the air and the gesticulating ants died. A long shadow falling across the vertical cliff gave the illusion of a hanging bridge in the emptiness. Von Hagen was sure that this was the location of the bridge of San Luis Rey. He wrote from nearby Estrella Hacienda and challenged the author. Wilder replied: "It is best, von Hagen, that I make no comment or point of it. . . ."

If von Hagen was right, then Wilder was using the freedom of literary license. The rope of the Apurímac bridge rotted through sometime after 1890, the bridge fell more than a century after 1714, and July 20 in that year (for new-style-calendar Catholic Limans) was a Wednesday, not a Friday as Wilder stated. When the curving, slatted pathway fell into the abyss nobody was killed; nobody was on the bridge.

Wilder, in his 1927 story, created an instant legend. Limans "identify'' the bridge as the one over the dry riverbed a few hundred yards northwest of the President's Palace in the Plaza des Armas. It is called Puente de Piedra, Bridge of Stone. Perichole's château is identified as a colonial structure, pleasantly situated in a secluded garden, three bus stops from the bridge. Doña Camila, the Perichole, reformed and became a nun. Brother Juniper was tortured by the Inquisition and burned at the stake for his heretical idea, that we live, Q.E.D., either by godly plan or by nature's caprice. Wilder, through the fictional mind of Brother Juniper, injected into the Western world a new thought, a startling thing to do to a civilization.

For me the choice of hotel was decided by a free-lance photographer-explorer, Tony Morrison. As a film director specializing in the South American tropics he was well known for his wildlife studies in the virgin forest of Manu, east of Cuzco. I was to meet him at the Hotel Bolivar, at the bar.

Tony was gaunt, a well-traveled figure in a blue-gray suit, neat striped tie, with blue eyes, a dried face, and hair the color of Peruvian sand. As he drank his *grande* beer, local brew, he seemed out of place with the high scrolled ceilings, the overhead fans, the Granada-like colonial tile—he was more suited to khaki shorts and open-neck shirt. Tony had crisscrossed South America by jeep from Yucatan to Tierra del Fuego. He knew the Peruvian deserts firsthand.

We moved to the lounge to have table-room for aerial photographs and maps. The pictures were large, glossy, and printed with contrast. The ground showed black with white markings—rectangles, wedges, long faint lines and black spots placed geometrically.

''How long are the lines?'' I asked.

''Five miles or more.''

''And the rectangle?''

''Eight hundred yards by seventy.''

''What are these black spots?''

''Piles of stones neatly stacked. Look, here is a pile at the end of the rectangle. On the ground it's a mound of boulders 30 yards across and 3 feet high. Lines radiate from it.'' Tony pointed to the features shown in

93

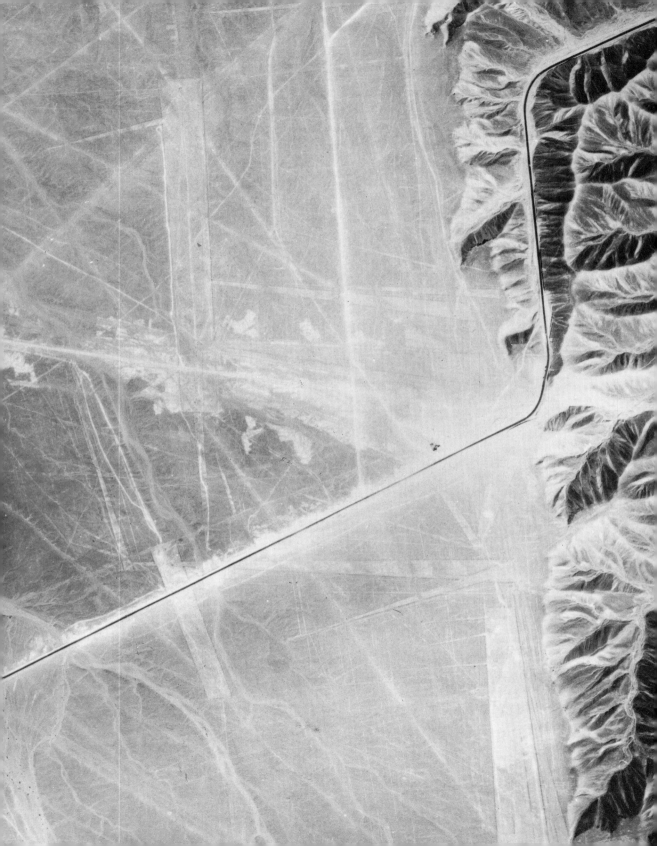

PLATE 16. (left) *High-altitude air photo of Peruvian desert markings, Pampa Jumana-Colorada, near Ingenio Valley. The large rectangle is 800 meters in length. The dark line is the modern Pan American Highway.*

PLATE 17. (above) *A complex of ancient lines and figures, and a modern car track, Nascan desert.*

95

Plate 17. "In some places the mounds are set out in rows, like a network or some type of grid."

The photographs were intriguing. Much labor had been needed to carve out those patterns in the endless desert. Tony likened the geometrical shapes to the runways of Kennedy airport. But, of course, the features are old, prehistoric, and placed vaguely in time by various archaeological authorities at 1,000, 2,000, or maybe 3,000 years ago.

A Western mind asks, "What is the purpose of these lines?" the puritan ethic regarding labor as semiholy, virtuous, and above all, purposeful. Since the discovery of the lines in the years immediately prior to World War II, one theory has been suggested and reinforced by repetition. The lines are an astronomical calendar. The direction of each line points perhaps to a star, or to the sun or moon. Standing on the desert and looking along a line at the time of construction, a person saw star "X" rising at the end of the line. Or the sun or moon; or a group of stars; or some other celestial object.

In the end chapter "Books That Cannot Yet Be Written," in *Gods, Graves and Scholars,* C. W. Ceram wrote excitedly: "Professor Kosok now claims that he has found the world's largest astronomical atlas. . . . He even believes that some of the lines define the movement of the stars. If he is right, we have gained a new insight into the cultural accomplishments of the old Andean peoples, after already having been filled with wonder by the Inca state system, destroyed by Pizarro as Cortes destroyed Mexico."

Stonehenge functioned as a calendar, not so much for counting days, but seasonally as the sun returned to its appointed place among the stones. Lines on the desert might, as Kosok suggests, point to midsummer and midwinter sunrise, marking the seasons of the year.

Geographically, Peru falls short of the equator by a scant 10 miles, and the changes in the seasons are not severe. But there are noticeable differences between winter and summer, particularly south. Nasca, the nearest center of ancient culture to the lines, is at latitude 15 degrees. There would be some utilitarian value (purpose?) there to marking the solstices. The lines, on investigation, might point to the sun.

A star rises in the same place on the horizon each day of the year. If a line points to Sirius, the "dog star" attendant of Orion the hunter, then

Sirius will be there tomorrow, and tomorrow, and tomorrow. It will rise four minutes earlier on each occasion as the star inches forward behind the sun.

This star-sun motion is a relative one. It is caused by the yearly orbit of the earth around the sun. The stars provide a backdrop. We can imagine the sun to move one degree to the left each day, or the stars one degree to the right. Either way it is no more than seeming appearance—the ocular proof, as Othello learned, deceives. It is the earth which is the true mover, with its cyclic track through space, compounded from the orbital motion around the sun and the passage of the sun through space.

It is possible to use stars for a seasonal calendar if the time of rising (or setting) is noted. Time, not measured by a uniform-rate wall clock, but time fixed by a natural, time-factored event. One of these nature-given times is the synchronization of the rising of a star with sunrise, the so-called heliacal rising. The Egyptians through many dynasties watched for the heliacal rising of Sirius, that first dawn in the year when the dog star hung in the golden glow, moments before sunrise. This was a calendar event, occurring close to Midsummer's Day.

The Nasca lines might, on investigation, point to the stars. Precession would have to be taken into account in the calculation.* The slow, conical motion of the earth's axis would shift a star from a line after one generation.

The town on maps and sign posts is spelled with an *s,* but earlier authorities give the option of a *z.* Since Peruvian Spanish is closer to Andalusian than Castilian, Nasca and Nazca sound very much alike. Some archaeologists draw a distinction and call the ancient culture of that valley, before Pizarro, Nazcan. In this book I have adapted the modern spelling for the town, river, and the ancient culture.

According to the writings of missionary-chroniclers who arrived on the heels of Pizarro, the Inca sun-god replaced a moon-god of earlier civilizations. Some Peruvian Indians at the time of Pizarro still claimed the moon-god to be more powerful. Logical reasons were cited:

* The sun and moon are not affected by precession as long as the angle of tilt remains constant. There is a small change (nutation), but the extreme position of the sun would not change noticeably in the lifetime of an observer. For example, Stonehenge still functions today after nearly 4,000 years.

97

the moon could be seen in the daytime as well as at night; the moon had the power to change its shape; the moon had the power to eclipse the sun, but the sun could not eclipse the moon. And so, with this pre-Inca interest, the lines might point to the moon.

Whether sun, moon, or star, observation along the lines would serve practically as an astronomical calendar, would signal religious feasts, crop planting, and harvesting, and would fix that critical period of the year when the rains fell deep in the Andes to make the normally parched riverbeds flow with life-giving water. A calendar in the desert— that was the suggestion, that was the hypothesis to be tested. We needed measurements, an air survey, and the computer time-machine.

We continued talking as we moved into the dining room. Tony was described to me as having a deep sensitivity toward South America and the ancient cultures of that continent. Confirmed. His stories were fascinating; his recommendations of menu delicacies and wine were good. We got up from the dinner table and walked over to the spread of buffet desserts set out in silver dishes (post-Inca) in the center of the floral red-carpeted room. In my mind's eye he changed from shot silk to travel-worn khaki. The dust swirled yellow at his boots. The table was a mound of black and red stones, the overhead lights were blazing suns. It was his assignment to take footage of the expedition. This, in color but without sound, was to be edited and produced for British TV viewers. My assignment, quite separate from his, was to collect data and examine the calendar, star-alignment hypothesis. I was to cover the *astro* in the astro-archaeology.

A team was at the desert site making preliminary measurements— astronomers, surveyors, and geologists, their work and the expedition being sponsored by the National Geographic Society.

I went to the air-survey department of the Peruvian Air Force, Servicio Aerofotografico National. The liaison was through the Peruvian Geophysical Institute. At S.A.N. headquarters, on the edge of a pleasant residential suburb of Lima, the officers were fascinated to be using their modern equipment on a puzzle of antiquity. They had just received the latest Mirage fighter from France, *La Prensa,* and they described it with glowing pride, but the survey would be made with the normal slower plane. A standard photogrammetric program—two clicks, stereo-projection in the machine, and then the accurate map.

We looked over a preliminary survey of the Nasca area at Pampa Colorada where the lines are located. A civilian operator put two films in the machine and handed me the stereo goggles, red and green. The ground showed in sharp relief. Pampa Colorada was a flat mesa at the foothills of the Andes, cut through at the north by the Ingenio river valley. The Pan American Highway ran across the pampa and twisted down a gully into the valley which showed deep under the exaggeration of the stereo. The mountains were craggy, barren, and devoid of life.

We drove south out of Lima down the Pan American Highway. At first it was posted "Autopista"—auto racetrack—but after about 50 kilometers the broad, modern, eight-lane freeway degenerated by stages into a two-way bumpy macadam strip. The road changed, but the traffic speed was the same—fast!

The highway, running the length of South America, is what the Nile is to Egypt, or the Santa Fe is to the West. It links the towns and villages in that strip between the Andes and the Pacific, bringing commerce and communication. The route today follows in many places the old empire-controlling roadway of the Incas. But the highway, unlike the Nile, does not bring to the villages what Peru needs most: water.

Without rain the hills and plains are in moonscape nakedness, a geologist's delight. A ridge of red sandstone shows mile after mile for exactly what it is. Limestone is stark white; basalt is dark gray. Nothing grows on the rock. The impression is of changelessness. Actually wind and sun erosion are at work. Slowly, relentlessly, the rock is cracked, ground down. Sand and dust blow across the landscape, making dry dunes and Sahara-colored deserts. Water, no more than two inches of monthly rain, would bring this land to life. If the highway brought water, not dusty traffic, the desert strip would be lush.

Seasonal riverbeds cross the highway at intervals. These valleys are the centers of distinct, ancient cultures—Ica (not to be confused with Inca) and Nasca. At a very early date in Peruvian prehistory, irrigation networks were made to nurse and spread the mountain water. Population growth has overloaded the system. Villages below now squabble with those above. Nothing reaches the sea, and the salt ocean laps at the dry river mouth. Between the rivers there is a parched plateau where a cactus starting from a random seed can perish in the drought.

99

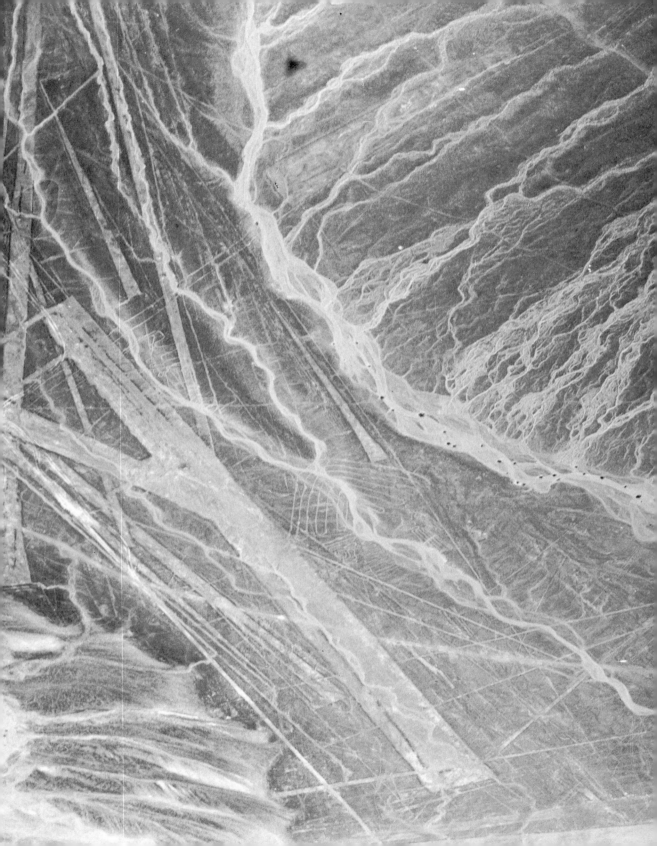

PLATE 18. (left) *Desert markings on the mesa above the Ingenio Valley.*

PLATE 19. (above) *Lines and triangles in the desert near Nasca.*

101

Maria Reiche, a German mathematician-geographer, spent twenty years studying the line complex near Nasca. Her conclusions favored the astronomical calendar idea. She reported, like Paul Kosok, the Long Island University discoverer before her, a number of lines pointing to the summer and winter sun. The Pleiades, known to the Aztecs and probably the early Peruvian Indians, show like a cluster of jewels in the autumn sky. Classical writers knew this star group as the Seven Sisters, one being Merope, daughter of the king of Chios. Dr. Reiche computed the direction and sky declination of the largest desert feature, the rectangle (Plate 16). It pointed to the Pleiades between A.D. 500 and 700.

Maria Reiche in her first pamphlet publication gave instructions for finding the lines by reference to kilometer posts along the then dirt-surfaced Pan American Highway. The first astronomer in the expedition to go to the area counted off the posts. He was baffled. The Reiche number fell in the town square of Nasca. Since Reiche's report the highway had been improved, adjusted, shortened. This is a continuous process. The kilometer posts keep pace with progress, moving up the shrinking roadway. The astronomer doubled back on his tracks and found the lines in their ancient positions.

No one, except Professor Kosok, noticed the lines from the ground. Spanish colonials went along the old Inca track; Pizarro and the eagle-eyed reporting missionaries passed through with no mention. A Harvard student majoring in medieval Spanish read the chronicles in the original to check this. Soldier Francisco Hernández was stationed in Nasca for a month, yet his diary, usually oriented toward terrain and natural history, makes no mention of the markings. Trucks, cars, and buses speed oblivious along the modern road. Occasionally a tourist asks the whereabouts of the lines in Nasca after having passed through them.

This is understandable. We pulled the eight-geared four-wheel-drive Land Rover off the highway. We drove over hard-packed clayey sand, across shallow washways, past a leafless sagebush to a spot no different from the rest of the desert. And we parked. This was it: Pampa Jumana-Colorada. A bare pampa, a shimmering pampa without a blade of grass. The dust from the stopped vehicle moved forward in the hot air toward the faraway violet-black mountains.

"Where's the rectangle?" I said, referring to that most obvious feature in the air photos. It was several moments before I realized I was standing in it. Because of the flatness of the area, because of the sameness, a feature 800 yards long could not be seen. Yet it was there, drawn out on the desert blackboard by the unknown hands of a lost civilization centuries before.

We walked past a mound, a low tumulus of blackened stones. The other one, 800 yards away, was too distant to see. We walked toward the edge of the feature, a sharp, clear, black line in the photograph. It was a low, long bank of piled stones. Within the rectangle, the seemingly white area, the surface stones had been removed, exposing the sandy clay. Beyond, stones covered the undisturbed surface which stretched out to meet the skyline many miles away.

It was a moonscape of dust and rock. Without landmarks there was a feeling of disorientation. As I walked, the distant hills moved with me. Like Alice's Queen, I ran but made no progress. It was an endless desert-sea, with an unreal coastline.

When Commander Edgar D. Mitchell and Captain Alan B. Shepard, Jr., stepped from Apollo 14 to walk to the cone crater they were disoriented. After exacting ground rehearsals they turned back on the moon 40 yards from the target. "They didn't know exactly where the cone [crater] was. They were misled," said Robin Brett, vice-chairman of the earth-bound analysis team.

I had the sensation of moon-blindness at Nasca, directionless walking. The sun was no help as an orientation mark—it was overhead, intense, white, swollen.

My companion wore suede boots with serrated soles. We walked looking down at the hot desert.

"Wait!" I said. I was looking at something that tingled the hair. "Your footprints—they go on ahead of us!" Was it a mirage? The future had already happened out there in front.

"Sure. I went along here twelve months ago. Nothing changes. No rain—a few drops now and again, but they dry up on contact. The wind's blown away everything that's going to blow away. Footprints stay here for years."

"The desert surface is not being substantially modified by either erosion or deposition," stated the geological report; "such a stable regime may have dominated the region for thousands of years.''

The underlying soil is a light-yellow mixture of sand, clay, and calcite. This washed down from the Andes before the climate changed. The alluvial fan is now covered with angular fragments of reddish rhyolite and other volcanic pebbles. The fragments are red-colored underneath, hence the name Colorada. The top is blackened with a thin coat of desert varnish—manganese and iron oxides—caused by long-term exposure to the atmosphere. Long-term for a geologist means a hundred thousand years. When one picks up a red-bellied pebble from the sand it has not been disturbed for millennia.

The lines come sharply into focus when viewed lengthways. Standing a few yards to the side makes a line invisible, but standing astride makes the faintest line show clearly. Plates 23 and 24 shows a typical shallow marking. It extends farther than the field of vision. It is perfectly straight to the limit of the human eye. This is a prodigious constructional feat for an instrumentless culture.

How were the lines made? Clearing the stones was a straightforward, though time-consuming, job. Working fast, members of the expedition cleared at the rate of 1 square yard in 3 minutes.* A line 5 miles long and 6 inches wide required on this basis 80 hours of work, two full weeks for one person, a day for a team. But this does not include time for the engineering, surveying, and/or the adjustments as the work proceeded. The large rectangle—80,000 square yards—took a minimum of 4,000 man-hours to pick off the stones, and more time added to carry and dump at the edges.

Large areas may have been cleared by a two-stage process. In the first stage pebbles were carried, scraped, or thrown to a pile. Several large areas exist that are partially cleared. Hundreds of small neat mounds cover the ground, rows of them in a rough grid pattern.

Dr. Maria Reiche considers these patterns to have meaning, not simply the abandonment of work between stage 1 and stage 2. According to her, the mound complexes were a record of numbers—statistics of the population or of provisions, or maybe a reckoning of time by the day, month, or year.

* This cleared area in the desert was marked ''modern'' to avoid confusion with the ancient workings. It will be visible for thousands of years if left alone to nature.

There are isolated mounds among the lines not connected with the clearing process. There are large mounds at the end of triangles and rectangles, and smaller mounds between the lines. Minipyramids, like the tumulus of England—but there are no burials on this desert.

Archaeologists have dug under Peruvian governmental supervision, legally; *huaqueros,* "nefarious, cunning treasure trovers," have dug illegally. No graves have ever been uncovered in this field of lines. A member of the desert team stumbled across a skull, bolt upright, on a black, spread-out Spanish lace mantilla. But it was fresh bone, a gruesome, recent trick. He left it there in the desert with its secret. As we discovered later, the ancient burials were in the valleys, in cemeteries at the edge of the irrigated area. The dead were not taken to the desert mesa; they were carried the minimum distance to the edge of the irrigation. The human remains were mummified in a crouched position, wrapped in brilliant-colored textiles, and buried with rich polychrome pottery vessels and gold and silver ornaments.

Near the edge of the mesa, a steep climb from the valley, we found 30 mounds set out in graveyard fashion. These were raised, 6-foot-long, coffin-shaped piles, set in rows 4 feet apart. The edges were flanked with upright stone. Two of the mounds had been dug into—the sand and pebble filling was out as if in haste, and the "dig" abandoned. Aerial photography later showed how this false graveyard, meaningless on the ground, fitted into a gigantic picture.

Nearby there were more holes, neatly and purposefully dug. Each one was a foot deep in the soft, yellow subsoil. The holes looked fresh, but in this ageless desert one could not be sure. Someone had been here previously, digging for treasure.

Farther on we found the abandoned camp of the *huaquero.* He had lived under a square sun blind—there were four post holes. He left behind a crude, but valuable, antique water amphora and fragments of richly colored pottery. Clearly, his leaving these behind indicated he had found something of greater value. But what? And when? A newspaper fragment in his hole-in-the-ground latrine was dated 1948, twenty years earlier.

We walked toward the hills where the mesa ran into the Andes. The large rectangle had a tongue that tapered off into a line, and we followed the line. It went up the hillside, continuing without swerving from the original direction, and ended at a small insignificant knoll. We continued up to get a panoramic view of the line field. We went up on foot; a pack mule could not have made it. The climb was steep and difficult. The rocks and loose rubble were angular, with patches of sand between where the once-in-a-blue-moon rain had washed down. One team member fell, and two others gave up the climb.

"Hey, what's this?" Now it was the turn for my colleague's hair to tingle. He pointed down to the imprint of a tire. There was no doubt about it. In the sandy patches between the red boulders there was a short, clear, single tire track. We theorized as scientists do. A motorcycle? No, one glance up at the fierce climb disposed of that theory. An old tire thrown down from the top? No, most unlikely for it to bounce and roll all the way down the hill. An Indian hopping down, goatlike, in Ho Chi Minh rubber sandals? With no better hypothesis we settled for that one and proceeded with the climb.

The top was like the lower slopes, angular scree of rusty-brown rock, cracked by thermal stress. The desert below was flat and formless. Only the rectangle stood out, and that was because it was large and pointed toward the mountain.

No. The line builders, whoever they were, did not get a panoramic view of their handiwork from the mountaintop. It was hot, dry, suffocating. The enormous sun beat down onto the peak of the mountain. I was a broiling meat chunk on the point of a shish. I stood in the blue-above, red-below silence of the place with my feet planted on a slab of the jumbled rocky scree. Apart from Ho Chi Minh, whoever had stood here before in the whole of history? The precipice of the mountain sloped down to the desert floor, steep, dangerous.

Hell! The rock gave way. It slipped like a toboggan. I fell. I crashed hard on my thigh. My cry rang out over the circle of desert into the faraway haze, echo-less, absorbed into hot nothing.

Too late, I realized the risk of the situation. I carried no water, no supplies except a camera, notepad, and pencil. That camera was now smashed, the pad gone down the scree. If my leg was broken how long would I last in the heat? How could the others, as inexpert as I on this loose, moonlike rubble, get me down to the base? Carry me? No wood for a splint or stretcher. We were high over the desert, miles from the road, miles from Nasca. Ah! I could move the other leg. A colleague came over and examined me. Bruised but not broken. I would be able to get down under my own power.

"Move over!" he said. "There's something under your leg." He pulled at a large, wedge-shaped boulder. There was a pottery fragment sticking out from a cleft in the rock, black on the outside of the bowl, terra cotta slip on the inside. We found seven shards from the early Nascan culture, dating back to the first centuries A.D. Three fragments were from the same pot, so the collection represented five different vessels. Why did the Nascans carry breakables up a Hillary hill? Surely, unlike Everest, it wasn't climbed "because it was there." Despite the difficulty of the climb, they left traces of ceremonies and culture at the top. The mountain must have had meaning to them.

We made a systematic survey along the 2-kilometer tongue, all the way back to the rectangle. The line was covered with fragments—polychrome pieces, brilliantly colored with fired pigments. The desert in all directions was equally rich—fragments scattered on the surface, on the mounds, and between the black-glazed stones.

We came across a patch of shards. Where the fragment was face up, the pattern was blackened by a thousand years of sun; face down, the pattern was as new. We dusted off the hundred pieces and reassembled the pot. It was the fierce jaguar head, the feline deity, the tiger-god, common to pre-Columbian religions. It was red-faced, white-eyed, with an orange tongue extended. The whiskers on close examination turned out to be pale faces with slit eyes and long extended hair. Typical of Nascan style, the jaguar wore a blue-gray, flat-brimmed, bowler-type hat.

Forest Indians worshiped a star which was a tiger in the sky. Its name was Chuquichinchay, according to Polo de Ondegardo. The Chiriguani Indians still believe in Yaguarogui, a fabulous green tiger-god that eats the sun and moon during an eclipse. I recognized the feline on the bowl as the most powerful of the Peruvian earth-sky gods.

The jaguar, the third form of the all-powerful sun-god, identified by ethnologists across the globe from Mesopotamia to the far Pacific.

The jaguar, found buried, sunset-red, with 73 jade spots at the Mayan observatory of Chichen Itza.

The jaguar—here on the blazing, sun-drenched desert for longer than the life span of a civilization.

It was a deep, ceremonial flared bowl, exquisitely thin, with a rounded

PLATE 20. *Fragments of a vessel almost 2,000 years old were scattered in the desert. When reassembled they show the jaguar face, one of the South American symbols for the sun-god. Black desert varnish has begun to form on those fragments which were upturned and exposed.*

108

base. Amazingly, that craftmanship was done without the potter's wheel. One hand was placed inside the wet clay vessel before baking, and it was tapped into shape with a paddle. That final shape was as smooth as a wheel-turned item.

Why a rounded base? A good question, answered by the archaeologist. On a table the bowl would tip over like a bobbing toy clown. But when the table is the sandy desert a rounded base is very sensible. Visitors to the special Peruvian exhibition held in 1968 at the Guggenheim Museum in New York saw vessels from private collections set out on smoothed white sand—utilitarian and richly artistic.

At the time of the exhibition no estimate of the total value of the Peruvian ceramics was given. All Nascaware was artisan-made. One 6-inch Nasca bowl, decorated with a simple pattern of colored seeds, was priced at $100 at that time by a New York dealer. The clever, happy caricatures of birds and animals were valued higher. A large anthropomorphic vessel would be $500 or more depending on its beauty, rareness, or uniqueness. Even for the Nascans, these delicate ceremonial items were out of the ordinary. One pot in a hundred, archaeologists estimate, was made to perfection, never to be used in the worldly sense. The remaining ninety-nine were thick, unpainted—destined for household use in drinking, stewing, and beermaking.

Duplicate pottery is rare; there is an individuality in each piece as if the creativity of the artisan were at stake. He operated within a framework of stylized symbols, a fanciful and not fully decoded hieroglyphic message, but he seldom made an exact duplicate. Ceremonial Nascaware is rare, and the fragments in the desert are mostly ceremonial.

The jaguar bowl pieced together in the desert was later identified by experts as Nasca type 3 or 4. This period runs approximately from 100 B.C. to A.D. 100, contemporary with the Roman invasion of Britain. Was this the time the bowl was placed in the desert—the time it was smashed? Are those markings in the desert 2,000 years old?

We moved forward to complete the traverse. Result: 523 fragments collected, representing 44 vessels. Most were Nasca 3 and 4; one fragment was Nasca 2; a few others had dates scattered from the time of the birth of Christ to the present. Conclusion: for the short span of two centuries there was intensive activity in this region. Jesus of Nazareth was foretold, born, and crucified while the lines were being drawn.

PLATE 21. *Peruvian survey team on the mound of the main rectangle.*

Valuable ceramics were added (given?) to the desert—a desolate area of
stark beauty, where no person could live.

I estimated that 225,000 museum-quality items once stood in that 150-
square-kilometer area. The appraisal on such treasure now would
amount to $15 million.

The plane of the Peruvian Air Force droned overhead like Hemingway's silver speck in *For Whom the Bell Tolls*—altitude 5,000 feet,
flight plan level and straight. It was too high to see the opening in the
belly, but I knew the surveillance lens was pointing down. Inside the
camera the photogrammetric shutter clicked. The wide film moved on
automatically for the next exposure.

PLATE 22. *Sighting to the distant mound in the large rectangle, exact direction marked on the mountain range. The rectangle points neither to a peak nor a cleft.*

I stood up and brushed off the dust from my sun jacket. Tony was at his work. Half-hidden by the camera tripod, he was taking footage of an assistant with multicolored pottery in his hands. There was no sound track, but the assistant was requested to say something to provide lip movement. Slyly, before he could be stopped, the B.B.C.-banned words came out: "You **** TV lip readers are too **** smart for your own **** good!" Anyway, he said it with a smile.

I began my assignment, walking over to the mound where the theodolite was set. It was necessary to obtain measurements of the sun to fix the exact north–south direction to be coordinated with the air survey

111

later. It was also necessary to measure the altitude of the skyline, those distant hills. Azimuth, altitude, photogrammetry—necessary data for the calculations.

I looked through the instrument, setting the telescopic cross wire on the distant ridge, that spot where I had fallen, that rocky scree with delicate pottery at the summit.

7 TESTING

The air maps covered four large desktop-sized sheets.

The scale was 1:2,000 with contours at every meter above sea level. The desert markings were drawn to scale—zigzags, radiating stars, parallel grids of lines. The stereo-plan, detailed though it was, missed lines narrower than 12 inches. But the map was sufficient to test the astronomical calendar theory. This was the most extensive set of desert markings in South America.

The basic Stonehenge program was used in the computer with adjustment for the new latitude. In this the machine calculates back to any chosen date in prehistory, and prints out whether or not the sun or moon can be seen on the horizon at the end of a line at one of the calendar extremes—midwinter setting, midsummer rising, etc. For Peru we added a new subroutine, a program for the stars.

The sun and moon change the position of rising and setting day by day. The sunrise halts on the horizon when the declination is $\pm23\frac{1}{2}$ degrees (24° in 2000 B.C.). This is an extreme fixed by the angle of tilt of the earth's axis. The angle does not change much over the centuries. The moon, when full, turns at declinations $\pm29°$ and $\pm19°$ every 18 or 19 years depending on the timing of the 56-year cycle.

A star rises approximately in the same position each night. It is carried on Aristotle's fixed sphere, constant and immutable. Constant, that is, except for the precession of the earth's axis, which conical motion causes the rising point of a star to change by up to $\frac{1}{2}°$ per century.

The first step was to measure XY coordinates from the ground plan of selected points on a line. We measured the center axis of 21 thin triangles, and 72 linear features—lines, bands, and edges of rectangles. We did not measure more than one line in a parallel grid (and there were several of these grids), nor could we measure those numerous lines visible on foot at the site but not shown on the map. But the 93 measurements were sufficient to test the theory.

The lines were indeed straight. The average bend was no more than 9 minutes of arc—a 4-yard deviation in the length of a mile. That figure was the limit of accuracy called for in the photogrammetric survey. The ancient lines were in fact laid out straighter than could be measured with modern air-survey techniques. (Maria Reiche had claimed extraordinary eyesight for the ancient Peruvians, with eyes like telescopes!) And this linearity continues for miles. It goes out beyond that circle of clear visibility set by ground-level dust haze. It picks up in the same unswerving direction on the opposite side of a gully, and can run, straight as an arrow, up a hill.

How could this be done? One can only speculate. A person could do it by driving stakes in the ground, moving and adjusting until the stakes appeared to line up. Or a team of men could stand in a row and step to one side or the other until that row was judged straight. Either way, it was no small achievement.

The first machine-question was: *How many lines point to the 18 Stonehenge directions?**

The machine was instructed to tolerate and print out errors of up to one degree. The print-out showed 39 sun-moon alignments from the 186 ground-marked directions (93 lines, each used twice, forwards and backwards).

This result did not favor the calendar theory. It was too close to the number expected by chance. Eighteen sun-moon targets, each 2° wide, gives a total target of 36°. This is one-tenth of the 360° circle of the horizon. From this we expect 1 line in 10 to point to the sun or moon by chance, i.e., 19 out of the 186 shots. The machine found a total of 39 alignments, which was only 20 above the number to be expected by chance. This was too slim a margin. Speaking nonmathematically, no more than about 20 out of 186 possibilities could be thought of as calendric.

We looked at the map to find those 39 sun-moon lines reported by the computer. These had no special significance in the pattern, nothing to suggest an importance over and above the other lines. And what of those others, the 80 percent which did not point to sun or moon? It is

* 6 for the sun (4 solstice, 2 equinox), and 12 for the moon (8 solstice extremes, 4 at the equinox).

114

essential for any theory to have *substantial* confirmation. As Fred Hoyle pointed out, all of the main architectural regularities at Stonehenge fit the theory. It should be so at Nasca. Certainly, as Maria Reiche and Paul Kosok suggest, one or two lines here and there might point to the sun, but unless an explanation, preferably an astronomical one, can be found for the unassigned lines, then the speculation is no more than that—a speculation. No, the lines did not point to sun or moon.

The second machine-question was: *What stars did the lines point to at any date between 5000 B.C. and A.D. 1900?* The machine was fed positions of 45 stars—those brighter than magnitude +2.0, and the brightest star in the Pleiades, eta Tauri, magnitude +2.9. It was coded to print out any alignment that occurred during this 6,900-year interval.

The date of the pottery was limited to the first centuries B.C. and A.D., but that date was not sure to a century or so. Nor could one assume without further evidence that the lines were laid out at the time of the placing of the pots. Certainly that time correlation between pot and line was the simplest assumption, but, conceivably, the lines might have come before the pots, or (less conceivably) vice versa. And it needed only a few seconds more to compute for the full 6,900-year span. If the pottery date was right, and *if* the lines were astronomical, there would be a star for every line at A.D. 0,* but not at other dates.

The print-out sheets were full, stars at the end of each line. But, disappointingly, no more in number than expected by chance. Taking account of precessional drift, a line should hit one of the star targets every thousand years or so. This was the luck of the blindfold marksman shooting in the dark. In any given century we expected 1 line out of 10 to connect. For 186 directions there should be 19 chance alignments in every century.

The computer average per century was 17.3 star alignments over the period 5000 B.C. to A.D. 1900. The centuries of archaeological interest were no better than the other centuries. As it so happened, those centuries were worse—only 7 stars from 100 to 0 B.C., and 6 from A.D. 0 to 100. Some centuries scored higher than others as Lady Luck played the

* Astronomers recognize A.D. 0 but historians do not. They count B.C. 2, B.C. 1, A.D. 1. . . .

odds. In the thirty-fourth century B.C. there were 31 alignments, but still only an unacceptable fraction of the 186 directions under test. Even ignoring the very improbable date of 3400–3300 B.C., there were far too many lines without stars. No, the lines did not point to the stars.

As a last resort we tested for unidentified sky objects, things seen when the lines were made but not visible today. A new star, a nova, shines brilliantly for a few months and then fades to invisibility. A comet glows ghostly in the early dawn light. A conjunction of two or more planets attracts attention. These and other transitory things are sometimes identified with the "star of Bethlehem."

The test for these objects was to compare one set of lines with another set. At Pampa Jumana-Colorada we compared the lines to the east with the lines to the west of the Pan American Highway. If a line in the eastern group pointed to declination "X," the unknown object, then one would expect to find a line in the western group also pointing to "X."

We also compared the Pampa Jumana-Colorada lines with a set near to the cultivation belt at Nasca.* Result: in both tests, no overlap. Conclusion: the line builders were not pointing to a set of celestial objects not now visible or recognizable.

Disappointed, we rejected the astronomical calendar theory. There was no time in the reasonable past when all, or mostly all, of the lines fitted a star at rising or setting. A few of the lines might point to the solstice extremes of the sun or moon, but not in sufficient numbers to account for the vast complex of grids, radiating centers, triangles, and isolated lines. No, the creation in the desert could not function as a time-clock calendar.

If there were to be any credibility in the calendar theory, the main rectangle taken by itself must work astronomically. The computer output was revealing. The feature did not line up with any star at the time of Nasca 3 and 4. It did point to the rising of the Pleiades in A.D. 610, as Maria Reiche suggested, but the revised radiocarbon-based date of A.D. 0 puts the time out of joint. It did point to the moon at the declina-

---

* This field of lines was measured on the first expedition. On the second, Tony went up a small hill to photograph the site. The lines had gone, were obliterated—sacrificed to the god of irrigation.

tion extreme of $+19°$, but for credibility one would expect to find matching rectangles marking other moon extremes. There are none such.

The star-sun-moon calendar theory had been killed by the computer.

In retrospect the result made sense. It would be difficult in practice to use a line to mark a star. Visibility on the horizon was affected by dust haze—a haze not thick enough to shield the blazing sun, but sufficient to make the seeing of a star difficult. Then again, a line on the desert pavement is not visible at night. It would need to be marked out by lamps. The pottery vessels in the lines were bowls, dishes, not lamps. Nor were the mounds (logical places for setting a lamp) located along the lines. More often than not these mounds were set to one side, or near curved lines.

Then what were the lines for?

Here we leave the computer print-out hardware and take up the software of speculation.

Flying saucers? I share the skepticism of my astronomical colleagues about so-called unidentified flying objects. I have seen no evidence convincing, authentic, and reputable. The case is not proved, and unless proved, UFO's are relegated to that Ilium of myth and legend. In fact, within the boundaries of science, serious doubts are raised against the existence of UFO's because of known hoaxes, because of misidentification of natural objects, meteors, weather balloons, Venus when an evening star, because of the growing evidence against the existence of life forms on Mars, Venus, and the other planets in the solar system, and because of the recognized difficulty of intelligent life surviving the journey over the enormous distances from the stars. Yet a Nascan UFO theory has been put forward by writers with a science-fiction leaning: "Extraterrestrial visitors came to Nasca and marked out the lines for a landing strip."

Proponents of the UFO theory have first to establish UFO's as real, then explain the large amount of man-made Nascaware, more than 200,000 items originally scattered over the area, then work out a rationale. Needless to say, we found no extraterrestrial artifacts. Nothing the least bit UFO-ish.

The world's largest scratch pad? Nature abhors a vacuum; man abhors an empty surface. Muralists glow at the sight of an unpainted wall. Architects imagine a new building wherever their gaze falls.

117

PLATE 23. *A typical desert line on the Pampa Jumana-Colorada looking south. The line, perfectly straight, made by removing the blackened stones, does not point to either a mountain peak or a valley.*

Doodling, a magazine article claims, is a major occupation of pyramid-climbing executives; 32 percent of paper used at committee meetings is filled with scribble; secretaries are bribed to smuggle pads out of the boss's office for psychological analysis. In the first expedition one team member was forcibly restrained upon arrival from writing out his name in giant-sized letters. Maybe, suggested a sociologist half-seriously, there was a prehistoric compulsion to scribble.

Skyline markers? Several writers have explained the lines as leading to a distant peak or valley. A few lines do this, but not all. It is the problem of the blindfold marksman again. A substantial score is needed

PLATE 24. *The same line as in Plate 23 looking north. Again the line does not point to a natural feature on the horizon.*

to be convincing. The computer was not put through the rigorous star-hit analysis for the hill targets, but sufficient "misses" were noted to belie the suggestion. In particular the main rectangle did not point to the prominent mountain peak, nor to the cleft on either side.

Ancient streets? C. W. Ceram refers to Paul Kosok's work when, flying near the old city of Nasca, he thought he had discovered a network of "Inca streets." Aerial photographs showed "that they could not be roads, for some of them led nowhere but to the tops of mountains where they abruptly ended." As a postscript, the pottery fragments show the network to be *pre*-Inca.

119

PLATE 25. *Piper Cherokee spotter plane touches down on the broad expanse of one of the ancient strips. The white line is recent, of unknown origin.*

Pathways? Some of the lines run, as though with a purpose, from one hillock to another. These hillocks rise up a low 10 meters from the plain. Perhaps they were sacred, important places—ceramic shards are thick there—and the lines are a connecting link. But only a few lines can be so accounted for. The majority begin unnoticeably in the desert and end, as Ceram says, nowhere. Some desert lines jump the span of a gully, maintaining the straightness. Footpaths, like the occasional donkey track in the area, tend to meander as the pedestrian selects the easiest route.

Ceremonial walkways? Perhaps. But what could be the ceremony—religious ritual, occult practices, sex-fertility rites?

Signals to the gods in the sky? Gerhart Weibe, dean of Public Communications at Boston University, suggested this as a motive for Stonehenge. The concentric pattern looked pleasing from above and thus the gods were satisfied.

The desert markings are on a gigantic scale; many features can be recognized only from a height of several hundred feet, a height the Nascans could not attain.

We flew a Piper Cherokee on the expedition. The view was impressive, the lines forcefully straight, the cleared areas gaining contrast from the higher viewpoint. The Cherokee made a Daedalus swoop over the terrain, banking tightly for the camera shots. We gazed down, and then suddenly, between the lines, in the maze, we made out the curves, the pictograms—too big to see on the ground, but clear from the air.

Some of our photographs are shown in the plates: lizard, spider, flower, monkey, a condor bird, and a huge beaked creature with two mounds at the head. Each figure was drawn with precision. Living representations. Life, in a Graham Greene hell of frozen mathematics.

The gargantuan artist employed an intriguing single-line technique. Careful inspection shows how a line commenced, turned, and wove the picture so as not to cross itself. The line of the spider returned to its starting point; the line of the monkey did not. It extended from the genitals and ended in a huge zigzag pattern covering 20,000 square meters. The same applied to the penis of the dog, though there was no zigzag in this case.

The lizard, 200 yards long, was cut across by the rebuilt Pan American Highway. It was not recognized by the construction workers. A civil engineer claimed he would need to start with a scaled plan and mark out the ground with rods, tapes, and telescopic sighting instruments to reproduce these drawings.

What was the purpose of these huge, invisible-from-the-ground desert pictures? Were they constructed at the epoch of the lines? Were they conceived and fashioned by the same hands that placed the pottery in this bewilderingly complex wilderness?

The CDC 6400, like other digital calculators, was capable of laborious, tedious arithmetic; of summing up data; of testing a theory against hard fact—and all this without the disconcerting slips and errors that a "human computer" makes. But the CDC could not penetrate the mind process of a lost civilization.

121

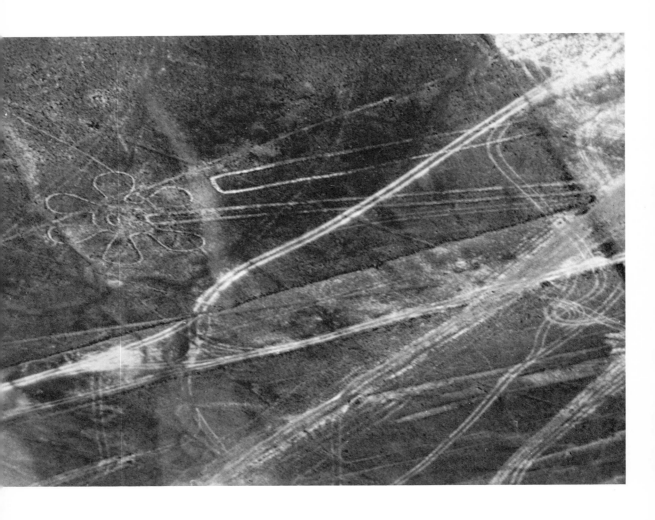

PLATE 26. (above) *Drawing of a flower. The stem may be a pathway leading through the pollen.*

PLATE 27. (right) *Spider,* Ricinulei, *with tip marked on the extended leg for copulation.*

123

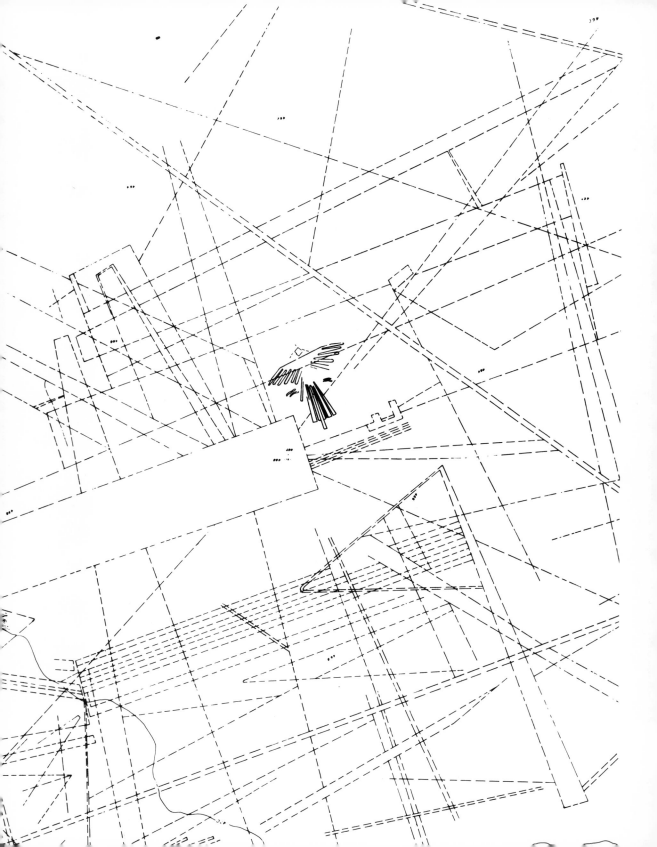

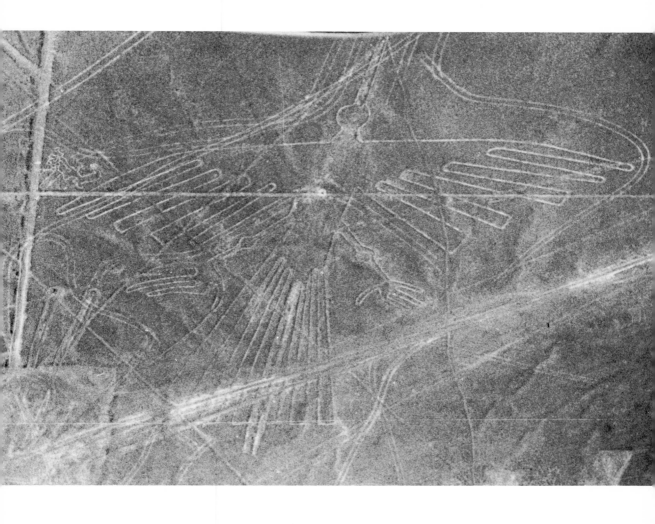

PLATE 28. (above) *Outstretched condor. Note the exaggerated knee joints and the mound at the center.*

FIG. 13. (left) *Part of stereo-plan of S.A.N.   The condor marks the   western end of the great rectangle.*

125

126

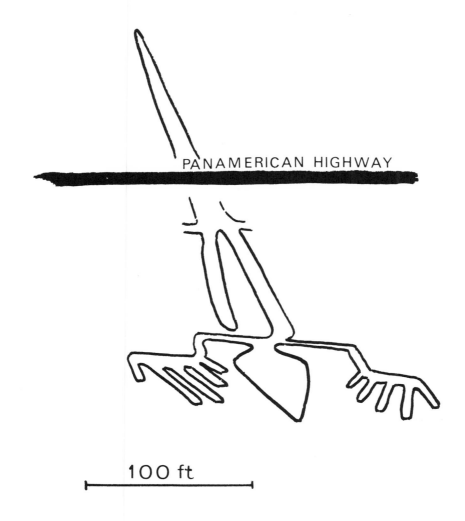

PANAMERICAN HIGHWAY

100 ft

FIG. 14. (above) *Lizard, cut across by the Pan American Highway, from Plate 29.*

PLATE 29. (left) *Gigantic lizard, drawn with a single-line technique.*

127

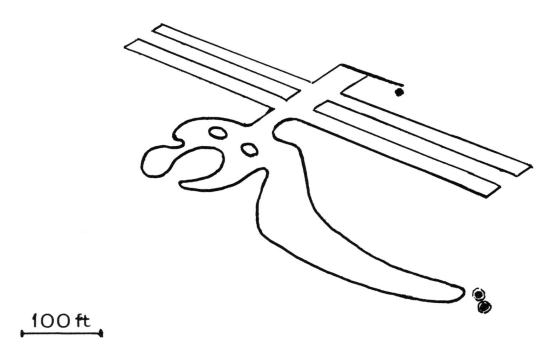

100 ft

FIG. 15. (above) *A beaked creature, drawn in perspective from aerial Plate 30.*

PLATE 30. (right) *A strange, huge, beaked creature.*

128

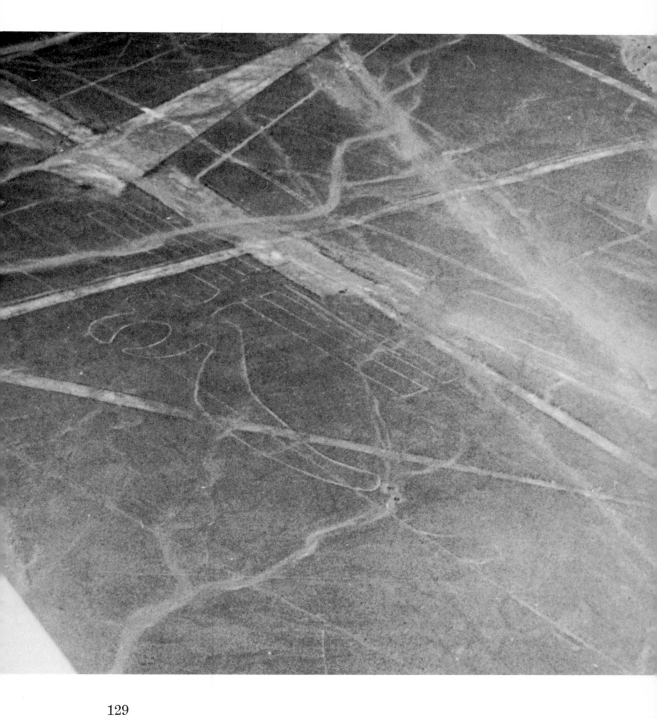

129

130

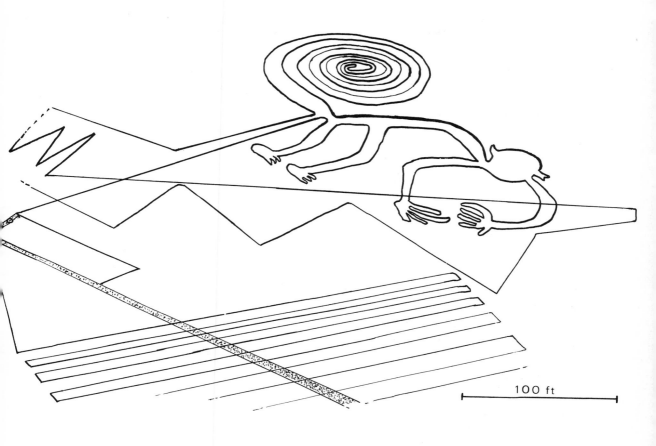

100 ft

FIG. 16. (above) *Spider monkey drawn on the desert plateau with zigzag pathway from the genitals.*

PLATE 31. (left) *Standing on the claws of a gigantic figure drawn in the Nascan desert.*

131

I circulated a preliminary report of the computer findings. The negative result was disappointing, particularly to Dr. Reiche, who had spent so much time on this mystery, "going out into the desert for weeks on end, alone," as one local Nascan put it. Another rumor from Nasca to Ica had Dr. Reiche's set of measurements and mathematical papers stolen and destroyed by bandits. Fortunately the rumor was unfounded. I corresponded with her in Germany, and with archaeologists in the United States, United Kingdom, and South America. Isaac Asimov chewed over the matter briefly, and then stored the 45-paged, 9-tabled report in his card-index brain.

No, Paul Kosok was not right, yet Ceram's hope of a "new insight into the cultural accomplishments of the old Andean peoples" was still there. According to the circumstantial evidence it was certainly the Nascans who were responsible for what we now see in the Pampa Jumana-Colorada. The desert markings and the pottery are the sum total legacy of that civilization, supposedly conquered by the Incas, who were in turn crushed by the conquistadors—"beheaded as a culture, as the passer-by sweeps off the head of a sunflower." There is no writing, and scant verbal folklore. Nothing survived. Modern scholars are separated in time and cultural background from those thought processes. A psychologist aptly described it as a "gulf of cognitive perception."

I was intrigued. I wanted to know more of the ancient Nascans—religion, mythology, beliefs and knowledge, philosophy. I turned to those few anthropologists who were pre-Columbian experts; to the present-day people in the Nasca Valley; and to those mysterious rogues who lived by plundering the graves—the *huaqueros*.

8 LOST CIVILIZATION

Palacio was the expert of the graverobbers.

His reputation was known far afield, from Lima to Arequipa. He had dug into more Nascan graves and charnal tombs than any archaeologist.

Huaqueros are naturally secretive, for professional reasons. They sell the gold and silver icon treasures, the jewelry, the richest-colored tapestry of the ancient world, and the ceremonial pottery to middlemen, with zero information as to where it was excavated, how it was located, and what was the setting of the treasure trove before the spade disturbed it. We wanted to meet with Señor Palacio. We wanted to get him to talk.

The janitor of the local mission church was a double convert—from paganism and from graverobbing. ("It is not right, señor, to disturb the dead, and besides, señor, the police are very strict now.") He took us to an enormous cemetery on the south bank of the Nasca riverbed. Barren sandy soil reached into the hills. It was as hot as the Valley of the Kings on the "death side" of the Nile. Every few yards we saw holes 10 feet wide and some of them, the freshly dug ones, 12 feet deep. the sand was slipping back down by natural erosion. Holes covered the entire area between the edge of cultivation and the low rocky cliff. There were upwards of 5,000 opened, plundered graves.

The burials were mummified corpses, in a knee-to-chin position, and wrapped in layers of coarse cloth and ceremonial textile patterned with designs of the mythical creatures of the Nascans. Skulls and bones littered the place. Some still bore tresses of hair. Only the coarse cloth and inferior textile had been left behind. The whole area was littered with scraps of Nascaware pottery. We began to guess at another reason for our guide's conversion—there was nothing left to dig!

Did our guide know Palacio? "Yes, it is possible," but it was better to take us to another *huaquero* who was currently active in the profession.

PLATE 32. *Five thousand plundered graves at the edge of the Nasca valley.*

PLATE 33. *Vandals took the treasures but left the skeletons.*

134

We followed the guide to a select house on Main Street, to a man in white shirt, belted black trousers, and tie. He had clean fingernails. We entered, and as he closed the door he looked down the street and drew the curtain over the window. He showed us a collection of artifacts: bowls, brushes, and a small jar with a powdered mineral found in a tomb and allegedly a glaze of the ancient pottery craftsmen. But this gentleman turned out to be an assistant bank manager who on the side was a prosperous, nondigging go-between. He had no firsthand information, or maybe he was choosing to keep quiet about the profession. Did he know Palacio? "Sí. . . ."

We followed his directions to a man in a two-roomed, bamboo-roofed cottage who said he "called himself" Palacio. He was slimy, toothless, with no air of self-confidence. Some of the ceramics on the bookcase shelving were poor forgeries. We suspected his integrity and questioned the high price he asked for one item. "But, señors, it is much work to find a pot—much hours of digging under the hot sun. And then bad luck if your shovel strikes the pot." This confirmed our suspicions. *Huaqueros* work at night. They know exactly where the treasure is buried in relation to the mummy. They don't ruin their profit margin with a careless spade. He gave us street directions to a "friend who also held pots," but we had little hope that these directions would lead to Palacio.

We walked through the square, across the earth-floored, grass-roofed market, between a stall of ripe papayas and a stand of bubbling Peruvian soup, into a back alley where ten thousand flies gathered at each garbage pile, along a white-washed adobe wall, and then finally through a thick doorway into a softly lighted room.

Inside we sat opposite each other on plastic-covered armchairs, so close that our knees almost touched. On the opposite wall was a framed certificate in Spanish, and I made out a long paternal-maternal name beginning with "Juan." No part of that name was Palacio.

The man in the room wore blue denims. He was in his mid-thirties and had that Spanish-Indian look of thick but handsome features with black hair and clear, curved eyebrows. His eyes were a warm dark brown in his browned face, and his manner was one of confidence.

"Juan" opened a wooden chest and began to place Nasca pottery on the tiled floor. The items were superb, better than those of the Guggenheim exhibition. He had examples of the twenty basic shapes ranging from dishes and flared bowls to cylindrical vases and the characteristic double-spouted, stirrup-handled jars. The earlier items, classified archaeologically as "proto-Nasca," were decorated with simple colors —black and reddish brown on a cream background. Later items, classified as "classical Nasca," showed as many as eight different colors with intricate patterns.

The Nascans were surely dedicated to nature, life, and living things. Their decorations showed this life-force motif. The rims of bowls were painted with a repeated design: skillful representations of a flower or sprouting seed; hummingbird, catfish, or jellyfish; condor or spider. Some typical patterns are drawn in the accompanying figures. The Nascan outlook was humorous, happy, carefree—at least the paintings seemed to reflect this spirit. The Disney-like duck had corncobs painted on, suggesting it was well stuffed. The bowl decorated with the U-shaped, catfish ran out of space, but "not to worry," said the artist: a straight and skinny fish was squeezed in to finish the pattern.

There was a jar with pretty girls. A smiling face with black hair was repeated five times: a white face, brown face, red, black, and yellow. Did this show the races of man? Was the artist integrating in symbols the different ethnic groups—a United Nations pot before the time of *Pax Catholica!*

Three items stopped my eye. First there was a tall jar with a wrap-around pictograph. The "unwrapped" picture (see Fig. 22) was startling. In my imagination it became a high priest standing at the end of a desert triangle with raised hand looking towards a star-god at the end of the lines. The priest identified himself with the star in the sky because he wears the same headdress as the star-god. Multitudes of people, represented by triangular, slit-eyed faces, are standing along

FIG. 17. *Beetle pattern on a Nascaware bowl. A four-legged imaginary creation, strangely inaccurate for those observant artists: insects have six legs.*

FIG. 18. *Hummingbird from a flared bowl.*

FIG. 19. *Jumping catfish, from a flared bowl.*

FIG. 20. *Duck filled with corn, from a Nascaware lugged jar.*

FIG. 21. *Stars of three colors from a flared bowl.*

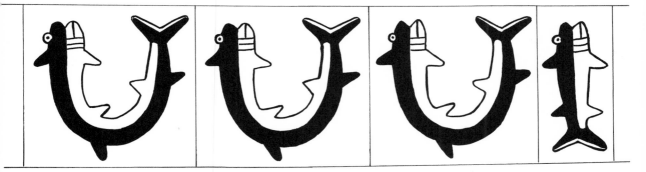

FIG. 22. *Pattern on a cylindrical Nascaware jar. Priest, desert lines, and a star?*

138

the line. At first glance this was to me a pictorial record of some ancient line ceremony. A Nascaware expert was later to correct me by identifying the "star" as a flower, and the "slit-eyed faces" as severed trophy heads. And what of the priest figure? He could not say.

Second, there was a large double-spouted vessel with a figure dressed in feathers. On the head a flat ceremonial hat and, maybe, a face mask. Was this a winged bird-man? Could the hat be a prehistoric crash helmet? Did the Nascans have the aspiration to fly; did they whirl from the top of high poles suspended on vines as did the Aztecs in Mexico; was this the way the Nascans viewed the figures on the desert?

Third, there was a bowl with a colored zigzag motif. We had picked up a fragment of just such a bowl on the west mound of the great rectangle. The fragment matched the bowl perfectly. Presumably a complete bowl had been placed in the desert 2,000 years ago. Where had the *huaquero* found the twin? He must have gathered a wealth of information from his digging. We pushed him to talk.

"Are you Palacio?"

"Sí! I am him," Juan grinned and his parted lips showed a pleasant curve of white and gold teeth. I glanced from him to the wall certificate—membership in some local club. Palacio was obviously a false name, but an alias he was proud of. I prodded him for information.

"We want to know where you found this bowl."

"As normal—buried in the sand at the mouth of the mummy."

"Where?"

"Beyond Nasca."

"Yes, but exactly where?"

"*No se*, señor." (I wouldn't know.)

We pulled back from this too specific questioning and generalized. Palacio told how surface clues, known only to him, gave the location of a burial. Important personages were buried with flanking, sentinel graves. These "companion bodies" signaled the unearthing of a good haul of treasure. Food dishes were placed near the folded hands of the mummy. He confirmed unknowingly the words of Pedro de Cieza de León in 1554:

I have frequently mentioned in this history that in the greater part of the kingdom of Peru it is a custom much practiced and cherished by the Indians

139

PLATE 34. *Nascan polychrome vessel showing girls of different-colored skin—white, black, yellow, and red.*

PLATE 36. *Nascan polychrome vessel in the form of the jaguar.*

PLATE 35. *Tall Nascaware vessel with priest (?) design. (See Fig. 22.)*

to bury with the bodies of the dead all their most prized possessions and some of the most beautiful of their women and those most beloved by them. . . . From the fact that they placed with dead all their goods and their women and servants, an ample store of provisions and numerous jars of *chicha* [corn beer], and also their weapons and personal adornments, one can gather that they had understanding of the immortality of the soul and knew that there was more to man than the mortal body.

The best pots Palacio ever found in the course of his trade were buried, so he said, just below the surface in the hard sand on the desert mesa. He showed us one, the not-for-sale pride of the collection. He had dug it out from a low pile of sand on the mesa, wrapped in woven textile. A mummified pot, preserved in mint condition!

I mentally figured that twenty years ago he was in his virile teens. I thought of the time-frozen relics of the hut on the mesa, the dated refuse. "Did you dig it up in 1948?"

He started, looked at us as if we were the secret police, then showed his gold in a grin. *"No se!"* he said.

We talked about the Peruvian "waca," that place inhabited by a spirit. The waca might be a tree, a spring, a mountain—any spot selected by folklore or some happening in the past to be a spirit place. The Spanish took the word from the Incas and transliterated it *huaco.* The spirit had malignant influence on any passer-by who did not leave an offering. Icons, jewels, and ceremonial vessels were placed at these spots and became part of the spiritual component of the place. Hence the name *huaquero,* a thief of spirits. And Palacio had gathered together many wacas in his narrow room. He scoffed at the taboo. For centuries the offerings had remained untouched, protected by the ghost of the waca. Now that power was broken.

The Spanish chroniclers wrote of these "pagan ideas." The Incas knew of hundreds of spirit places; they thought of them as lying on lines radiating in all quarters of the compass outward from the temple of the sun in the capital city, Cuzco. Some lines connected together as many as fifteen wacas. Every Inca was supposed to have a twin brother, a genie, a guardian spirit called a wawki (*huauqui*). A person knew the abode of his protective wawki. Presumably he kept the location a secret.

It was reminiscent of that old Egyptian tale of Aladdin, whose genie in the lamp came out with a rub to serve the master and to satisfy his

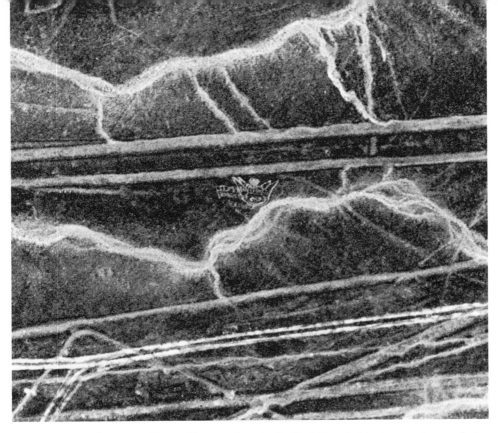

PLATE 37. *Modern markings, Nascan desert. Dotted line indicates marks made by a galloping horse several years earlier. The shield is the coat of arms, the national emblem of Peru. (See flag, Plate 38.)*

PLATE 38. *A fiesta procession, Nascan town.*

every desire. A fanciful notion, but did the Nascans place their wawkis in a ceremonial pot in the desert? Did they, like Aladdin, rub the pot when in trouble, or when there was a desire to be satisfied by the genie? My mind's eye went back to that mysterious desert, the markings, the estimated 225,000 pots standing among the lines two thousand years ago.

"We found only broken pots up there. Who broke them?"

Palacio was ingenuous in his reply. "The best ones were taken. The inferior ones were smashed to keep the prices up."

"How were the large figures drawn in the desert?"

"Never have seen them. I don't know."

We opened the file of pictures at the monkey. Palacio quickly lifted out a vessel with the motif of a monkey. It was similar to the ground drawing with ears and a spiral tail.

We showed him the air photo of the spider. He held up a spider painted on a bowl. Similar, yet there was a difference. Both were spiders, but the desert one was more exact, more forceful. The sand spider was drawn in plan with a single, continuous line scratched into the hardened sand, the shape 150 feet long, the meandering line almost half a mile. Pedipalpi were at the head, and it had eight legs, with the third leg deliberately lengthened and extended. At the tip of the extended leg was a small cleared area. Did this distortion of the third leg have meaning?

Spiders have a sex problem. To quote the *Encyclopaedia Britannica* (1960 ed.): "It [the problem] consists in a complete separation of the male copulatory apparatus from the reproductive system proper." The male overcomes this handicap by transferring sperm with other methods. It is deposited on a blade of grass, or on the thread of a web, and the female is maneuvered backwards in a sexual dance routine. "How such an arrangement could have originated remains a mystery."

The *Ricinulei* spider of the Amazon jungle is unique in the world of spiders in the way reproduction is enacted. The tip of the third leg is used for copulation.

Ricinulei is the rarest of spiders and probably the rarest of all the orders of the animal kingdom; until the mid-century no more than 32 specimens were known. It lives in the darkness of tropical caves and in

143

PLATE 39. *Spider monkey in the Amazon jungle. Compare the giant desert drawing, Figure 16.*

the humus of the jungle floor. It is blind (no eyes) and no more than ¼ inch in length. Its method of reproduction was not recognized by modern science until the mid-twentieth century. The copulatory device on the tip of the leg requires a microscope to be seen.

Did the Nascans know of this Amazon spider? This jungle basin is on the other side of the Andes, but tributaries do run into the Amazon from Peru. The journey on foot would be arduous but not impossible. The thin-limbed monkey, drawn in the desert, has the features of a spider monkey—another species of the Amazon jungle.

One of the Nascan pots showed a thumb-sized, white-breasted, black-backed penguin. How did the Nascans know of the penguin? This sea-bird inhabits Antarctica, although specimens are found as far north as the Galapagos Islands in the Pacific.

A biology colleague at Boston University later confirmed these insect, animal, and bird interpretations. But he was surprised. He commented that for the ancient Peruvians to find *Ricinulei* and spy on its sex life was a remarkable achievement, as remarkable as the Stonehengers

144

PLATE 40. *Nascan polychrome pottery—penguin, mice, and man.*

finding the 56-year moon cycle, more remarkable intellectually than if the lines in the desert had pointed to the stars.

There was a decorated pot in the Carlos Belli Archaeological Museum at Ica, the provincial center north of Nasca. To my eyes, as an astronomer, it was a mixture of bird forms and undeciphered symbols. Nothing more. But Maria Belli de Leon, daughter of Carlos Belli, the archaeologist, saw it differently. Writing in the *Voice of Ica,* she said:

This *huaco* [shown in Fig. 23] symbolizes the moon. It is divisible into 4 zones.

Zone 1 is the curved handle and spout. The handle is decorated with a series of ritual steps making a bridge or chain-link through the space from the earth to the moon. This symbolizes a voyage to the moon and the voyage is possible from any place on the earth.

Zone 2 is the upper third, decorated with 3 different signs, each containing a dot. The sign nearest the spout is a fundamental sign. The other signs represent evolution and the power of the cosmos that makes the surface of the moon inhabitable.

145

Zone 3, the center band, shows again the fundamental symbol, and birds and subterranean forms. The black bands represent atoms and chemical elements from which life is created.

Zone 4, the base, is the inner nucleus of the moon.

This archaeological testimony is an important proof of a great prehistoric civilization that had the courage to forge a lost, linking chain.

Another flared vessel showed "Lemurians, gigantic in stature, almost without faces, large ears, short necks and very long arms." Every other figure had large genitals (or was it a G-string?), and there were three toes on the feet. "The inhabitants of Atlantis were descended from the Lemurians . . . the contact with the spiritual world is lost. . . ."

Atlantis, Lemurians, prehistoric giants—these were beyond the limits

FIG. 23. *Vessel described by Maria Belli de Leon as lunar.*

of my assignment. On the basis of the limited hard facts, I would not agree with these interpretations. But I could agree with Enrique Vallis, commenting in the same issue of *La Voz:* ". . . one thing is certain: South America is a prodigious spawning ground for archaeological puzzles, of lost civilizations which now, little by little, come to light. . . ."

The markings in the desert are dead, unspeaking, geometric patterns—rectangles, triangles, zigzags—but the figures are of living things. Most of them can be directly linked to fertility. That third leg of *Ricinulei,* the genitals of the monkey, and dog, the hairpin pathway leading into the pollen of the flower. The life signs in the desert seem to show a preoccupation with nature, and the same awareness is in the motifs on the Nascan ceramics. This is nothing more than a speculation. Fertility symbols in the dead desert? Was there some rite of fertility on

PLATE 41. *Strange figures on a Nascan flared bowl.*

147

those ornamental pathways—a sex-cult orgy, working for life in the life-destroying desert?

It would be a major expedition for a group of people to stay for long out there on the plateau. Water, food, and all provisions would have to be carried because there is nothing to pick or forage. We did catch a glimpse of a coyote in the mountains. John Harvard (a student of, but not related to the founder of, Harvard University) attracted two buzzards out of the blue when he lay prostrate on the bare soil. He got up, so he claimed, just as the birds were about to tear his flesh. Maybe Ian Fleming's scorpion was sting-poised under that isolated, dust-dried bush, scared by the thud of our feet, "its senses questing for the minute vibrations which would decide its next move." And maybe there was that small beetle passing by in the sand, "and the swift rush of the scorpion down the slope gave him no time to open his wings." But there were no diamond smugglers, no machine-gun-firing helicopters. All in all, the Pampa Jumana-Colorada was a desolate, inhospitable, lonely place, and to carry out these vast projects on the parched wasteland—giant drawings, miles of linear marks, cleared areas, larger-than-life-sized figures, and the setting out of valuable pottery—required some deep drive welling from the spirit and the mind of those people.

PLATE 42. *"Did that lost civilization at Nasca progress from incising gourds and clay to incising the desert?"*

The lost civilization that conceived of and executed the decorating of the desert might have been far-reaching in its experience and knowledge. If it was Nascan, it reached far beyond the Nasca Valley, to the Amazon and the Galapagos Islands. Someone mentioned the Paracas peninsula, that barren, waterless spur of land jutting into the Pacific, the burial place for a culture dating back 4,000 years. Woven textiles reached a peak of perfection then. The rare Paracas ceramics are decorated characteristically with lines cut in the clay, the spaces filled with colored resins. Incision decoration began before the age of ceramics, ivory and stone engraving in ancient Central America and Ice Age Europe. There are wooden gourds from Paracas decorated in this technique. A gourd in my own collection has triangular heads very similar to the lizard at Pampa Jumana-Colorada. Did that lost civilization at Nasca turn from incising gourds and clay to incising the desert?

All the clues were there. Work left untouched for 2,000 years, lines to measure, to study, and to base calculations on. The computer had searched for an astronomical purpose and failed. The lines were not made to point to the heavens or the horizon, were not roadways or footpaths, would not irrigate, and do not mark anything buried in the desert subsoil. Maybe tomorrow's graduate student, with or without computer, will go over the data and find a fresh insight into the mystery.

I could believe that the mesa, suspended below the violet mountains, was an ancient Peruvian holy place, an abode of spirits. A line or giant geometrical shape might have been made as a penance to please the gods. Whatever the intent of the builders, the lines did serve mundanely as a navigation grid for placing and relocating ceremonial vessels. The body might be buried in the valley tomb with a bowl and the soul placed in a matching twin bowl in the desert. Or the offering might be commemorative of a tribal or family event. Perhaps the waca vessels held the power of life, fertility, and the unknown future—a genie, a guardian spirit to be communed with in the solitude of that unworldly place.

When there is a cognitive gulf we lose that element of myth, legend, and philosophical perspective. We reach for the mind in the soil, as Richard Atkinson said in the *Mystery of Stonehenge,* and it "slips through our fingers."

I suddenly noticed that the moist, sweet-earth smell did not come from the opened chest as I had at first supposed. It was the house. There was one door in the wall of the small, tiled-floor room, screened by a streamer curtain through which one glimpsed a kitchen with a floor of beaten earth. The roof was matted bamboo with mud spread on top. It had squeezed through the cracks before hardening. The shadeless electric bulb hung down over the *huacos,* a sun with planetary moths.

As Palacio put the treasures back in the wooden chest I reflected on the Indian stories. In the beginning they

lived like wild animals without religion or polity, without house or cities. . . . Like beasts they ate wild plants and roots, the fruits which were produced by the bushes without cultivation, and human flesh. They covered their bodies with leaves and bark and skins of animals; others went naked. In a word they lived like wild animals and like the brutes they even had their women in common. . . . (The Inca Garcilaso de la Vega, 1722.)

They say that the creator was in Tiahuanaco and that was his principal abode. Hence there are there superb edifices deserving of wonder in which are painted many dresses of those Indians and many stone figures of men and women whom he turned into stone for not obeying his commands. They say that over all was the darkness of night and there he created the Sun and the Moon and stars, and that he commanded the Sun, the Moon and the stars to go to the island of Titicaca which is nearby and from there to ascend to the sky. [Then] the Creator . . . or Ticci Viracocha, which means the Unknowable God, went along the highland road and visited the tribes to see how they had begun to multiply. . . . (Cristobal de Molina of Cuzco, 1873.)

Ticci Viracocha is the Inca (Quetchua) name for the ancient Peruvian sun-god. According to Thor Heyerdahl, the name before the time of the Incas was Kon-Tiki, the same god that cropped up in historic legends current among the natives of the Pacific islands. Heyerdahl followed the legendary path of Kon-Tiki from Callao, the port of Lima, across the Pacific to the Tuamotu Islands. Perhaps Kon-Tiki's influence touched Nasca.

Cieza de León, in 1554, wrote of the Indians of the Lake Titicaca region: they ''say the same as all the highland peoples that his [Ticci Viracocha's] principal abode is in heaven . . . and among the natives are men of good understanding who show their intelligence when questioned. They keep count of time and know something of the movements of both the sun and the moon. . . .''

Palacio lifted a small pottery idol to place it in the chest. There was a symbol on the headdress: ▭ . "That's the Chinese symbol for the sun!" someone said. Some of the faces painted on the pots looked slit-eyed and vaguely Oriental. Perhaps the mystery of Nasca had a broader reach than the desert mesa.

There are several rival migration theories. Heyerdahl, of course, proposes a raft colonization from South America westward. During the Ice Age, migration across the (dry?) Bering Strait is thought to have taken place, with prehistoric Asiatics slowly traveling through Alaska, Canada, the United States, Central America down to Peru, and beyond. There again, trans-Pacific voyages eastward have been proposed, from Asia, island-hopping to the Americas.

Franz Caspar, Swiss ethnologist, lived with the Stone Age Mato Grosso Indians for four months. On the edge of the steaming Amazon jungle he learned of their beliefs about earth, sky, and man. There were magicians in the sky who had animal form, a capuchin monkey, a black monkey, a howler monkey, and many others. "Ordinary people cannot see these dwellers in heaven. Only our magicians have dealings with them during the raising of spirits."

The Incas prayed to a cosmic god:

> Viracocha, Lord of the Universe!
> Whether male or female,
> Commander of heat and reproduction,
> being one who, even with his spittle, can work sorcery,
> Where are you? . . .
> The sun, the moon; the day, the night; summer, winter,
> not in vain but in orderly succession
> do they march to their destined place, to their goal.*

Emperor Pachacuti, before Pizarro's conquest, is credited with the building of eight towers to the east and west of Cuzco. Viewed from the throne in the center of the square, the towers marked the sun at the solstices and equinoxes. J. Alden Mason believes "the Inca probably knew the length of the year and that of the lunar month, and possibly the period of Venus, with considerable accuracy."

---

* P. A. Means, *Ancient Civilizations of the Andes.* New York, 1931.

151

COTADOR.MAIOR.ITEZORERO
TAVANTIN.SVIO.QVIPOC
CVRACA·CON DOR·CHAVA

con tador ytezorero   con tador

FIG. 24. *Inca with knotted quipu in his hands. At the lower left, a binary colored counting device with a core memory of 20 compartments.*

152

Palacio put a tassel of colored knotted cords back in the chest. This was a quipu, an ancient memory bank for storing numbers. A knot on one string stood for 10; a knot an another stood for units. The "number" strings were tied to a line, and the whole made up a tassel. It was a place-value system, decimal, like the Arabic system we use in Western culture. The first string of the tassel carried knots XX, XXX, X, which I read as the number 231. There were more numbers tied into the strands, each one placed there neatly, purposefully. Was this an astronomical period? A cosmic, magical number? Or was it the total inhabitants of a village, a census, or bookkeeping record?

Baron Erland Nordenskiold* deciphered those special quipus found in the tombs. He claimed the quipus to be calendric and astronomical. He found sums and totals which agreed with the rotation period of certain celestial bodies.

Garcilaso de la Vega, born of an Inca princess, fathered by a conquistador, wrote of the quipu reckoning system: " [it] caused wonder to the Spaniards, who saw that their own best accountants made mistakes in their arithmetic, while the Indians were so accurate. . . ."

The Spaniards should have looked further. The Incas used a computer. We do not know how it worked or how the calculations were made, nor do we know what they were calculating. The device was a box with twenty compartments placed in four rows of five. Stones were placed in the various compartments, some black, some white. A compartment was filled when five stones were in it. Padre José de Acosta watched the Incas manipulate this abacuslike device and drew a sketch. But that was back in 1590. He was unable to follow the computing procedure. None of these 20-core memory banks have been found by archaeologists. Were they destroyed as worthless, pagan magic?

Chronicler Fernando Montesinos wrote of "wise men and astrologers and, with the king himself (who was deeply learned), they all studied the solstice with care. There was a sort of shadow-clock by which they knew which days were long and which were short, and when the sun went to and returned from the tropics."† Montesinos was referring to

* *Comparative Ethnographic Studies*, Gottenburg Museum, Vol. 6, 1925.
† On Midsummer's Day the sun, rising at the extreme northerly azimuth at Stonehenge, is at declination +23°.5. On this day it stands vertically overhead at noon on the Tropic of Cancer, the small circle which runs at geographical latitude +23°.5 north.

the *intihuatana,* those modern-art-shaped stones ruthlessly destroyed as pagan by the missionaries. Only one of these sun markers now survives—the one at Machu Picchu, high above the jungle of the Urabamba River where the conquerors never penetrated.

Perhaps there were clues to the Nasca mystery to be found outside of the Pampa Colorada.

Plus ultra.

9 KON-TIKI

We changed planes at Lima airport from an international flight to a local one on Peru's Faucett Airline. On this second expedition we did not have time to make the 600-mile, bumpy jeep ride over the historic mountain roadway. Faucett had pioneered the trans-Andean flight with oxygen masks for the passengers. Today we would go in the luxury of a pressurized cabin and would swoop down into the Cuzco Valley like the legendary Inca Ayar Cachi, "coming in the air with great wings."

Originally we had been summoned to an audience with the president of Peru in the Government Palace. We were to discuss and answer questions about our research into Inca lore and Peruvian antiquities. But the president had been deposed between expeditions 1 and 2, and now the country, the palace, and the airport transit lounge were in a temporary state of emergency, controlled by dark green uniforms, steel helmets, and submachine guns. However, the direction of the research, international in its reach, timeless in its quest, was unchanged. Our project, a study of the greatness of ancient Peru, was nonpolitical, archaeological, scientific.

I was amazed to see the passengers from the New York flight dragooned in the lounge, sitting in rows and looking blankly at the officers. Each passenger had a thermometer in his or her mouth. It was the height of the Hong Kong flu epidemic in the States, and this was a medical control check to find those who were infectious. Their stay in Peru would be cut short. I was apprehensive. My schedule was tight. Three days before the flight I had been laid low with the bug. I wouldn't take any chances—I would pull the thermometer out when it reached normal. The thermometer was placed in my mouth. By squinting my eyes I could bring the graduation marks into focus and watch for the thin line of mercury. Curse it, it was a Centigrade scale! I was too fatigued to convert 98.6°F. into Centigrade—minus 32, times 5/9. The mercury moved up untampered to somewhere near 37. I passed the test.

Cuzco, the oldest inhabited city of South America, is a cluster of red Spanish tile roofs when seen from the air. The color blends with the rock and the verdant green of the high valley. The Renaissance cathedral, built on Inca ruins in 1560, is a russet brown. Ancient stone terraces line the steep sides of the valley to hold the soil of the orchards and fields in place. These fertile strips have produced the same crops for centuries. The flow of mountain water is controlled by sluices engineered in stone. Aqueducts lead water from high springs into the city. Some of these ancient stone-lined pipes run with pure water from faraway, forgotten, untraced sources. Stony pathways climb the hills, breaking into steps where the going is steep.

Cieza de León questioned the Inca noblemen in 1550 about the origins of the city. His inquiry must be rated as the world's first research project in social anthropology, though he called it "an exercise to escape from the vices caused by idleness."

Manco Capac (the first Inca) . . . raised his eyes to heaven and with great humility besought the sun that he would favor and aid him in forming the new settlement. Then turning his eyes towards the hill of Huanacauri he addressed the same petition to his brother (Ayar Cachi) whom he now held and reverenced as a god (after having just killed him by walling him up in a cave). Next he watched the flight of birds, the signs of the stars, and other omens. . . . In the name of Ticci Viracocha and of the sun and of other gods he laid the foundations of the new city.

Clearly the founding of Cuzco was connected with astronomy and the sun, linked to the sky. The Inca kings, like the pharaohs of Egypt, claimed to be born of the sun. The growth of the Inca empire, spreading a full thousand miles from the equator at Quito down to modern Chile, was a crusade to spread the worship of the sun as the supreme god.

Heavy stonework without machinery is remarkable in the thin air of Cuzco. The city, 11,400 feet above sea level, is only a few hundred feet short of the agriculture line, the limit above which no crop will grow. It takes three weeks for the human body to adapt to the altitude as the oxygen capacity of the bloodstream gradually increases to the viable amount. Until that time the visitor is recommended to rest and avoid physical strain.

The Cuzco hotel carries notices to warn tourists of altitude sickness.

Oxygen equipment is available from the hall porter. Yet in the tourist rush, particularly on a one-day sightseeing jet trip, the warning is often read too late. After deplaning at sunrise, breakfasting, climbing the fortress of Sacsahuaman, lunching through five courses, rushing to buy llama-skin rugs at 10 percent more than the price in downtown Lima, one sees the wife at the phone by the reception desk: "Yes, Doctor, come right away, I think it's his heart!"

We did not wish for *la seroche,* the altitude sickness which strikes with a migraine headache, palpitation of the heart, nausea, and blackout. James Glaisher found these symptoms the hard way when in 1862, as the world's first guinea pig, he ascended by balloon to 29,000 feet from the Wolverhampton gasworks. We spent the first day quietly speaking with the Cuzco Indians in broken Spanish and in Quechua with the help of an interpreter.

Even so I did suffer mild effects—heavy-headedness, fatigue, and the ground coming up to meet me with each step as I plodded forward. I needed a drink—something stronger than the refreshing pause of Peru called Inca-Cola. The bell captain in the hotel recommended a local medicine. I drank hot, almost colorless tea brewed English style in a pot with long dark leaves. Good. "What do you call this?" It was cocaine. The leaves were *Erythroxylon cocae,* the Peruvian coca bush. Native Indians have chewed the coca leaf for generations, getting their kick despite the intervention of the Spanish conquerors and later the national government. In small doses it produces pleasant hallucinations, stimulates the mind and body, and anesthetizes the stomach. In excess it produces a paranoiac psychosis, emaciation, and convulsions. Historical perspective excuses the cocaine addiction of the high Andes as a natural response to the oppression of the Spanish colonizers, the harshness of the climate, and the pangs of ever-present hunger.

I do not have a cellophane-wrap, antiseptic fetish. I enjoy local foods, nights on the town, *vinos de la casa.* But to become ill during field work is a loss of time, a gross misjudgment, scientifically unforgivable. I stick to an expedition diet of beer, bread, peeled fruits, and stews (boiled and bubbled to sterility). Nor do I have to watch my weight, usually losing 10 pounds on an expedition. I once saw a tourist moaning in a hotel lounge in Mexico City, struck by "Moctezuma's revenge," and a sightseer in Spain with "Torquemada's tummy." Not that foreign bugs are to blame. "Señor," said the manager of the hotel in Mexico City, pointing to the tourist, "it is not my cuisine. He arrived yesterday. What passes? Our city is 3,000 meters high. He had a three-course breakfast, brandy, coffee, lunch, a pile of tortillas, cognac, wine, red peppers. Milk of the mother of god! I myself would be sick, and I'm a Mexicano!"

The center of Cuzco is virtually the same as in colonial days. On the outskirts the Peruvian government has added apartments and schools, and the new airport, but the town square dates back to antiquity. One of the streets, steep and paved in rough stone, is still known as the road of the conquistadores, and folklore affirms it as the way of entry of Pizarro and his men. The lower courses of walls and buildings are constructed of limestone and granite-type blocks, set without mortar, interlocking with precision. One such block has twelve sides and angles and is cut to fit perfectly into eleven surrounding stones. These foundation walls are Inca, for the colonizers destroyed and then built on top of the ruins.

T. Athol Joyce, a South Americanist, rates the Incas and their lost ancestors as the master masons of prehistory. They carved hard blocks with exactitude to make a three-dimensional jigsaw puzzle. Each stone was cut for one position only. This unique interlocking has preserved the structure against storm and earthquake. It was achieved with nothing more than stone tools. The Peruvian stonemasons did not have iron, steel, or hard metal. There were no instruments, no blueprints—the fitting was done by sight and touch.

Architecturally the builders mastered the rectangular corner, the ellipse, and the circle. The temple structures have a classical simplicity, devoid of fanciful decorations. The keyed archway was not known, and so windows and entrances were spanned by means of a single-slab lintel, Stonehenge fashion.

The Spanish chroniclers did not wish to praise anything pagan if this could be avoided. They passed off the superb workmanship as witchcraft—the Peruvians, they said, had a process to soften stone so that it could be cut as easily as cheese! And the weight of those stones, some up to 100 tons? Perhaps, like the doctor in H. G. Wells's *First Men in the Moon* they cheated with antigravity plates, temporarily removing the pull of the earth!

The Great Square was impressive. I stood where the emperor once held sway on religious feast days; where singing, dancing, and initiation ceremonies took place, where chicha beer was the drink. These events were time-factored, following the priestly calendar, controlled by the sun, moon, and perhaps the stars. Each day at the instant of sunrise a sacred fire was kindled from carved and incensed wood. Food was thrown in with the accompaniment of a communionlike liturgy. "Eat this, Lord Sun, and acknowledge thy children." On the first day of the month 100 llamas were paraded in a circle before the emperor and his court and the animals were allocated into lots for future sacrifice—30 lots, one for each day of the moon.

The chroniclers give us only a garbled account of the time-factored system. There were 12 months in the year, so they say, and each month began on the day of the new moon. Agricultural and other seasonal events were recognized at the appropriate place in the calendar. But 12 lunations, each averaging 29.53 days, do not make a tropical year, 365.2422. They fall short by nearly 11 days. To correct this is an exacting problem. Extra months must be inserted in accordance with a prescribed calendar round. The Babylonian round takes place over a period of 19 years, and from this the Jewish calendar has been developed. The old prerepublican Chinese calendar was also based on a 19-year cycle. The successful development of a lunar-solar calendar must be preceded by several centuries of observation to determine the correct periodicities. While the chroniclers were suppressing the calendric knowledge of the Incas, Gregory XIII was establishing a papal commission to look into the then intolerable error in the old-style Julian calendar. In 1582 our current, Gregorian calendar was introduced. It is accurate to 26 seconds through the solar year, but it takes no account of the moon.

Knowledge of the Inca calendar was held by the *orejones* (the long-ears), the select class of noblemen-priests who were related through the royal line to Manco Capac. Emperor Huascar was killed as Pizarro arrived, together with his entire family of eighty children, wives, and brothers. The murders were ordered by the Inca Atahullpa, who himself was led to the stake, baptized, and then garroted by the Spanish. The last lineal descendant, Tupac Amaru, was beheaded in the Great Square in 1572. Unless the knotted quipus contain calendric information which can be deciphered, the Inca knowledge may be irretrievable.

159

The missionaries give only scant information about the ceremonies. The most important event took place when the sun was at the southern extreme, —23°.5, corresponding to midsummer in the southern hemisphere. This was the month of Capac Raimi, or December by the Gregorian calendar. At that time there were puberty initiations for boys of noble rank, athletic competitions, and a mock battle. The ceremony for the month of June, winter solstice, was directed to the adoration of the sun, with a fiesta for the populace, sacrifices, and the solemn ritual of the making of a new fire.

I looked from the Great Square to the rugged skyline. Pachacuti's eight towers were gone. There was no archaeological trace of the original positions. Historians record how one of the towers of this ninth emperor marked the midwinter sunrise; another, midsummer. In one of the legends Pachacuti built the towers to obtain a correction to the 12-month calendar set up by the eighth emperor, Viracocha Inca, but it would not have been possible to initiate and calibrate a lunar-solar calendar in so short a period of time. The towers and system of time reckoning might date back before Pachacuti and Viracocha.

The astronomical sun-sight from the square to the skyline could be calculated, and with this process the site of the tower perhaps located. This would be astro-archaeology in reverse. One could then determine the alignment error in the placing, could say whether the whole orb or the rim was observed, but the investigation would not be in the main thrust of research. It would not yield data on pre-Columbian scientific knowledge. Those other towers are the lure, the ones that did not mark the solstices. Did they mark the equinoxes (J. Alden Mason, the Philadelphia-based expert on Inca civilization, doubts this), or did they mark the moon or stars? Would there be by some remote chance a relationship to the directions of the lines at Nasca? Here we must await the archaeologist's spade.

I walked across the square to the place where Manco Capac first settled with his sister-wife. The great Temple of the Sun (Coricancha, meaning gold circle) was built on the spot to sanctify the site. Here 3,000 men and women priests attended to the rituals of *inti*, the Quechua title for sun-god. The hall of the sun was 93 feet by 47 feet, according to the estimate of Americanist John H. Rowe, comparable in size to the sarsen circle. The outer perimeter was 1,200 feet long, comparable to the outer circle at Stonehenge. The hall was hung with rich ornaments, notably the enormous gold disk of the sun which disappeared without trace before Pizarro got his hands on it. Golden-eyed speculators have dug for it in the surrounding hills, but without success. The disk could be likened to the Aztec calendar stone, though the Incas did not have a developed system of hieroglyphics. Bundled, mummified bodies of the emperors were kept in the hall to be brought out into the sunlight on fiesta occasions.

There were rooms and buildings within the perimeter for the temple staff—astrologers, judges, weavers, and medics. The royal cloth was fine-threaded, patterned, the best in Peru, and ergo the best in the world. The medical staff successfully performed bone transplants, amputations, and brain trephining under anesthetic (cocaine from coca leaves), and with postoperative drugs. There were rooms for the women of the temple, the *mamacuna* (who were virgins of the sun), and the so-called chosen women (who were not). Girls were selected from the four corners of the empire for the honor of Cuzco. They were, so the Spaniards found, matched in features and proportions, the result of a national beauty and talent search.

The temple was the hub of the empire. Imaginary (?) lines radiated from it to the wacas, or spirit places, to the hills and towers. But it is impossible at the present time to tell whether or not directional information was built into the temple structure. The layout is obliterated. The monks reconsecrated the consecrated site. The church and monastery of Santo Domingo spreads over and through the Inca temple. Only portions of the original walls are visible, notably the curved section at the west. This might have been an observing platform.

There is a circular platform at Pisac, on a hill near to Cuzco. It carries the fragments of an angular stone, the *intihuatana* ("sun's hitching post" in Quechua). The Inca priests measured the shadow of a central gnomon. Observations were carried out up to the time of the conquest. The work was of critical importance to the *inti* religion, and stone instruments were set up at temples throughout the empire. The Spanish men of the Renaissance had no interest in or respect for "pagan" science. Concerning the nature of the temple astronomy we have nothing more than the brief statement of Montesinos: they all studied the solstices with care. But the conquerors recognized the power

161

of the ritual. They smashed the stone at Pisac and destroyed all other *intihuatanas,* methodically, relentlessly. All, that is, except the one at Machu Picchu.

Somewhere in the jungle was a refuge, a hidden city of the Incas, the Shangri-la of the New World. The rumor was persistent. Hiram Bingham, a Yale archaeologist, believed it. The prospects were exciting. He searched and explored the torrid eastern edge of Peru where the rivers flow into the Amazon. If he found the city would it be inhabited? Would there be artifacts, a golden sun disk?

In July, 1911, after many disappointments he was led by an Indian up a steep path at the edge of the rain forest. On the top of the mountain at 8,000 feet elevation his search ended. He walked along grass terraces, through stone gateways, and up flights of steps. He looked at crumbled buildings blooming with poinsettias, at a tower of white granite blocks and a high temple. He had found Machu Picchu.

If there are seven wonderful places in the world, Machu Picchu is one of them. The natural beauty is comparable to the Victoria Falls of central Africa, the Isles of Greece, or the Grand Tetons, Wyoming. The high pinnacle is surrounded by a distant cauldron of yet higher mountains, forest-green, uncut by roads or habitation. The sky has tropical brilliance, yet the altitude produces a moderate, stimulating climate. It would be difficult for man to pollute this inaccessible spot. If the aerosol smog ever reaches Machu Picchu then it will have touched every place on earth.

The Incas had selected a place of natural abundance. Food crops were plentiful on the extensive soil terraces, watered by the Florida-style rain showers. There was a drinking well and a catchment area. Natural fruits were there for the picking in the jungle at the mouth of the gorge. Llama and vicuna herds provided wool for garments. The lower slopes gave wood for fuel.

Today a small diesel train rattles down the Urabamba river valley from Cuzco. A jeep waits at the station to take passengers up the hairpin-bend dirt road cut on the western slope of the gorge. When one

PLATE 43. *Machu Picchu, lost city of the Incas, perched high on the edge of the Amazon jungle.*

looks up from the gorge, the ancient city is invisible, hidden by the almost vertical forest slopes.

Archaeological digging has exposed the full extent of the settlement. It was not a city; it was a temple complex. The purpose was religious, ritualistic, not secular. The focal point was a pyramid on the western edge of the precipice. This pyramid was probably natural in origin, a hillock shaped with stone terraces, for the Incas did not build pyramids like the Mayas and Aztecs.

I walked across the plaza and climbed the stairway to the summit. This, of course, was the place of the *intihuatana,* and it was intact. I studied and took measurements of the device. The post, or vertical gnomon, was 1 foot high with a slanting top. The eastern face of the stone was cut into with slanting and horizontal planes, so that the edges were straight and ran in various directions. As far as I could tell without digging, the stone was a natural outcrop, carved *in situ.* Without doubt this was a prehistoric scientific instrument. The shadow cast by the sun or moon could be read to ½ centimeter, corresponding to an angular error of about ¼ degree for the longest shadow line. The solstice, equinox, and displacements of the moon could be observed. At this altitude Venus also would cast a shadow.

How would *we* do it? How would we take shadow measurements? The question does not help because the *intihuatana* is constructed on principles alien to present-day science. We would draw a north–south meridian and make radial lines from the gnomon like spokes in a wheel. We would have elliptical curves symmetrical about the meridian. But the Inca stone is not symmetrical. The north–south line runs diagonally across the top surface from one corner to a small facet. I took measurements and planned an analysis. It would require the machine to compute the numerous three-dimensional shadow direction. While the main directions were obvious in the Stonehenge architecture, it was an abstruse and detailed problem to find those significant directions in the *intihuatana.* The investigation is proceeding at the time of writing.

How did the settlement of Machu Picchu come to an end? It was not war, or famine, or pestilence. The graves are predominantly female. The few males were probably eunuchs. The temple was an isolated, pure community of virgins of the sun. I overheard a guide discussing this

PLATE 44. *Intihuatana at Machu Picchu. A stone fashioned to read the movements of the sun.*

165

with a group of French tourists: "And so you see it went under with—how you say it?—zero birth rate."

We traveled across the high, desolate plateau of the Andes, the roof of the world, the Altiplano—13,000 feet, 14,000 feet and higher . . . the altitude, like the stretching of a rack, increased. At one village I felt inert, dead, pressured into the ground. The height was given on a sign: 17,400 feet above sea level. Yet here in the highest village life continued. The genetics of the region have produced a special physique. Doctors speak of the great size of the altitude lung. The body contains 2 quarts more blood than normal, the hemoglobin count is 8 million instead of 5 million, and the heart rate is slow. As I stood there, turned to stone like Inca Ayar Cachi, I saw children playing soccer on a rocky incline above the village.

Apart from a few potato patches agriculture is impossible in the Altiplano climate. A research team was sure that the inhabitants must be severely undernourished. The diet was way short on calcium, and by all the laws of nutrition the natives should be hairless, weak-boned, and convulsed with muscular spasms. The team watched the intake of food, the monotonous diet of gruel, potatoes, etc., which confirmed the hypothesis. Then for no reason an Indian crushed a piece of tasteless limestone rock into a fine powder and sprinkled it on his food. It was an age-old Altiplano custom. It added no flavor or seasoning, but it did supply the dietary requirement of calcium.

We did see four-year-old children employed in minding the llamas in the bleak pasture, and families where only the man could afford sandals, but we could not agree with the ethnographist who wrote: "Their dark, heavy, patient faces are set in perpetual sullenness, their eyes subdued, it seems as though these native folk had been oppressed by eternal grief." Nor did we believe the allegation that the Altiplano is a ghetto and law forbids the offer of a ride down to the cities and coastal lowlands.

Titicaca, the highest navigable lake in the world, was the prehistoric center of the sun cult. Legend hints at this (the birthplace of the sun and the place of all creation), and archaeology confirms it. There was an important temple on the Island of the Sun, and a palace of priests on the Island of Coati. The megalithic site of Tiahuanaco was built on the shores of the lake, though the waters have receded now.

166

PLATE 45. *The gate of the sun-god, Tiahuanaco.*

167

The edifice of Tiahuanaco was once called a "rectangular Stonehenge."* There are indeed similarities. The stones weighing up to 100 tons were transported to a ceremonial location, the blocks have tenons and notches as if made of wood, and the main rectangle, 445 feet by 425 feet, is marked off with standing stones. But there are differences. The megaliths are carved, mostly in the shape of human figures, and there is no enclosing ditch. The entrance to the rectangle is through the famous Gate of the Sun. This solid-block archway is carved with a godlike figure and 48 symbols, 24 on either side. Much speculative hot air has risen over Tiahuanaco—that it was once an island which sunk Atlantis-like beneath the Pacific to be raised intact on the back of the Andes—and the 48 symbols have been cited as proof of a 48-month year when the moon circled the earth every 7½ days. But this cannot be so. The moon might have been close to the earth in the past with a period of about 10 days, but celestial mechanical calculations give the time as at least 1 billion years ago.

It would be interesting to survey the position of the monoliths around the rectangle to investigate possible alignments with sun, moon, or stars. On the other hand, J. Alden Mason considers these monoliths to be nothing more than the remnants of a wall.

Although the Incas claimed to be a new race created by the sun, they were probably descendants of the Tiahuanaco culture which flourished between A.D. 200 and 600, some 700 years before the Inca rise to power. The Tiahuanaco culture possibly came from, or was influenced by, Nasca. The connection has not been formally proposed in a professional journal, but the evidence is suggestive. The Tiahuanaco pottery is painted with colored designs, rich polychrome, similar to Nascaware. The style is bolder, more dramatic, and would be a natural evolution from the style of Nasca 2, 3, and 4, which were several centuries earlier. At the time horizon of A.D. 700, the influence of Tiahuanaco shows up in most Peruvian archaeological sites. The cultural lens spread wide from Titicaca and overlapped the desert regions between the mountains and the ocean.

When science stops, imagination begins. Concerning the ancient civilizations of Peru, archaeology has not yet produced enough threads to

* T. Athol Joyce, *Wonders of the Past,* Vol. 2 (London: Hammerton, 1925), p. 719.

spin a theory on. We do not know the basis of the legends or the development of the culture. "Archaeology," said Sir Cyril Fox, "is incapable of dealing with myths."

Thor Heyerdahl sat by the palm trees on tropical Fatu Hiva in the Marquesas Island group. He was on a beach one starry night listening to the roar of the invisible surf as it ended the long roll across the Pacific driven by the easterly trade winds. An old wrinkled man, bark-brown and weathered, crouched by the red embers of a fire on the coral sand, and his voice mingled appropriately with the sound of the waves. He told how his ancestors were carried to the island paradise from a distant land many generations before by the sun-god, Tiki.

Heyerdahl's imagination took flight. He coupled Tiki with a pre-Inca sun-god, Kon-Tiki; he joined in his mind the human effigies on Easter Island and the Marquesas with the statues at Tiahuanaco, and the pyramids on Tahiti and Samoa with those in Peru. He saw a great chieftain spring from Lake Titicaca, journey to the dusty coast, and sail westward in the wind and current on a balsa-log raft to the South Sea Islands. His theory of the settlement of Polynesia was born.

He turned imagination into reality. With five companions he sailed in a replica of a Peruvian raft from Callao to the Tuamotu Archipelago. But Heyerdahl was the first to admit that the adventure on the high seas did not prove his theory (as with the Stonehenge theory, it waited for acceptance, not proof Q.E.D.); the voyage proved that a balsa raft can float from Peru to Polynesia, no more.

I am not an ethnologist and do not wish to enter the controversy over Heyerdahl's theory of race migration with the spread of a sun cult westward across the Pacific. Rival theories have South America populated by ocean passage in reverse of Heyerdahl's voyage, from Polynesia to Chile (the great circulating Humboldt Current flows from west to east on its southern leg), or alternatively by overland travel from China via the then dry Bering Strait, down the North American continent, across the Isthmus of Panama. But there are some interesting hard facts to consider.

Item: Polynesians use knots in strings for record keeping, similar to the quipus of the Inca.

Item: Counting back through the family histories as recorded in the quipus, and allowing an average of 25 years for a generation, the date

PLATE 46. *The solar observatory markers on Rano Kao, above Orongo, Easter Island.*

of commencement of the several Polynesian genealogies comes out to be about A.D. 500. This is the approximate climax of the lost Tiahuanaco culture (and a few centuries after the Nasca lines).

Item: On Easter Island in the mid-Pacific there are large stone figures of long-eared, legless men (*orejones?*), set in the turf or on flat platforms by the shore. The platforms are made of stone blocks, cut and fitted together without mortar, precisely and masterfully. The nearest equivalent is in Cuzco, in the Inca walls where stone was cut "as though it were cheese."

Item: Heyerdahl's colleagues carried out a survey of the orientation of the 300-foot platform at Vinapu. The wall, and the statues originally on it, faced the equinox direction to within the limits of measurement.

Item: There was a sacred village at Orongo, romantically perched on a narrow ridge, overlooking the vista of the blue ocean. Forty-eight stone chapels, unique to Polynesia, were decorated with colored figures and designs. Sockets were found carved in the lava of the wall of the volcanic crater high above the village. When a stick was set in the central hole the shadow was observed to fall on the marks in the rock at the summer and winter solstice. (Several years later, however, another ethnologist was unable to locate these features at the Orongo observatory.)

Long before Admiral Jacob Roggeveen discovered the island on Easter Day, 1722, the natives made fetishes with supposed magical powers. The items were carved stone figures and pottery vessels. When Heyerdahl arrived he was shown these "akus," some hidden for protection in caves. Like the Peruvian "waca," the aku was the abode of a spirit. Like the Inca "wawaki," the aku-aku was a guiding spirit, a benevolent genie, a conscience. Thor Heyerdahl was swept up by the idea, transculturized. On Easter Island one restless night he thought he heard the voice of his own personal aku coming from the depths of his archaic subconscious. The aku talked with him, argued with him about his theory of trans-Pacific migration. It liberated his wildest thoughts!

The origin of the Polynesian race is under discussion as I write; theories circulate with the great Humboldt Current, east to west, west to east; ideas blow from this school of thought and that, breezy as the trade winds. But beyond the ethnology there is the clear possibility of a pan-Pacific, pan-American sun cult. Astro-archaeology already exists in the islands. The tools of physical science can fruitfully be applied to Pacificana when, in the aftermath of the world economic recession, research money flows again.

In 1968 I received a scientific communication from Taufa'ahau Tupau IV, king of the Tonga Islands. His Majesty reported on the investigation of a stone trilithon—prehistoric, of unknown age—on one of the islands in the archipelago. Careful observation of two incised lines on the top of the lintel reveals that they point to the sun on the horizon at the winter and summer solstices. The midway marker for spring and fall was not so exact, but ancient people, the king suggested, could readily count 91 days from the solstice.

While the antiquities of the Pacific and South America await the astro-probe, we must stop short at the words of Cristobal de Molina of Cuzco: "And at the moment when the sun was about to ascend as a man all shining and resplendent, he called to the Incas and to Manco Capac

171

and said: 'Thou and thy descendants are to be lords and subdue many nations. Regard me as thy father and yourselves as my children. . . .' ''
The Incas did subdue many nations and with them the oral culture and heritage. They were themselves cut short as "the passer-by sweeps off the head of a sunflower."

Mound Builders, U.S.A., Inc.

From the Rocky Mountains to the Appalachians, from the Great Lakes to the Gulf of Mexico, the mound builders have left their mark— huge geometrical earthworks, circles, squares, and perfect, nesting octagons. Nineteenth-century explorers were awed by these structures which collectively and individually required greater efforts of organized labor than Stonehenge or the Gizeh Pyramids. A distinct, specialized, highly civilized race of people must have been at work on the North American continent before the arrival of the nomadic Indians— so theorized the scholars. It was supposedly a whole race eliminated, in the modern phrase, with extreme prejudice.

But the slow accumulation of data, of facts and artifacts, proved the theory wrong. The skeletons of mound builders are similar to the remains of Sioux, Apache, and other tribes. There is a continuity of style in copper and silver jewelry, and in stone implements. There was no previous, distinct ethnic group. For some unknown reason, group dynamics, psychocompulsion, the North American Indian from about 1000 B.C. to A.D. 500 was engaged in vast, architecturally planned, imaginatively conceived building projects.

There were thousands of prehistoric constructions across the prairie, some now obliterated by railroad and turnpike, some flattened by the suburbs. Moundsville, West Virginia, takes its name from the large mound nearby at Graves Creek. This is an example of prehistoric building that has not, at the time of writing, been fully excavated.

Small mounds found in Ohio are like the British burial tumulus. They contain interments. Some have a depression at the top, 3 or 4 feet across, and the surrounding clay is baked hard by fire. Archaeologists have collected a rich yield of artifacts, flint knives, arrowheads, and jewelry, from these so-called altar mounds.

But the geometric earthworks are not for burials and are too big to be

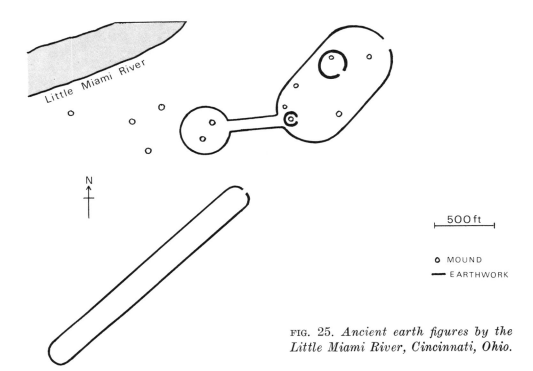

Little Miami River

N

500 ft

o MOUND
— EARTHWORK

FIG. 25. *Ancient earth figures by the Little Miami River, Cincinnati, Ohio.*

called altars. The patterns are vast, eroded by the centuries and over-grown with vegetation and farm crops. They are difficult to recognize from the ground. The would-be discoverer is better off in a light air-craft. A few business executives have taken to figure-spotting, using the company's plane. On the ground citizen groups have banded together to measure the structures, to survey and test for astronomical alignments.

Little Miami, Inc., is a group concerned with a set of ancient figures located 10 miles south of downtown Cincinnati. There is a circle joined by a graded way to an enclosure, and there is a longer enclosure to the southwest. The lines are marked in raised causeways of earth 20 feet wide and 2 or 3 feet high. Mathematicians have no name for the shape of the enclosures, though they are clearly in the class of definite geo-metrical figures. They are rectangles closed at the narrow end by semicircles, enclosing an area $a \times b$ plus πb^2. It is difficult to compre-hend the size when looking at a small-scale map. The circle and great enclosure contain more than a mile of earthworks; the narrow enclosure is 600 yards long. Little Miami, Inc., suspects that the 600-yard-long feature was built to point to midwinter sunset, but measurements at the site are difficult because of the intrusion of gravel pits.

On the banks of the Scioro River, Ohio, E. G. Squier and E. H. Davis in 1846 surveyed a circle joined onto another Stone Age mathematical novelty, a square with sides pushed outward in the form of flat triangles. The length of the diagonal across the corners of the "square" is equal to the diameter of the circle. The circle and square enclose a total area of 38 acres—enough room for 60 house lots.

Nearby, on a tributary of the Scioro, is another site. Circles and squares have been built across a field of mounds. The mounds were arranged, equally spaced, in rows of ten. The outline of the mound field is rectangular, with the sides oriented north–south and east–west. No explanation for this pattern has yet been offered.

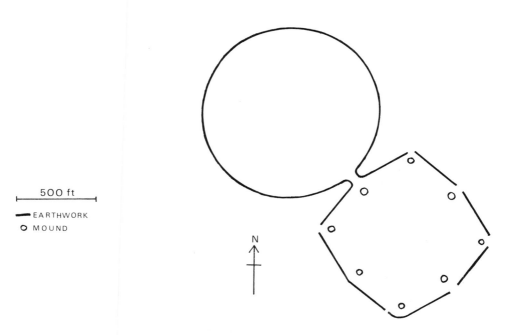

FIG. 26. *Geometric embankments near the Scioro River, Ohio.*

175

On the bank of the Mississippi east of St. Louis are the remains of the largest city-temple complex in the United States. It was in use from A.D. 800 to 1550 according to radiocarbon data, and was abandoned shortly before the French explorers went by in their canoes. Archaeologists are working on the problem of why it was abandoned—whether because of whim, war, or white man. There were hamlets, house clusters, and cornfields separated by lakes and creeks. There were five ceremonial plazas and large, flat-topped pyramids with temples. The eroded remains of one of these is known as Monks Mound. It is comparable in size to Silbury Hill. Archaeologists have discovered four circles of post holes ranging in diameter from 240 to 480 feet. One circle has been accurately surveyed to date, giving evidence of astronomical alignment. The circle contained 48 equally spaced posts with an "observer's" pole set 5 feet off center toward the east. By squatting on the top of the pole, the observer would see the sun over the east post on the first day of spring and fall. It would set over the west post also on those days. At midsummer it would rise over the fourth post to the north; at midwinter, the fourth post to the south.

FIG. 27. *Oriented mounds in rows of ten near the Scioro River, Ohio.*

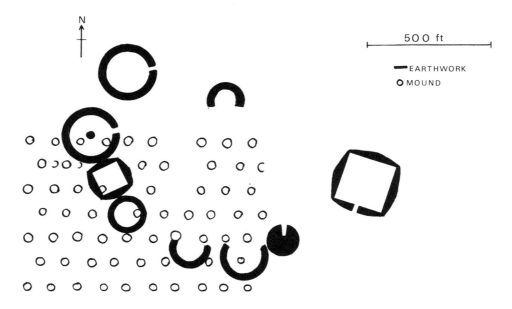

FIG. 28. *Flat-topped "Monks Mound" and related structures, Cahokia, Illinois.*

The largest and oldest geometrical figure found so far is on the banks of the Arkansas River near where it joins the Mississippi Valley. The radiocarbon date is 800 B.C. with a spread from 200 to 1300 B.C. Clarence Moore went down the river at the turn of the century in his steamboat *Gopher,* and he saw unusual "swales" in the ground. Aerial reconnaissance in 1953 showed the true nature of the feature. It was a set of six perfect octagons nesting one inside the other. The outside octagon measured three-quarters of a mile across. The geometric earth lines were ridges, 4 to 6 feet high, flat-topped, and 80 feet wide. The meandering of the river has removed about 25 percent of the structure over the centuries.

The site is known archaeologically as Poverty Point. One theory has it as a planned township with huts spaced at 100-foot intervals along the six ridges. This would make 600 huts with a population of 3,000 at five to a family. But even with extensive digging, no post holes, foundation walls, or other evidence of dwellings was found. The people who lived there left no mark of a city, and under the narrow definition were therefore "uncivilized." The artifacts are hand-thrown darts, bolas

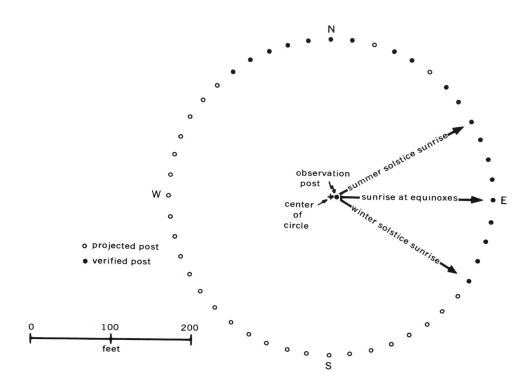

FIG. 29. *Plan of the "American Woodhenge," Cahokia, Illinois.*

with iron weights at the end of the strings, and fired clay balls (for dropping red hot into a stew)—typical items of a hunting culture not dependent on the raising of crops. And so the township theory is not easy to accept. Why not choose a natural clearing for the settlement, one with natural, ready-made ridges? Why move 500,000 cubic yards of earth, scooped by hand and carried by basket? Why build geometrical octagons? No group today would voluntarily do this work.

The ancient geometers never saw the enormous patterns from above. It would be surprising if they had evolved far enough to be doing art for art's sake. Their efforts have been categorized by one archaeologist as "nonproductive labor." To find a reason boggles the imagination. Some markings were "astro," connecting by sight lines the ground with

FIG. 30. *Raising the posts of the American Woodhenge.*

the heavens; some were temple platforms, altars, or burial mounds. But if the psychology of a prehistoric group followed the rules of group psychology today, then some all-persuasive drive was present, a single idea that "caught on," a common rationale which could not be challenged by any member of the group for fear of being ostracized.

If we can rely on the radiocarbon data, then the culture—Mound Builders U.S.A., Inc.—began in the lower Mississippi Valley and spread northward and eastward along the tributaries into Illinois, Ohio, and West Virginia. The earth markings are mostly on the banks of rivers, and the Poverty Point date is 500 years earlier than the dates in Ohio. The people who built these vast geometries, or perhaps the idea compelling people to build them, seemed to enter through the Missis-

179

sippi Delta from somewhere across the Gulf of Mexico. Current opinion places the origin of the culture on the southern shores of the Gulf, in the Yucatan Peninsula, land of the Mayas, the lost civilization discovered almost accidentally and credited with the most advanced knowledge of pre-Columbian America.

John Stephens, one-time New Jersey lawyer and amateur archaeologist, gets the popular credit for discovering the vanished Mayan civilization. While in the pay of the State Department he broadly interpreted his post of commercial attaché and went off into the hot, steaming jungle of Honduras on the trail of a rumor. He cleared the growth of vines, scattered the howling monkeys, felled trees to expose again to the sunlight the pyramids, temples, and statues of Copan. It was 1839, the year Daguerre announced the invention of photography in Paris, and it would be a long time before the camera went to this jungle city. Stephens forced an engraving artist to draw the details of the stonework, over complaints about conditions—mosquitoes, mud, poor light—and a total unfamiliarity with this strange art form—grotesque faces, serpents, jaguars, convoluted patterns.

A year before, F. de Waldeck had published a book on exploration in Yucatan, but his claim to fame was eclipsed by Stephens, who not only produced the visual impact of the etchings but used his legal training and the mesmerizing power of his jungle-damp, brass-buttoned, official U.S. jacket (with the trousers missing) to purchase the ruined city for $50. Actually it was a poor bargain. The Indian seller had no proof of ownership and said, as he disappeared, that $50 was way too much.

Twenty years went by; other sites were discovered in the jungles of Central America—Chichen Itza, Uxmal, Uaxactun—and scholars discussed and admired the spectacular art. Then a long-forgotten manuscript turned up in the Royal Library of Madrid: "Things in Yucatan," by Bishop Diego de Landa, written in 1566; it was a clue to the intricate stonework, based on interviews with a Mayan prince. The ornamentation that the scholars were looking at was not art; it was science. Every symbol, picture, and stone relief was representative of an astronomical number. The two crosses over the eyebrows of a serpent's head, the single jaguar claw at the ear of a god, the rows of shells, the pictures of gates, the steps of the pyramids—all stood for a number associated with this or that time-factored event. A cabala, cunningly woven in stone to look like an art form. Without clues, such as Bishop Diego's manuscript, the problem in astro-archaeology might have been impossible to solve. As it is, the reading of the ornamentation has come about slowly and much remains to be decoded.

The numbers relate to calendar events. The Mayas were obsessed with the notion of the flow of time: Is it continuous? Will it come to an end? These questions are fundamental to modern physics in the theory of relativity. They used two calendars, one made up of a year of 365 days, the other 260 days. The origin of the dual calendar system is not known at the present. From a practical point of view, a second independent day count would eliminate errors, but this is not a full explanation. The two calendars came into step once every 52 years (exactly 18,980 days), a convenient check point, at which date the end of time itself was expected (unless averted by ceremonies and sacrifice).

The months of both calendars contained 20 days apiece. The 20, not being astronomical, is probably due to the Mayan habit of counting everything in "scores." The seasonal year was made up of 18 months of 20 days and an extra nineteenth month of 5 days.

When Stephens climbed the ornamental stairway at Copan he was looking at something more than art. The carved relief, repeated 15 times, showed the passing of 15 years of Mayan history. The 75 steps of the stairway showed the totality of extra days added in the short months (nineteenth) of the period (5×15). The grotesque faces at the gateway were hieroglyphics which stated the date of construction of the moment.

A calendar year of 365 days needed careful watching. The seasons would slip by $\frac{1}{4}$ day each year, 25 days in a century, 1 full year in 1,508. The problem of calibration was the responsibility of an elite group, the priest-astronomers. They used astro-alignment—earth and sky were joined in the projection of the foundation lines of the pyramids, temples, and plazas.

The solstices were marked not with heel stone, trilithon, or Pachacuti tower, but with temples, and in a not so obvious way. Uaxactun, in northern Guatemala, is the best example of the Mayan approach to the Stonehenge problem, and illustrates what was done at several other Mayan cities. A raised platform was built due east of the main pyramid. There were three small roofed temples on the platform. The priest-

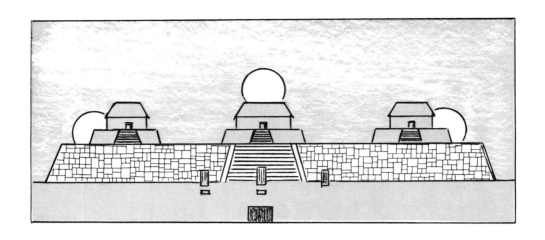

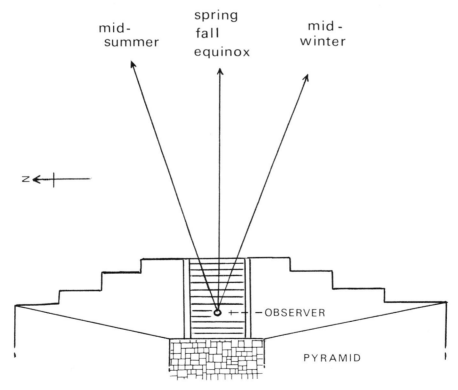

FIG. 31. *Three temples marking the seasonal sun at Uaxactun, Guatemala.*

observer stood on the steps of the pyramid at a height which made the distant skyline appear level with the roof of the temple. At each dawn he saw first the rosy glow and then the disk of the sun appear somewhere along the silhouettes of the three roofs. At the equinox, sunrise was centrally placed over the roof of the middle temple, and it also lined up with a stele (carved monolith) in the plaza at the foot of the stairway to the temple. On Midsummer's Day, sunrise was level with the end wall of the "summer" temple on the left; at midwinter the alignment was with the end wall of the temple to the right. To my mind, this was an odd way to do it—not to use the center of the roof of the end temples with perhaps a small, raised, godlike effigy to mark the spot—but no doubt the Maya had a rationale within their own culture for this. The summer/equinox/winter, triple-temple system was used at more than a dozen of these sites, at different epochs in the Mayan history.

Uaxactun was built in the classic period, around A.D. 300, when the Mayan civilization was well developed. Pyramidal observations began earlier at other sites. The earliest known is at Monte Alto, Guatemala, date about 500 B.C. in the preclassic period. Here the observer walked up the stairway of the pyramid and faced east, looking over the plaza; sunrise was marked by carved stone pillars, one for the equinoxes, two for the solstices. There were other stelae placed in the forecourt of the pyramid which might have been for moon extremes. Research is in progress as I write. Throughout eight centuries and more the brilliant sun-god was marked—first by simple monoliths, then by temples.

Sun watching was that method of season-calendar regulation. At Stonehenge there was no yearly calendar—at least, no evidence shows up in the circle of holes—and midwinter festival would be celebrated as it came, with no counting off of the days. In Yucatan there was a calendar, but it was not, as is often said, more accurate than the one we have today. The length was a simple, constant 365 days, with no leap years.

It was necessary to make observations to check on the appropriate date for a seasonal event, say midsummer, the spring equinox, or fall. Observationally the priest would always come out right (because the sun cannot be wrong), and the day of the equinox would slip in its celebration date by an average of 0.2422 days per year. By analyzing the long stone-chiseled record of the slippage, the priest would know the correct length of the year better than did Clavius when he advised Pope Gregory XIII. Nevertheless, the Mayan priests continued to use the traditional, formal, 365-day year.

Every five years the Maya carved a "timestone." The symbols and notation in the rich carving gave the date and other numerical facts. The continuous run of time was marked out, irreversibly, for all to see. At Quirigua, Guatemala, the blocks took the form of 7-ton "earth monsters," a double-headed serpent with the image of the sun-god held in the jaws. The all-important sun-god was sometimes represented as a human face, not unlike the Kon-Tiki that was painted on Heyerdahl's sail, and sometimes as a jaguar with pierced ears and extended tongue, reminiscent of Nasca polychromes.

Chichen Itza, Mexico, was one of the last cities to be built. The sun temples on the eastern platform were replaced with an observatory with a dome 41 feet high, entered inside by a spiral staircase. The building (called the Caracol because the spiral staircase reminded the Spanish colonists of a snail's shell), now half-ruined, must have looked very much like the telescope dome at Mount Wilson or Palomar. The telescope, of course, was unknown to the Maya, who observed through tunnel windows in the masonry. Only the southwest portion of the dome remains. Three tunnel windows mark due south and declinations —29° and +29°. These are the extremes of the moon over the period of the regression of the nodes (18.61 years), the same declinations as were marked at Stonehenge. The sunset position at the evening of the equinox, 0°, is also marked. Presumably there were other windows in the southeast quadrant.

The Mayan astronomers knew the exact period of the moon, 29.53 days. A Mayan statement on the walls of the pharaoh tomb in the pyramid at Palenque says: "81 moons make 2,392 days." Here we must be careful with our mathematics. Heyerdahl, in the *Ra Expeditions,* divides 2,392 by 81, "giving them [the Maya] a month of 29.53086 days, which deviates by only 24 seconds from the real length." In mathematics it is well known that you cannot get out any more significant numbers than those of the weakest number in the calculation. Presuming they counted 81 months exactly, we have an accuracy of only four figures in the number of days. And so the month cannot be quoted any

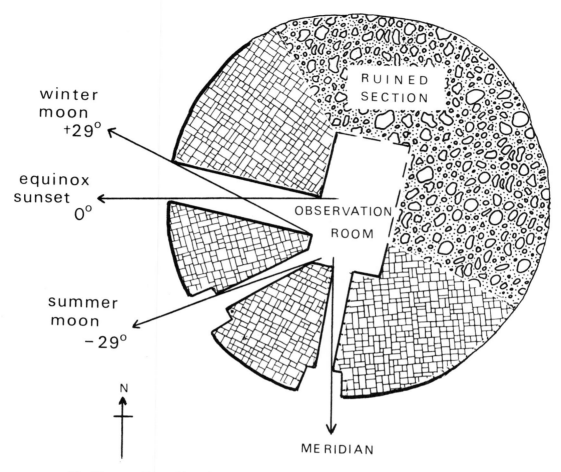

winter
moon
+29°

equinox
sunset
0°

summer
moon
−29°

RUINED
SECTION

OBSERVATION
ROOM

N

MERIDIAN

FIG. 32. *Moon and sun lines in the ruined Mayan Caracol at Chichen Itza, Mexico.*

further than four figures: 29.53. Actually the moon is not regular from month to month, and the Mayan count could well have been 2,393 in some series and 2,391 in others. Their determination would then come up with the result: month = 29.53 ±0.01. What is truly remarkable is that the Maya did come up with the correct *average* number of days. This is equivalent to the counting of many periods of 81 moons. The simple statement on the tomb wall would be read less simply by an astronomer: "The duration of 81 synodic revolutions of the moon is 2,392 days, sometimes more, sometimes less. The reason for the variation is unknown." Or was it?

185

They knew the number of years and days for the giant planet Jupiter to pass once around the zodiac. They recorded the pattern of numbers for Venus as an evening star—580, 587, 583, 583, and 587 days—and knew that this series of five apparitions repeated after the passing of eight years.* They knew that Mars was a brilliant midnight star every 780 days. This might have been the reason for the hitherto unexplained length of the religious calendar, 260 days—three sacred years equaling one synodic revolution of Mars.†

Knowledge of periodicities gave power—power to predict eclipses, to predict the bright shining of Venus, the future movement of the planets —and it gave confidence in the sky environment, the cosmos—the reliability of nature, of god.

Mayan civilization collapsed, revived, and collapsed again. The cities were jungle-covered ruins, populated by scattered, low-culture tribes at the time of the Spanish conquest. The way of life of a millennium, the industry, knowledge, came to an end according to some law of natural consequences. To us, when America is celebrating only its second centennial, the question "Why the collapse?" is a good one.

At Copan, Uaxactun, and other centers we find an abandonment stone, a hieroglyphic record of the date. Simultaneously a new city was founded somewhere else. The population, priests and artisans, moved *en bloc* to another location. The most obvious explanation is an ecological one. The agricultural system of slash and burn failed to provide the food needed by the population. After centuries of intensive cropping with little or no replenishment the soil became exhausted. The elite class of scholars were too absorbed in the heavens to attend to the more earthly sciences of agriculture, forestry, and ecology. Decline, on this theory, was a natural consequence of overspecialization. On the other hand there was a series of debilitating wars. A Mayan peace organization akin to the United Nations was formed, but this led to diplomatic intrigue and more wars. Toward the end of the civilization the priests were extracting a tribute of two-thirds of the gross produce of the

* $580 + 587 + 583 + 583 + 587 = 5 \times 584 = 8 \times 365$.
† $3 \times 260 = 780$.

farmers. Perhaps when the tax rate hits 67 percent social disruption inevitably follows.

The Aztecs, in Mexico City, were at the apex of power at the time of the conquest, but their days as a civilization were numbered. The Aztec calendar stone and system of time reckoning is Mayan in all its main features; their astronomical knowledge was great. But the time-factored ceremonies had developed a moral decadence of torture, heart ripping, and unspeakable inhumanities. They were essentially a military state, and their power was feared throughout Mexico and Yucatan. They would have come to a violent end at hands other than those of Cortés.

The Aztecs were probably responsible for the destruction of Teotihuacan, the largest city of classical Central America. The ruins are 30 miles north of Mexico City, covered with yards of hand-carried earth.

I learned of this wonderful site through James Dow of Brandeis University. Greater Boston has the largest concentration of academic institutions in the United States—50 colleges and universities, 200,000 students—and cooperation among them is frequent. Dow was a member of an archaeological digging team, but he had his eye on the possibility of star alignments. He sat in my office where Jay Williams had listened to the clatter of punched cards across the corridor. We used his careful measurements in the astro-archaeology program and computed for sun, moon, and star alignments.

Teotihuacan, at its climax, was an immense city, 4 miles across, population perhaps 100,000, with a ceremonial plaza and two pyramids named one for the sun, the other for the moon. Streets and avenues were laid out in a U.S.-type grid system, but with intriguing anomalies. First, the streets did not intersect at 90° but at 89°; second, the grid was skewed from the north–south direction.

The east-pointing street was at azimuth 106.°9 east of north, and with the altitude of the distant hills being duly allowed for, the machine printed out a significant alignment with alpha Canis Major—Sirius, the dog star, the Sothis of the Egyptians, the brightest star in the sky. In the westerly direction there was another sky object; the street pointed to the setting of the Pleiades, the "Seven Sisters" of Western culture, known as *tzab,* the rattle of the rattlesnake, to the Maya. The northerly street pointed to alpha Ursa Major, the brightest star in the Big Dipper.

Was the city built on a cosmic framework? Dow's findings have been challenged professionally: the builders were not exact, a 1° deviation from a right angle is neither here nor there; a skew of 16° from the cardinal points is a matter of caprice. But a symbol has been found carved into the southeast face of Cerro (hill) Colorado, and a similar mark in the floor of a house on the main street. These are like modern surveyor's marks, and a line between them is parallel to the Sirius-Pleiades axis. A river was rechanneled to flow along the line of the streets—and the grid is continued, inconveniently, Nascan style, up the sweeping contours of a hill.

The cosmic orientation, it would seem, was chosen, measured, and forced onto the shape of the landscape.

The four-tier pyramid of the sun has a square platform built onto the western face. This platform juts out from the base of the pyramid at a skewed angle of 6°. "Sloppy workmanship!" muttered an anthropologist at a colloquium where this was being discussed. But not so. The walls point to where the sun sets when the declination is 19°.7, a fundamentally important value for Teotihuacan. At that declination the sun makes its highest sweep across the sky, and at noon shines down vertically on the city. It is on the "tropic of Teotihuacan."

As the story of ancient America unfolds, the Maya take their place at the beginning of things. Mayan ideas were present at Teotihuacan, and later in the Aztec empire. Judging by the hardware, those solid things left for us to look at, the Maya led the New World in scientific knowledge. Perhaps the culture did find its way across the Gulf of Mexico and up the Mississippi to create the enormous geometric figures of North America. Perhaps it did influence the Nasca community in their line building, and the ancestors of the Incas at Tiahuanaco. But here we spin theories without proof, without facts. All that we can say is that South, Central, and to some extent, North America followed the same sweeping hands of the prehistoric clock. For a thousand years before the birth of Christ it was the time for development; around A.D. 0 the classical phase began—the founding of pre-Inca Tiahuanaco, Mayan astro-glyphs, and the Nasca desert lines. Finally by A.D. 1000 the New World became decadent in art, near to becoming ecologically unbalanced, torn between militaristic empires.

Thor Heyerdahl has launched a bold hypothesis. It shakes the world picture. It penetrates, stilettolike, into the minds of archaeologists, anthropologists, and scholars concerned with the past, with the roots of civilization. Heyerdahl said the great pre-Inca race came across the wide Atlantic from Egypt.

He took account of the universal cult of the sun, an obsession with the sunrise and the pattern of movement of celestial orbs. Kon-Tiki, in his theory, spread as the great sun-god from Peru across the Pacific. Now the mythical link was traced eastward to its place of origin. He related Kon-Tiki to the most important god of ancient Egypt, Amon-Ra.

It is not for me to stir the whirlpool of controversy. As an astron-omer I limit myself to the astronomical facts: Was this temple built to point to the sunrise? Is this ancient number related to the periodicities of the cosmos? Heyerdahl's arguments have been well summarized and added to by the South American experts:

- There are pyramids in the New World and pyramids in Egypt.
- Bodies were mummified in Peru and also in Egypt.
- The Incas counted history by the reigns of royal god-chiefs; ancient Egypt counted by dynasties, by the reigns of pharaohs.
- Pharaohs and Inca kings alike were regarded as divine, as "sons of the sun."
- Pharaohs and Inca kings had the unusual habit of marrying their sister.
- Peruvian cotton seed is genetically related to Egyptian cotton.
- There were reed boats on the Nile and reed boats on Lake Titicaca, hieroglyphics in the Middle East, hieroglyphics in Middle America.

Counterarguments erupted as soon as Heyerdahl's book was off the press: Pyramids in the New World are built in stepped tiers and have outside stairways, but those in Egypt are flat-faced. Egyptian pyramids

189

are royal graves, American pyramids are not.* There is no resemblance between Mayan and Egyptian hieroglyphs. The last pyramid built in Egypt was some thousand years before the first in Yucatan, so what went on during the time gap?

One archaeologist was vehement. He said to me over his afternoon cup of tea (it was at a university in England, in that noisy free-for-all before a colloquium), "Damn it all, the fellow's crazy. All he has shown is that if you float a reed boat off the coast of West Africa, sink it, try

* With the exception, as Heyerdahl rightly points out, of the mummified sun-king buried deep in the chamber under the pyramid at Palenque.

PLATE 47. (left) *Lake Titicaca. Reed boats on the roof of the world.*

PLATE 48. (right) *Harvesting Peruvian cotton, genetically related to Egyptian cotton.*

again, have a tow for the last fifteen miles, then you can just about finish up in Barbados. Barbados, mind you, not Yucatan. But why aren't there pyramids across the Sahara, eh? There's three thousand miles between the Nile and Morocco. And what's more, the ancient Egyptians were no bloody astronomers; their temples don't point anywhere.''

Amon-Ra . . . sun-god . . . their temples don't point anywhere. . . . I watched him bite into a digestive biscuit. He was excited and the words came out in a shower of crumbs. ''Look here, I say, we know all there is to know about the Egyptian mind. They could write, it's all in

191

the hieroglyphics. Now take the *Book of the Dead* . . .''

I could hardly hear him over the noise in the room. In my imagination I was flying with United Arab Airlines, eastward to the sun, altitude 37,000 feet, on a great circle course over Paris, Rome, Athens, to the land of the pharaohs.

11 AMON-RA

I met with Gamel in the Cairo Railway Station.

Gamel means ''handsome'' in Arabic, and one-third of the men in Cairo are so called. One-third of Cairo seemed to be in the station— upcountry fellahin in turbans and tunics, wives in peeping-black veils, chickens in crates, businessmen in suits. It was an immense, echoing, high-vaulted concourse. There were bazaars, offices, and cafés set in the distant walls.

Gamel was the quintessence of experts. He was an *Egyptian* Egyptologist. He had kindly joined with me on my plans for an astro-survey of the Temples of the Nile. He was short, bronze-faced, and amiable, with disappearing white hair and a dark gray mustache. He was absorbed by the wonders of his ancient country; intelligent, fluent in French, German, English, and that archaic tongue carved on the walls of the tombs but now unspoken. His eyes would dart into a quick question and then relax into a pale blue, kindly absent-mindedness.

''If we sit here we must drink,'' he said. It was a table outside the café, and the waiter had the right to serve whoever sat there. It is the same in most countries.

The waiter brought two lemonades in short, thick glasses. I paid, but I did not drink. Gamel drank mine for me. He had no sympathy with my ''expedition diet.''

I was anxious to be going. How long to departure time? Yet I remembered the advice of the old Arabic saying—''Only the devil makes haste.''

Another train came in and the crowd moved toward the sun-bright portico which led to the city.

I saw parallels between Cairo and Lima. Both are desert cities; dry, rainless, with sprinkler-fed lawns and flower beds. Both have sand-colored buildings, plazas, and statues, a mixture of the old and the very new, a colonial feeling in the older hotels, European and indigenous costume on the streets. At dawn in the center of Cairo I had heard a cock crowing from a roof pen on an apartment house. In Lima, the same. And in both cities the same 6-inch-square, thin, hard-surfaced paper napkins arranged fanlike in a glass on the table. Modern paradoxes to be added to the 60 ancient parallels between Egypt and Peru!

In the city I had received excellent treatment from the minister of culture, minister of science and research, minister of antiquities, and various officials of security. One minister in a chocolate-brown pinstripe suit, who a year before had sped Thor Heyerdahl on his way in *Ra,* the papyrus raft, was interested and most helpful in this new project to investigate the astronomical pointing of the Great Temple of Karnak, the temple of Amon-Ra.

I explained the nature of the intended project—a study peaceful and international in scope; humanistic, scientific. The original plan had been to make an aerial reconnaissance down the Nile with high-resolution overlapping pictures, but by necessity that request was deferred. It was a time of emergency. There were brick blast-walls at the doors of buildings and the Museum. The desert sand which, historically, blown by the wind, constantly tried to enter the capital, was in at last—sandbags were piled high at the windows. Egyptian fighter planes zoomed along the river mast-high; guns and rockets were fused, primed, and in position east and west of Suez; invasion, war seemed imminent. Yet both sides were linked in the distant haze of prehistory. Before the canal, before the Bible, before the Koran, before the pharaohs, the sky-gods, with different names, were a common heritage.

It was good progress to be at the railroad station at this time. I had a triple-stamped pass in my wallet. I could take the train up the Nile Valley with no stop-offs. Luxor only. I could take photographs, but only of the temples.

Gamel gave me a tropical sun hat, the old type worn by the British army in colonial India. My face showed my recalcitrant feelings. "The heat, you know," he said. "We'll have to work through the middle of the day. Professor G——— collapsed last year. Wouldn't take good advice."

He was anxious to complete the expedition as quickly as possible. Not to "make haste" as only the devil does, but an urgency to avoid the dreaded khamsin. It was that 50-day period near the spring equinox when the dry southern wind was apt to blow. With the wind came the

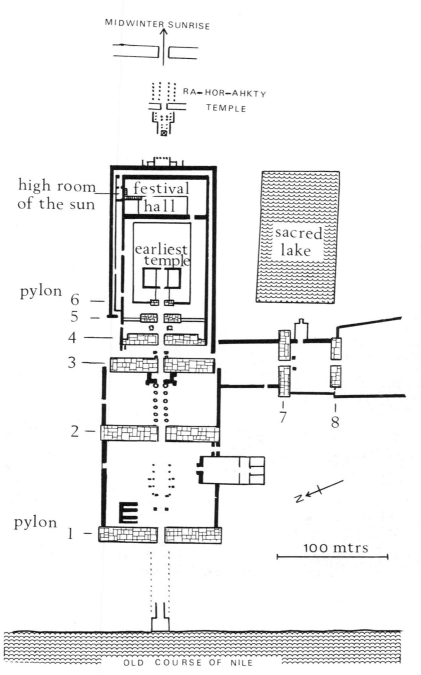

MIDWINTER SUNRISE

RA–HOR–AHKTY TEMPLE

high room of the sun

festival hall

earliest temple

sacred lake

pylon 6

5

4

3

2

pylon 1

7

8

100 mtrs

OLD COURSE OF NILE

FIG. 33. *The Great Temple of Amon-Ra, Karnak, Luxor, Egypt.*

195

PLATE 49. *Excavation in progress, Luxor, Egypt.*

sand—fine dust, grit, blown from the desert and hurled at the temples and cities as if to make them part of the desert again. When the khamsin blew, so I was told by an ex-army officer, transportation stopped, people holed up, and animals lay low; to be caught exposed in the blast was hazardous.

The train was air-conditioned, well equipped, built, as the little white plate said, by the "Hungarian Railway Carriage and Engine Works." People wonder how much Soviet influence is in the Land of the Pharaohs. The Aswan Dam, of course, was rated as impractical by the consortium of the International Bank for Reconstruction and Development way back in the '50's, opening the way de facto for Russian financial support and engineering and now the dam is built and functioning. However, I did not see evidence of influence. As a scientist I was intent on the science; nonpolitical, astrophysical, neutral.

The railroad followed the right bank of the Nile until it reached Farshut, then it switched to the left. It is a journey from Lower Egypt to Upper Egypt, from the land of the papyrus flower to that of the lotus blossom, from Suez warfare to flowing, graceful Nile peace, from things modern, nerve-jangling, to a simple vista of oasis, palm trees, and cultivation. The pharaoh required several weeks for the journey by royal barge. The train took less than half a day.

Donkey cart. Waterwheel. Cotton. Village square. Charcoal fire. Royal palms. Girls bathing in the river. Railroad crossing. Carts. Bare feet. Head-carried bundles. Eucalyptus. Mosque. Lawns. It flashed by.

It is difficult to imagine how narrow and sinuous Egypt is. The lush green on either side of the rail track, the farms, villages, neat gardens, and fields, these fresh abundances of the living Egypt ended abruptly just beyond, where the eye could not see. The other Egypt, the huge expanse of wadi, sand dune, and rocky plateau, mysterious, impenetrable desert, was always there, running parallel with the train, as the moon moves with you as you drive along, challenging the life power of the Nile, reaching to within a mile of the riverbank in places.

From Luxor station we drove in Old World style in an Edwardian carriage. It was dark but fragrant along the river embankment. The sails of the dhows hung limp under the cool sky. The pinpoint jewels of heaven contrasted with the warm flickering candle of the coach lamp.

197

Beyond the lamp the driver sat with his legs on a pile of grassy reeds, food for the horses. Reeds, not papyrus, for papyrus no longer grows wild in Egypt—reason, some unknown imbalance of the ecology which took place last century. We turned to follow the path of the Sphinxes from the Nile to the citadel El Karnak. Here within a mud-brick temenos wall as thick as the Great Wall of China is an assemblage of sacred places—temples, chapels, plazas, pylons—dominated by the god of the sun, Ra, and the unseen god, Amon. The largest temple in Egypt and ergo the world.

I stood there absorbing the atmosphere. Amon-Ra, the temple of the brilliant sun, was dark. The sun's disk, Aton, was clutched by the evil ruler of the underworld, Set. The moon was full and lunar-god Khon-su's pale light filtered down between the giant columns of Ra and cast soft shadows on the ground.

Our work would begin tomorrow at daybreak. Tonight we were to stay by kind invitation at an archaeological headquarters overlooking the Nile, a superb, time-worn, academic facility which echoed with the voice of scholars renowned for spade and book—though not Howard Carter, the discoverer of Tutankhamen's tomb; nor Flinders Petrie, the measurer of the pyramids. Carter lived in a private villa built in the Valley of the Kings; Petrie made his home in an excavated tomb on the Gizeh plateau.

Sir Norman Lockyer had worked at Stonehenge before me, and also at Karnak. His measurements of the heel stone were exact, verifiable, constructive. His survey of the Amon-Ra axis was not. Lockyer wrote how looking westward through the gateway-pylons the sun could be seen setting on Midsummer's Day.* Army engineer P. J. G. Wakefield set up a theodolite in the chancel of the temple on June 21, 1891. The change in the angle of obliquity since the founding of the temple was less than ½°, and Wakefield expected to see the sun's disk, red, framed in the openings between pylon 1 and 2. But he did not. The sun was totally blocked by the Theban hills on the west bank of the Nile, and would have been so blocked in antiquity. There was something wrong with Lockyer's survey. The "great temple of the sun" was not solar oriented. Furthermore, the sun has never shone down the center line

_____

* J. Norman Lockyer, *The Dawn of Astronomy* (Cambridge: M.I.T. Press, 1964).

of the temple from the day of its building to the present epoch.

Could this be? Was the temple line aimless, *no tiene Norte,* as the Spanish say? Was the foundation cord set to point, as it were, at a whim? One scholar at the breakfast table said over his eggs and bacon: "It points to the Nile, that's all, and not exactly either. Those fellows couldn't line things up better than a few feet, and what's more they didn't care!"

But a second look was in order. Something might have been missed.

The main temple is 350 yards long, 120 yards wide. Approaching from the west, from the Nile, one sees the enormous Ptolemaic pylons, 142 feet high, which form a decorated end wall on either side of the entrance. There are six twin pylons along the length of the structure, built at different periods in its history from the fifteenth to the first century B.C. These pylons separate by intent the various sacred areas.

Four pylon-framed gateways lead out at an angle from the south wall of Amon-Ra to the Temple of Mut via an avenue lined with sphinxes. The complex of shrines, chapels, and subsidiary temples within the main temple are set precisely to conform to the rectangular pattern and are aligned parallel to the Amon-Ra axis. There are two subsidiary temples within the Great Court of Amon-Ra, built by Rameses III and Seti II, which are perpendicular to the axis.

The Hypostyle Hall competes with Stonehenge in its megalithic grandeur. The hall, constructed when Stonehenge was falling in ruins, took the resources of three consecutive pharaohs: Rameses I, Seti I, and Rameses II. The lintels on top of the columns weigh from 10 to 20 tons. They were placed there by sliding the block up an earthen ramp, and the soil was removed afterward. The central columns are 80 feet high, and the flared tops are 25 feet in diameter. The mirror of the 200-inch telescope on Mount Palomar would fit on one of these great pillars, and there would be enough room left over for 70 men to stand around the edge. The 12 central columns are flanked by 122 smaller pillars, the whole assemblage being roofed over to make a cathedral within the temple. The rows of pillars run parallel to the axis of the temple, the alignment being precise to better than 5 inches.

The columns are decorated from top to bottom with hieroglyphic inscriptions and tableaus. Traces remain of the once rich colors on the stone. The lintels and roof blocks were similarly decorated. When first erected, the hall must have dazzled the eye with its polychrome beauty. The floor, perhaps, was covered with sheets of silver, as was the temple at nearby Luxor. There would be crowds here on feast days, for the Hypostyle Hall was built to show all mankind the power of the pharaoh and his almighty father, Amon-Ra, the sun-god. Those who could not read the hieroglyphics could see the story in the tableau pictures. Yet the fellah did not need to read. He understood by word of mouth the intricate religion, the magic, the multiple theologies cemented together by fierce pagan superstition.

The modern scholar does not have the word of mouth, only the inscriptions. And the hieroglyphics are difficult to read. The symbols are alphabetic letters (not picture writing) with 24 signs for single letters, and about 50 signs for double letters such as *sm, sb.* The words are those of the ancient Egyptian language (which resembles modern Arabic less than Chaucer's "Nonnes Preestes Tale" resembles English). Extra signs, not read, indicate the nature of a word. One sign, for example, shows that the preceding word is a person's name, another the name of a place of habitation. With letters, signs, and the special indicators, there are about 400 different symbols to be learned. All vowels are omitted. Scholars argue for different renderings. Amon-Ra can be read as Amen-Re, Amun-Ra, or Aman-Ra. Without reviving a mummified scribe it is difficult to say which is the correct rendering. Papyrus writing tends to be hurried; monumental hieroglyphics are the most exact, the most precise. Superfluous signs are added quite frequently. A single *b* is often spelled with a string of three different signs, but it is to be read as *b,* not a stammering *b . . . b . . . b.* Scribes delighted in homophones, the spelling of the same sound in different ways—night, nite, knight. Now and again they enjoyed the creative urge to carve a new, self-invented set of symbols into the inscription. If we can guess the meaning the new phrase is called "sportive writing," if undeciphered, "mysterious" or "secret." Two scholars reading the same inscription will seldom come up with exactly the same translation, but the general meaning will be clear. Difficult though it is to read, we

PLATE 50. *The view along the central axis of the great temple of Amon-Ra, Karnak, Egypt. The photograph was taken at the end of the Hypostyle Hall, looking toward the inner sanctum. (See Fig. 33.)*

200

PLATE 51. *Inner sanctum, Amon-Ra temple.*

must not criticize this beautiful way of recording in stone the spoken words and thoughts of ancient Egypt. Our own language has had standardized spelling for less than two centuries; the 26 alphabetic letters represent 40 spoken sounds, more than 2,000 syllables with confusing homophones. Sir James Pitman was driven to introduce ITA, the Initial Teaching Alphabet, in English schools in 1959 because, he claimed, the complicated illogical rules, with their many exceptions, were a stumbling block to children in their mother tongue.

We walked through the fourth and fifth pylons, past the slender obelisk of Queen Hatshepsut which seems to penetrate the deep-space blue of the sky. There were hieroglyphics reaching up on all four faces. The shadow was short and compressed, reflecting the height of the sun. Gamel waved his hand along the inscription on the wall of the third pylon. He translated from ancient Arabic to English:

O pharaoh [Rameses II] you see your father Amon-Ra, god of the gods, lord of the thrones of the two Egypts, you see your father each time that he rises from out of Ipet Sout. His rays form together in front like the rays of the horizon at the point of dawn, after having illuminated the double door of the horizon of the Universal Master. The *rkyt*, the men [observers?], are happy that his beauty is risen, and they rejoice. . . .

From another culture, from another age, a beautiful description of sunrise. When there are low scattered clouds, especially in a desert climate, the sunlight shines through gaps, upward over the head of an

PLATE 52. *Beyond the Hall of Festivals, Amon-Ra temple, looking through the ruins of the temple of Ra-Hor-Ahkty, built by Rameses II, toward the southeast gateway which framed the midwinter sunrise.*

observer; the rays form together in front like the rays of the horizon at the point of dawn.

I thought of Homer centuries later in classical Greece: "Aurora, rosy-fingered dawn, now tinged the east. . . ." And of Heyerdahl in our own era, floating on a papyrus raft: "Resplendent lancets which no royal crown could match radiated like a diadem from the sea's edge into the sky."

Rameses' hymn was to the sun—the rising sun. The inscription was on the east face of the pylon. To me this was a clue. Ipet Sout was the name for the earliest temple at Karnak, a temple built about 2000 B.C. Ipet Sout was *east* of the pylon, in the direction of the sun*rise*. Could Lockyer have been wrong in thinking that the temple pointed to the west, to sunset?

We walked through the Ipet Sout temples, the holy of holies where the golden bark of the sun was kept, where as commoners we would not have dared to walk in the days of ritual and sacrifice.

I could see why Lockyer had calculated for a western orientation. The line of sight eastward from the central altar was blocked by an enormous building, the Hall of Festivals, erected by Thutmose III around 1480 B.C. This porticoed, roofed structure was a labyrinth of rooms, chapels, ritual temples. The walls, doorways, and window lintels were profusely decorated and inscribed.

There were astronomical clues beyond the Hall of Festivals. A small temple, back to back with the hall but not deep enough to give a measurable astronomical axis, carried hymns of praise to that god that appears at dawn. Some of the hieroglyphics, here and elsewhere in the temple complex, were filled in from a standard reference book, because the original stone carvings had been removed to museums in Cairo and cities outside Egypt. Farther along there was a temple dedicated to Ra-Hor-Akhty. This composite god title is roughly transliterated as Sun-Rising, Sun-Brilliant on the Horizon. These words brought to my mind Stonehenge—black architraves, the flame-shaped stone of Hardy, the purple-golden dawn. Nearby in the ruins an archaeologist had found fragments of a statue, a group of four monkeys. It was a tradition in ancient Egypt that monkeys greeted the dawn.

The Ra-Hor-Akhty temple was on the same long line of the main axis,

PLATE 53. *Statue of the four monkeys that traditionally greet the dawn at the foot of an obelisk, Luxor.*

a line which began at the Nile, ran along the center of the avenue of the sphinxes, through the opening of the six pylons, and through the altar of the earliest temple, Ipet Sout. This axis cut through the temenos wall; the opening was a huge gateway built at the end of the history of the monument by the Ptolemaic pharaohs. The gateway bore the words: "House of the tree *im*, of the living god (Amon)." Gamel could not say what was meant by the sign *im*.

I looked through the empty gateway. The line of sight went out toward a few scattered palm trees. Beyond the trees the distant low cliffs massed themselves formless and glaring, marking the edge of the hot, yellow desert. The statues of pharaohs and gods stood there gazing into the eastern distance with stony eyes. I was sure the line pointed to some sky object. The statues were poised for a celestial happening—an event which took place every day if it were stellar, each year if solar, and at some point in a 56-year cycle if of the moon. We needed a measurement of the eastward azimuth of the temple axis, an estimate of the height of the distant skyline, then to the computer, and those eyes would come to life.

Not that the computer was new to the pharaohs. Ray Smith of Philadelphia was using a digital machine to solve the jigsaw puzzle of the Akhenaten mural. That stone picture was a jumble of broken blocks in the outer courtyard of the temple and lodged in distant museums. They were numbered and classified as to size, shape, and pictorial content, and a computer was now testing one piece against another to find the fit. Smith was later to find Queen Nefertiti dominating the picture. (Was she the first of the "liberated," the brains behind the pharaoh, the real source of the Aton sun-disk heresy?) A second research team had set up cosmic ray counters in the tomb of the Gizeh Pyramid. A computer analysis of the counts could reveal secret chambers, if any, at the top of the pyramid. (The computer was to produce a negative result, solid stone, no hidden chambers.)

And the computer could turn the clock back through the ages of history to the time of Egypt's glory, Rameses, Thutmose—1400, 1500, 1600 B.C.

Archaeologists at the Franco-Egyptian Research Center at Karnak have jointly excavated the temple for many years. Napoleon Bonaparte invaded Egypt not so much for territorial gain for France as to satisfy his interest in archaeology. Before the campaign in 1798 he addressed an assemblage of scholars at the Institute of France, and embarked for Egypt with 175 astronomers, antiquarians, chemists, and the then greatest library of books on Egypt, scientific apparatus, measuring instruments, etc. Egypt has long since regained her independence, but scientific cooperation with France still goes on.

I was fortunate in this international atmosphere. The center had a large unpublished stereo air map of the 1-square-mile citadel which was kindly made available to me. I measured the azimuth, choosing the best straight line from the Nile avenue, through the pylons, the altar, and the eastern temples of the gods Ra-Hor-Akhty and "Amon-who-hears-the-prayers." Result: 116°.90 east of north.

Next I determined the altitude of the skyline. Here again I was indebted to international cooperation, but of a bizarre nature. I located a map from World War II. A topographical map with heights at meter intervals, a map drawn with Panzer precision for Field Marshal Erwin Rommel, the "Desert Fox," it showed *tempelen, Flugplatz, Schlacthaus,* and, accommodating, the exact position of a Cook's Tour rest house. According to Rommel the skyline hills were 25 kilometers distant, height 350 millimeters, and the altar of Amon-Ra was 77 millimeters above mean sea level. For an exact result we would need on-the-spot theodolite measurements executed by professional surveyors. But the map readings could be used for a reliable preliminary value. The result, allowing for refraction at an air temperature of 50° F., was 0°.53.

116.90 + 0.53: this was the critical data for the astro-archaeology program. Through the air, across the Sahara, trans-Atlantic, fast as light. The computer spoke for those staring stone faces.

The axis points to the rising sun when the disk stands tangent on the distant hills and when the declination of the sun's center is −23°.87. This was the position of the sun at its southern extreme at the winter solstice during the epoch of Hatshepsut and Thutmose, between the years 2000 and 1000 B.C., if the declination uncertainty is ±0°.05; on the basis of the data supplied the alignment is exact; the error is zero.

So Amon-Ra points eastward and not westward. It is like a Gothic cathedral entered by passing through the great west door, and with the chancel directed toward the east.

Gamel was not convinced. "Paul Barguet worked here for years. Barguet said, like you, how Amon-Ra points away from the Nile. He came to this conclusion by studying the archaeological evidence, the architecture. But no one could see the sunrise here after 1480 B.C., not unless he could see through that stone. The Hall of Festivals was in the way."

We went into the temple courts again. The heat was intense. Perspiration trickled out from under my tropical hat. The dust rose as if with heavy moon footsteps. The lion-headed goddess Sekhmet, carved in black stone, was hot to the touch. She was the power of the sun to ancient Egyptians.

On that wall, blocking the view, was a long mural. It dated to the

207

PLATE 54. *Position of the sloping stairway which led to the roof temple, the High Room of the Sun.*

period of Queen Hatshepsut and King Thutmose. It showed the sun-god in his yearly journey, carried around the sky on a boat. Ra, Horus, Sokaris, Khepri, the sun-god in all his names was, apparently, born each year at a special location in the temple. An inscription dating to 840 B.C. said: "One climbs the *Aha,* the lonesome place of the majestic soul, the high room of the intelligence which moves across the sky; one now opens the door of the horizon building of the primordial god of the two countries in order to see the mystery of Horus shining."

"What does *Aha* mean, Gamel?"

"Here the writer is very poetic, very fanciful. He refers to the old battlefield between Upper and Lower Egypt."

"Where was that?"

"In old Cairo."

"But what other meaning can this sign have. This spear, this four-

PLATE 55. *Aperture window for observation of the rising of the midwinter sun. The distant temenos wall of mud brick is of later construction.*

pointed circle?''

''Literally it could be read as 'place of combat,' but I am sure that the writer is poetically bringing the old and famous battlefield into a shrine in the temple here at Karnak.''

''But we're 300 miles away from Cairo. . . .''

We climbed a stairway—steep, narrow, without sides—into a small open-to-the-sky chamber, the so-called High Room of the Sun. There was a square altar of alabaster in front of a rectangular aperture in the wall. This roof temple was dedicated to Ra-Hor-Akhty, the sun-god rising on the horizon. The wall carried a picture of the pharaoh, facing the aperture, one knee to the ground, making a gesture of greeting to the rising sun: Make acclamation to your beautiful face, master of gods, Amon-Ra. . . .

Was this the *Aha,* the lonesome place of the majestic soul, high room

209

of the intelligence which moves across the sky? The platform was elevated, the view clear of obstruction. Here the priest-astronomer could make his observations to check that the sun was on course.

There was a long wall running under the middle of the roof temple. It was profusely decorated with scenes of the pharaoh, Thutmose III, stretching the surveyor's cord to mark out the line of the temple. The pharaoh was aided by Sechat, the wise and beautiful goddess of writing, of foundation ceremonies, according to Lockyer, and of the dawn. "This is the very wall, Gamel. This is where the pharaoh made his sun observation. The room above us was built to check out the sunrise in the following years. The other shrines, the main axis, were struck off from this line here. It all hinges on the turning place of the sun."

"Maybe. . . . Maybe."

We went back to the coolness of headquarters and talked over the discovery. The alignment began to make sense. It threw meaning into the ancient poems and myths. In Kherouef's tomb, circa 1400 B.C., it says: "The doors of the underworld are open, O Sokaris, sun in the sky. O reborn one, you are seen brilliant on the horizon and you give back Egypt her beauty each time the sky is pierced with rays, each time you are born as a disk in the sky." There were more references to a "place of combat." It occurred several times in the hieroglyphics, and it applied to the sun-god. What could it mean? I began to draft a paper for a scientific journal: "And so we see at Karnak it is the extreme southerly sunrise that is marked. There is a correspondence with the marking of the winter solstice in the great trilithon at Stonehenge. This has double significance. The sun overcomes the powers of darkness in a combat in the underworld each night, and overcomes the threat of the solstice each year. The new god is born free in victory at dawn on Midwinter's Day. . . ."

Plutarch said, in *Isis and Osiris:*

At the time of the winter solstice they [the Egyptians] lead the cow seven times around the temple of the sun . . . seeking for Osiris, since the goddess in the wintertime yearns for water; so many times do they go around, because in the seventh month the sun completes the transition from the winter solstice to the summer solstice. . . . Horus, the son of Isis, offered sacrifice to the sun. . . .

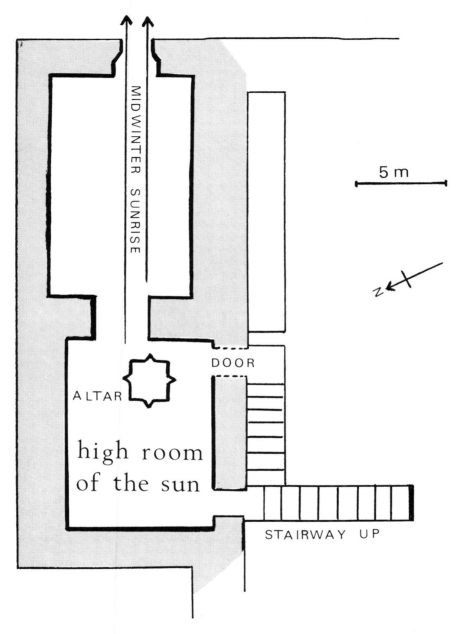

MIDWINTER SUNRISE

5 m

ALTAR

DOOR

high room
of the sun

STAIRWAY UP

FIG. 34. *High Room of the Sun. Dedicated to Ra-Hor-Ahkty.*

211

Every day they make a triple offering of incense to the sun [remember the Inca priests in the square at Cuzco], an offering of resin at sunrise, of myrrh at midday, and of the so-called cyphic at sunset. . . . They think that by means of all these they supplicate and serve the sun . . . there are those who declare Isis is none other than the moon . . . and in her dark garments [invisible period before the new crescent?] . . . she in her yearning [sexual] pursues the sun. For this reason also they call upon the moon in love affairs. . . .

I did not wish to get involved with the religions of ancient Egypt. My expertise is not in the religious or metaphysical. There were 15 inter-related deities at Karnak with Amon-Ra at the head, and the fantasies written about these gods are complex.

But, finding the temple linked purposefully to the sky, I could not agree with the well-known encyclopedia that rated the Egyptians in religious matters as barbarous and savage in origin, that claimed it a mistake to look for truth enshrined in the hieroglyphics, that said the brief period of worship of the physical sun (or even less likely, of a god behind the sun) as the giver of life was too simple and rational for the Egyptian mind and after Akhnaton's brief reign was soon "thrown to the winds."

No. Amon-Ra with his solar manifestations was the most important god of Egypt, the national deity for centuries. The underlying concept was solar, was cosmic, from *before* the time of Akhnaton and Nefertiti to the decline of the civilization with Cleopatra. The brief Amarna period was not a new heresy; it was a reaffirmation of the union of the sun-drenched ocher land with the cognitive universe. *O Ra, Amon-Ra, you give back Egypt her beauty each time you are born as a disk in the sky*.

A theory cannot hang by a thread. If Karnak was astro-oriented there must be other similar temples.

We took the ferry across the Nile. Chickens, bicycles, baggage, fez, veil, cotton tunic; harem and fellahin. Girls from the Thebes village on the west bank walked down to the river erect, with vases on their heads, to collect the pastel-colored water for drinking, cooking, washing. In Muslim tradition they must pass a man so as to be unnoticed. But with the movement of the figure within the silk, the seductive brown eyes over the veil, this was not possible.

We were visiting the Colossi of Memnon, a short, loping-stride camel ride from the river.

These statues, standing isolated in the fields, are most unfortunately named, not for Amenhotep, the architect who designed them, not for Amenhotep III, the pharaoh who built them, but, by a gross error on the part of the conquering Greeks under Alexander, for Memnon, son of mythical Aurora, who died at Troy. They are colossal: seventy feet high, cut from red sandstone, floated in eight ships from Edfu, and built, as Amenhotep claimed, to "last as long as heaven."

One of the statues scared the Romans. It wailed and moaned at sunrise. This is verified by inscriptions on the stone. The mysterious sounds occurred until about A.D. 195, then ceased when the earthquake-shifted blocks at the top of the statue were adjusted. Emperor Hadrian heard them with his wife Sabina, and Septimius Severus and Gallus also. The chilling sound was known as the "voice of Memnon" and its cause is unknown; it may have been air or adjacent rock surfaces expanding with the heat.

In 1400 B.C. there was a temple behind the statues dedicated to Ra-Hor-Akhty. The temple is now gone, but the direction of the axis can be estimated from the statues. Azimuth 117.

"The Colossi appear sentinent," wrote Francis Aiken, "as if gazing across the Nile valley for some new divine manifestation." Yes, indeed. Gazing at the sunrise. The temple and the statues pointed in 1400 B.C. to that "place of combat" of the sun, the turning point on Midwinter's Day. Memnon faces the holy Nile, and Amon-Ra faces away from the Nile, yet both are coupled to the same point on the celestial sphere.

There was clearly an astro-archaeological basis for the temples, beyond the writing, beyond the architecture. There might be more solar, and perhaps lunar, extremes in other temples. Egypt seemed to fit into the global, prehistoric pattern. I wanted to visit Heliopolis, the City of the Sun. Those temples are dedicated to Ra, and in them the priest-pharaoh first took upon himself the title Child of the Sun. Cleopatra's Needle once stood at Heliopolis. The twin obelisks, now in Central Park, New York, and the Thames Embankment, London, were erected by Thutmose III (not Cleopatra), builder of the roof observatory at Karnak. The tops were capped with gold, symbolic of the richness of the sun; the sides were inscribed to Ra. Astronomically the obelisks make a vertical gnomon, a shadow device for measuring time, seasons, latitude. I would expect the shadow of the tip to trace a course over lines and marks on the ground. Unfortunately, the original position and orientation of the needles are not known. They were moved by Caesar in 14 B.C. and then to New York and London in 1878 and 1880. Excavation would be required to determine where, and how many.

Engineering-wise, the obelisk had to have been made in one piece, monolithic, because it was levered up into position as a telephone pole might be set up in a hole in the ground. Also the slender proportions would not be strong against earthquakes and the elements if made from an assembly of blocks. In engineering and in quarrying the Egyptian stonemasons excelled the ancient Britons and the Incas. The Needles are 68 feet high and weigh 200 tons. A large obelisk lies unfinished in the quarry at Aswan. A flaw showed in the granite, and work stopped. This monolith was planned to be 137 feet high, 1,170 tons in weight. And the quarrying was done without metal tools. They used round, stone dolerite mauls and the crude bashing method of the Stonehengers.

Although it was astronomically intriguing, it was not possible for me to visit Heliopolis on this expedition owing to the shortage of research funds and the desert khamsin, which brought a blast of silica fog, brown, impenetrable, choking. The wind-slick sand stuck to the road like snow in a blizzard. Dust from the storm rose to 5,000 feet, and Sahara particles were picked up days later by air-filter planes over Central America. Another fraction of a millimeter was eroded off the face of the Sphinx and blown to the winds.

I circulated a tentative preliminary report and lectured on my findings in Cairo. There could be no reasonable doubt about the pointing of the axis of the Amon-Ra temple: it connected with the shortest-day sunrise; that alignment was a hard fact. But scholarly questions would be raised—the acceptance gap was ahead, maybe a heated controversy.

One Egyptologist said bluntly that the alignment was accidental, not intended; despite the hieroglyphical reference to sunrise, sunrises in general were meant, not *a* sunrise in particular. Furthermore, as everybody knew, temples pointed toward the Nile, which was a holy, north–south meridian for the ancient Egyptians, and so temples would naturally line up east–west. True in general, or at least one could in general reduce the problem to these simplistic terms, but at this juncture that commonly held viewpoint was too simplistic. Specificity was needed. Temples in Upper Egypt do tend to face the riverbank; there is a second preferred direction parallel to the bank, and there are temples set at an angle. Amon-Ra is in the first category of being perpendicular to the Nile (though astronomically facing away from it, not toward it). The Nile at Thebes takes a huge meander. It does not run north–south. Now, and in 1500 B.C., the direction is approximately NNE–SSW, approximately at right angles to the winter sunrise line. The temple aligns exactly, within the limits of modern measurement. This poses a question similar to that at Stonehenge. There the right angle of the sun-moon rectangle depends on the latitude. Did the builders seek out this latitude, or, living at the site, did they happen to notice the right angle and make use of it? At Amon-Ra, Karnak, in ancient Thebes, was the site chosen because of the meander, where the temple from the Nile would be on the sun line, or did they notice the alignment after the temple complex was begun? A devil's advocate would have to stick to the argument that the meander, the hitting of the winter sun target, was a happenstance, and that having hit a solstice sunrise, the builders did not notice this alignment, even though there is a roof temple, high room of the sun, with a sunward aperture window, and other temples, back to back with Amon-Ra, pointing toward this singular spot.

It must not be overlooked that the temple points to a critical calendric extreme of the sun, a position at the end of a more than 50° annual arc. If the builders were blindly hoping to hit the general direction of sunrise I would have expected them to have finished up more eastward, nearer to the center of the arc. Yet the axis is at the far extreme. A fraction of a degree farther south, and the sunrise would never be seen along the axis.

A more serious problem was raised by the words on a stele found many years ago in one of the courts of the temple. It describes how Thutmose III carried out the foundation ceremony, presumably of the Hall of Festivals, on the last day of the second month of winter. From our knowledge of the ancient calendar this would be nearly 40 days after midwinter, and the sunrise would have shifted about 6° to the

215

east. Clearly some further research would be needed on this and other hieroglyphic statements. Astronomically the data implies that the critical sun observations were made ahead of time, maybe by the priest-astronomers, not the pharaoh, and that the stele-described foundation ceremony was more a formal groundbreaking affair, not a mensuration.

I wanted to go to Shimish, beyond the Strait of Gibraltar, on the northeast coast of Morocco, but as with Heliopolis this again was not possible. The ancient Moroccan city was originally known as Maqom Semes, City of the Sun. It was ancient when the Romans arrived and built their town of Lixus on the ruins. Recently archaeologists have uncovered huge megalithic walls beneath Roman Lixus. The stone craftsmanship is equal to that of Egypt or Peru; the walls are carefully laid out according to the sun. Who built Maqom Semes is presently under debate—Phoenicians, Egyptians, prehistoric Moroccans—but the site is a critical one in the global pattern of astro-megaliths. Could the winged sun have touched this legendary burial place of Hercules on its way from the Nile to Titicaca? Heyerdahl makes great store of the existence of papyrus rafts on the river at Shimish, Heliopolis, and on the Inca lake.

I made a brief visit to Gizeh. Volumes have been written about the pyramids. Thirteen acres on the base, 6 million tons of limestone blocks, angle of the faces 51°52′, the largest-volume building in the history of the world, equivalent to St. Paul's, St. Peter's and Westminster Abbey combined and more. The sides of the Gizeh Pyramids run exactly east–west, azimuth 90°, accurate to the limit of human-eye measurement. How this was done by the builders is not known. It was not done by sighting the pole star, because in 2800 B.C. there was no star visible to the naked eye at or near the celestial pole. No matter how it was done, the sides of the pyramids do point to the sunrise on the first day of spring, the vernal equinox.

The Sphinx stares toward the horizon like the Colossi of Memnon. The direction of the gaze is reducible to a numeric: 90° E of N. An astro-orientation toward declination 0°, the position of the sun at the dawn of the equinox. On that day the sun rises and sets along the axis of the Sphinx, and at midday reaches an altitude of 60°—the good-luck, "sextile" angle of the ancient astrologers.

The Sphinx is not taken to be a sun-god by modern scholars. It is considered by some to be an effigy of King Khafra, who built the second pyramid. But Thutmose IV in antiquity thought it was solar. The young prince lay down in the shadow of the Sphinx one day. Wearied with the hunt, tortured by the sun, he slept. He dreamed. The Sphinx spoke to him, entreating him to clear away the encroaching sand, promising to make him pharoah. He did so, and down between the paws he uncovered a temple. He planted an engraved stele at the base of the Sphinx to tell this amazing story. After his death, the wind-blown sand again covered the stele, and it lay there for more than 3,000 years until it was excavated in 1818. The stele refers to the sun-god and his chosen place or position: "Great and exalted is this figure of the god [sun-god Khepre], resting in his chosen place; mighty is his power, for the shadow of the sun is upon him. . . . The temples of every town on both sides [of the Nile] adore him; they stretch out their hands to him [orientation toward the sun?]."

Gamel wanted me to make one last visit before I was due to leave Egypt. He took me through the bazaar, along earthen alleys to an adobe house with long window curtains and rough furniture. We were calling on a dealer in antiquities, descended, so I was told, from Abd-el-Rasul, the most famous of all tomb robbers, who came across the Deir el-Bahri cache of forty secretly buried pharaohs. El-Rasul drew on the spoils of this rich tomb for many years, using it as a sort of mummified bank account. Egyptologists do not despise the trade outright. Pertinent information can come to light this way. Truly precious items can be smelled out before they fall illegally into foreign hands. In return, an Egyptologist will occasionally give an unofficial stamp of approval to a less important but genuine item to distinguish it from the mass of counterfeit.

Our host was old, bearded, and upright in stature. He had the air of a sheik who had enjoyed but outlived his harem: composed, satisfied, regal. He placed statues, amulets, and papyrus scrolls in front of us from out of a dusty back room. He brought forward the unavoidable hospitality—two glasses of lukewarm brownish Nile water with an unidentified leaf floating on the top.

217

Our host retired to the back room. Gamel spoke, his lips ventriloquist-still: "You must drink; this man sees everything. He is the most important dealer in Egypt. I will not allow you to offend him."

I slid my glass toward Gamel. He slid it back. The bearded sheik returned and fixed me with his stare.

I drank.

Gamel said, "We have an old saying: He who drinks from the Nile will return again to Egypt."

There was a twinkle of Heliopolis in his eyes.

12 ART, MAGIC, AND NUMBERS

There is much from the past to be decoded, more to be found out than has been found out so far.

Sir Arthur Evans dug at Phaistos. His spade uncovered the Minoan civilization, named for ancient Crete's famous King Minos. These people flourished in art and intellect when Stonehenge declined. Knossos on the northern coast was more beautifully splendid than the cities of prehistoric Greece.

Two archaeologists came to my office with a copy of a ciphered disk discovered by Evans. The Phaistos Disk. It was found in the ruins of a house at Minoan Phaistos, buried in the last layer of debris when a natural (or unnatural) conflagration destroyed the city.

It was a clay disk, about the size of a 45 rpm phonograph record, with a spiral pattern between the grooves on both sides. The clay had been marked when wet by scratches and by the press of seals or special dies. The series of pictures around the spiral were divided off into groups by incised cross lines. The groupings contained from one to seven pictures. I could recognize a face with erect topknot of hair, a bear (?) skin, a flower, a bald head, a fish, a bird and the number 7 shown by dots in a circle.

"Obviously a message of some sort," said archaeologist No. 1.

"The fellow who made this had a printing kit, and must have stamped out a lot of these disks with different messages on them. I believe it's a phonetic language, a poem, or religious code. There's no telling what the language is because the Minoans imported from all around the Mediterranean. The disk might have come from outside."

"No, I believe it is an inscription with a scientific basis," said archaeologist No. 2. "It's a set of sailing instructions, a coded navigational aid based on the rising of the stars in the constellations. We think it was manufactured in 1600 B.C.; that's about two centuries before the development of the Linear B writing."

PLATE 56. *Phaistos disk, side A.*

Linear B was deciphered in 1956 by architect Michael Ventris, just a few years before his untimely death in a road accident. His brilliant work showed the language to be ancient Greek, even though the letters were not like ancient or modern Greek letters. The symbols stood for whole syllables, like the 400 or more Egyptian hieroglyphics. The marks were scratched into wet clay tablets which were then dried in the sun, adobe style. Only the chances of war or disaster preserved them, when fire raged over and baked a set of tablets into hard pottery. Otherwise adobe plates would dissolve away in the rain. Tablets showed up in great numbers in Evans's dig in Crete, and also on the Greek mainland in Mycenae. Consternation followed the decipherment, not so much because of the messages, which were lists of stores, livestock, place names, and other scribal regimentalia, but because the words were Greek. It raised the question of the diffusion arrow: Which way did it

PLATE 57. *Phaistos disk, side B.*

point? Was Greece, that stronghold of classical civilization, a mere offshoot of the Minoans; and if so, how great was the lost, preliterate culture of the Minoans? That debate continues today.

But the disk was intriguing on three counts. First: it was not scratched by a scribe. The pictures were pressed into the clay with a clean-cut die. There must have been a set of at least 45 stamps, easy to use without the rigorous training required of a professional scribe. The picture images were neater, more exact than the spiral groove and cross-line separators—it was movable type, 3,000 years before the Gutenberg Bible. Second: it was not a decorative art pattern. The order of the symbols was more important than the orientation and exact placing in the spiral. There was undeciphered meaning. Third: the disk was unique in the ancient world, the only one of its kind in the whole of prehistory.

221

They left me with the copy. "Put it on your computer," said No. 2. It was a barbed challenge, because a problem cannot be placed on a digital computer when the nature of the problem has not been formulated. The machine is a tireless, uncomplaining worker, but it must have numbers, equations, and clear operational instructions. Preceding the allocated seconds of machine time is the time of human looking, figuring, scratch-padding, gazing out of the window, pencil chewing. The Phaistos Disk had never broken out of this limbo stage of speculation for the full fifty years of its exposure.

I looked and I puzzled. There were 31 groups on side A, and 30 on side B. The disk seemed to me to be an example of a common object, even though only one had been found. It was marked deliberately—no erasing or errors—and the spaced spirals, 30 groups on one side, 31 on the other, fitted exactly on to the disk, finished off at one end with a row of 5 or 6 dots. Free art for free art's sake might not have come out so precisely correct (reference the goofed patterns around the Nasca bowls). My first thought turned to the calendar with events, astronomical, religious, or secular, marked off for a period of 2 months. It did not seem likely to me that sailing directions would be divided up into groups of 30 and 31 "words." If it were a written language then the problem would be out of my ken. The philologists must guess Ventris-wise, or hope for a Rosetta Stone.

I decided, like many before me, to investigate side A with the pencil-and-paper approach. If I found anything on A, then I would look to side B for confirmation. Since the pictures faced counterclockwise I figured that the "message" was to be read starting at the center. The first group was "flower-head-arrow." I converted the pictures into a numerical code to facilitate the work. The first group was repeated again at group 4. That made three intervals before the repetition occurred. There were five more repetitions, making six repeats altogether. Group 3 (rake? blossom, leaf, skin, skin, seven, head with topknot) was repeated at group 15, an interval of 12. Group 10 repeated at 13, interval of 3; 11 at 17, interval of 6; 12 at 18, interval of 6; and 13 at 16, interval of 3.

The spacings were in intervals of 3, 6, or 12—numbers divisible by 3. And there were 2×3 repetitions.

This was most intriguing, something not to be expected of a language with words following the sequence of a sentence. I clumsily tried to force the English language to do it:

$\overset{1}{Decoding}$ $\overset{2}{\text{tablets}}$ $\overset{3}{is}$ $\overset{4}{decoding}$ $\overset{5}{\text{with}}$ $\overset{6}{\text{great}}$ $\overset{7}{\text{difficulty}}$ $\overset{8}{\text{especially}}$ $\overset{9}{\text{when}}$ $\overset{10}{the}$ $\overset{11}{disk}$ $\overset{12}{like}$ $\overset{13}{the}$ $\overset{14}{\text{shell}}$ $\overset{15}{is}$ $\overset{16}{the}$ $\overset{17}{disk}$ $\overset{18}{like}$ $\overset{19}{\text{that}}$ $\overset{20}{\text{of}}$ $\overset{21}{\text{Phaistos.}}$

Nonphilologist as I am, I could not imagine any language having a base of 3!

The disk, I began to think, might respond to a programmed mathematical test. I counted the total number of stamped pictures—123, again a number divisible by 3. A cabala? A meaningful numerical series?

In case a reviewer criticizes me for unprofessional speculation, let me hasten to point out that this is an example of how a scientist works before the definite, dogmatic solution to a problem is published. It was the process of the self-questioning mind moving down the dales of acceptance, well aware of the danger of accidental interpretations. Many samples are needed to test a theory. There were more than 400 tablets available for the testing of Linear B. For the Phaistos Disk there was only the other side. Would it work?

I quickly numbered the various pictures on side B and repeated the scratch-pad analysis. It was a spiral of 30 groupings of 119 pictures. There was one repetition, the series which ran headdress, bell (?), bush, dog's head, and legs-and-torso. These occurred at group 5 and 10—a spacing of 5, not the ubiquitous 3 of side A!

Ariadne's thread was broken. To have meaning there should have been a cabala, base 3 or 5, on side B. The idea did not work. The copy of the disk went into my "unsolved" file, a challenge for prehistorical detectives of the future. Perhaps a second disk lies awaiting the spade in the black-humus cultural lens; perhaps a clue will be found in other civilizations—Amon-Ra Egypt, *Iliad* Greece. I describe it here as a cognitive challenge between an ancient and modern culture, and as a warning of the frustrations and disappointments of limited data.

There is more to go on when the detective turns to cave markings. These mysterious symbols are more plentiful in the southern caves, and La Pileta, 40 kilometers from the Spanish Mediterranean, contains the most. It is difficult to imagine that the animal pictures and the sim-

223

plistic dot and line patterns have been done by the same hand, yet this is the finding of the experts. It is a dualism, a chosen second medium of expression. Between the colorful bisons and the geometrical abstracts there is what anthropologist Paolo Graziosi calls a "veritable chasm, a deep and definite gulf." There is no switch from realism to abstract as the art develops; the designs occur with the earliest art, and the styles run parallel through time. Was there meaning in the geometry, magic beyond magic? Was there a cave rabbi who could read the cabala?

When man is shown on the walls of the cave, the figure is almost unrecognizable. Anthropomorphic figures are distorted in shape, unnatural in posture, and are painted deep in hidden niches. Experts have given opinions about this: "The artist was skilled at painting animals, and the zoological style carried over to the human portraits." "The artist observed species of animals clearly, but was myopic concerning his own." "The artist was painting gods, not men." "The artist was gripped by a magic or taboo; his hand was stayed from painting realistic humans."

The abstracts have been classed variously as "shield signs," "boat signs," "weapon signs," and flags or blazons of particular tribes.

FIG. 35. *Enigmatic drawing from the cave of La Pasiega. A two-storied house? Flat feet? The astronomer's symbol for the sun?*

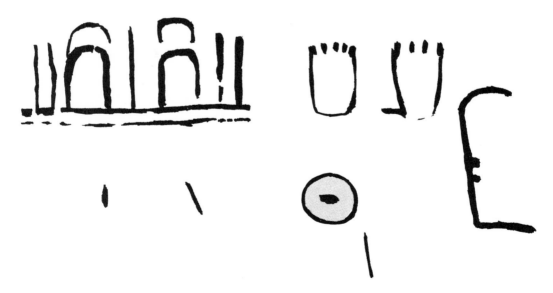

Squarish shapes, some invitingly ready for a game of tick-tack-toe, are taken to be huts, or animal traps, or traps for evil spirits. The house, if it is a house, drawn in the cave of La Pasiega has two doors, a central pillar, impressions of two flat feet (human?), the letter E, and a shaded circle with a central spot (the astronomer's symbol for the sun).

Sex has been read on the walls. No doubt this impulse does lie behind some of the abstracts, but surely not all can be accounted to sexual impulse. The cave men were probably free of the frustrations caused by modern taboos. In the paintings of humans there is nothing in the art erotic or provocative as in those notorious paintings of Roman Pompeii (shown by discreet tour guides only to the males in the party).

The interpretation of abstract art is colored in the eyes of the beholder. Across the ocean from Europe, in the caves of the Amazon basin, the German ethnologist Jesco von Puttkamer discovered geometrical markings: triangles, and triangles with a line drawn from one corner to the center. To a hippie the shape might look like a peace medallion. To one anthropologist it was a female sex symbol. A triangle within a triangle represented pregnancy, two triangles side by side lesbianism. The area was suggested to be the home of the Amazon women, the fierce, "liberated" culture met by conquistador Francisco de Orellana four centuries ago but not seen since. Five miles from the caves a platform was discovered, raised, smooth, and flat, approached by a long, carved stairway. On the platform were more carved triangles and a single, long, blunt rectangle. This was read as male phallus and female triangle in juxtaposition; the platform instantly became a one-shot, flute-orgied, compulsory love nest for the disposable male.

My training is in physical science—quantitative, numerical—and naturally I tend to look for these aspects in prehistoric art. The cave art should be looked at through all types of eyes, because by a composite integration we may approach something toward the original meaning. The Mayan carved friezes and decorated pyramids would still be regarded as pure grotesque art if numerically minded scholars had not looked at them.

As Halam L. Movius said at a New York Museum of Primitive Art lecture: "It is patently obvious that the documents . . . whether paintings, engravings, or sculpture, must be deciphered. To allude to them as 'probably for ceremonial purposes' . . . begs the issue. . . ."

225

In La Pileta I saw a circle with 12 radiating lines, another with 10. To me, these were sun signs, but of course, taken by themselves, I could not be sure of the interpretation. An anthropologist took the signs to be the all-seeing eye, like the eye on the prow of old Portuguese fishing boats, the protection against dangers ahead, the magical radar. Astronomy in the cave art would be difficult to prove.

La Pileta was more numerical than artistic, more mystical than real. If rows of dots, strings of vertical dashes, and pairs of strokes were numerical, then La Pileta was a number cave. The "if," I must admit, is debatable; many experts deny it. To them the marks are patterns, doodlings to achieve a pleasant result. Cave man was making guttural noises, was concerned with no more than feeding and breeding, and was close to the animals of his environment. Speech, thoughts, and pseudo-religion would be a surprising level of intellect, a concept of numbers even more so. The educational "R's," in the accepted order of difficulty, are reading, 'riting, and 'rithmetic. Numbers are the end point in educational development and, ergo, cannot exist in a culture until a high level of intellect has been attained. This argument was used against the Stonehenge theory: the numbers in the circles and horseshoes could not be conceptual constructs; they were "ritualistic."

I disagree. The underlying meaning was found at Stonehenge. The idea of the progression of the 3 R's is within our own culture system. A child can learn numbers before he writes, and he can write before he reads. The educational arrow can and does fly in reverse—arithmetic, writing, and reading. It is quite possible for a culture to understand numbers and their meaning, arithmetic and geometry, without being what we would call "literate." It is wrong to push comparisons between neolithic man and the brain of a present-day child. Their brains might be very similar at birth, but thereafter the stimulation is vastly differ-ent, and we do not know the full environmental stimulus of 20,000 years ago. We tend to overlook the subliminal influence even today. I tested my daughter for her concept of numbers (this was when she was a preschool TV watcher and, of course, preliterate). "Would you rather have one hundred and two candies, or two hundred and one?"

"One hundred and two."

"Why?" I said apprehensively.

"Because candy gives me cavities, and I don't want cavities."

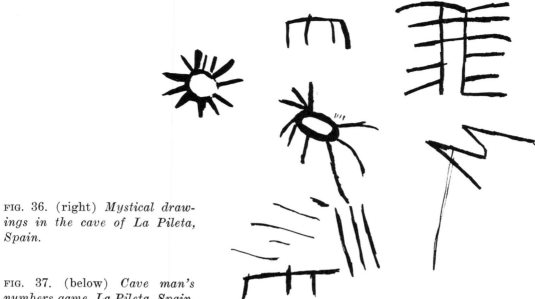

FIG. 36. (right) *Mystical drawings in the cave of La Pileta, Spain.*

FIG. 37. (below) *Cave man's numbers game, La Pileta, Spain.*

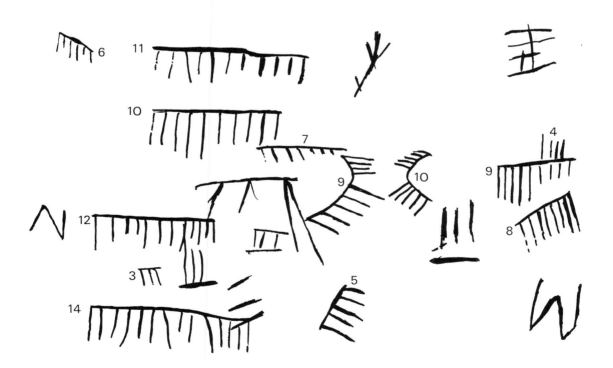

227

I looked over my copies of the drawings of La Pileta. There was a long hairpin serpentine figure, made up of close-spaced red marks, 63 on one leg of the pin, 65 on the other. These numbers and their total, 128, were large. I could find no astronomical interpretation, unless it marked off a series of days. There were other serpentine figures with several hundred carefully placed marks. If the artist were drawing a snake figure, I would expect him to use the quick single-line stroke of the animal figures, not a series of dots, painstakingly applied to the rock. The most frequently used pattern was almost certainly numerical, short lines in a row, comblike, connected across by a line at the top. This was a distinctive motif, unlike the hut signs, shields, and blazons of other caves. Taking the teeth of the comb as units, I could read 3, 4, 5, and all numbers up to 14. The larger numbers appeared on the bent or curved combs. In one area of the artwork the numbers 9, 10, 11, 12, appeared close together. It seemed to me that the artist was counting off something, or recording data, or experimenting with mathematics.

A tall, excited, work-pallored man came into my office, fresh from the New York–Boston air shuttle. He put down two zippered black vinyl travel grips. His wavy-gray Brillo-pad hair did not move as he leaned over and jerked out pages of typed manuscript onto my desk, the first draft of a book, with diagrams and large high-quality photographs. He spoke excitedly. He picked up a piece of chalk and drew a maze of cave signs over the blackboard to the right of my desk. When he ran out of blackboard he continued on the cinder-block wall. It was a whirlwind of chalk dust and speculation, those flights of scientific fancy before the hard-core facts are published. Through the whirlwind I grasped one fact clearly. He had found the sky in the caves. A record of the phases of the moon, day counts for moon months, month counts for the seasons of the year. The discoveries filled in the vacuum before Stonehenge, before Egypt. Man was preoccupied with the magical moon from the earliest beginnings. Even the rock markings of Neanderthal man were astronomical, inspired by the sky environment. The claim stunned me. I did not know what to say. I pressed the "go" button on my desk calculator to complete the multiplication which had been interrupted when he stepped into the room.

My caller was Alexander Marshack, journalist, producer-director of plays, and science writer, a singular background for astro-archaeological research. I swung around in my chair to look out the window. I thought over what he was saying. In the normal run of things a piece of scientific research is presented at a conference or symposium so as to air the theory and give those experts who are interested a chance to comment. A written paper is communicated to the appropriate scientific journal, where usually, upon receipt, the editor sends it out for review. One or two referees (who remain anonymous) look it over, criticize, and recommend (or sometimes veto) publication. I advised him to simplify, write it up as a short paper, and use a limited selection of his samples. I put him in touch with my colleagues at the Peabody Museum, promised to do a number-frequency analysis of the results when I could, and turned to the unfinished figures still showing in the windows of my desk calculator. Six discussion-packed years later the book was to come out, enlarged and title-changed, as *Roots of Civilization*.

The clearest example of moon markings come from Spain. Omnipresent Abbé Breuil exposed the ocher sign from Canchal de Mahoma. At first the central mark was taken as a war club, and the 27 spots plus 2 lines were "ceremonial." Now, with a new look at the old pattern, Marshack identified the club as a god symbol, and the spots as observation of the phases of the moon.

The moon goes through a complete period of phases in 30 (sometimes 29) days: first crescent, yellow, thin, and curved on the western horizon; first quarter, half a silver dollar, bulging to the left, high in the south at sunset; full, a brilliant, blinding orb; last quarter, late to rise and bulging eastward, and then, before final extinction, the last crescent which, milkmanlike, thinly flits at sunup. "Full" is that instant when the moon is exactly 180° in longitude from the sun. It is a split-second phenomenon astronomically. In practice the instrumentless observer can see no change in the fullness for three nights in a row. There is a period of invisibility between the old and the new crescent when the moon passes in front of the glare of the sun. The dark of the moon. The ancient Greeks called this gap the "ενη και νέα," the day when the old changes to new. Plutarch wrote: ". . . the years of Osiris's life . . . were 28, for that is the number of the moon's illuminations." The month contained 27 or 28 phases, plus 1 or 2 no-phase nights, making a total of either 29 or 30, and averaging out to 29.53. Modern astronomers put the time of new moon at the instant when it is in conjunction with the sun and, therefore, dark. Religiously and pedestrianly it is "new" sometime later, on that first evening when the thin crescent is seen by the high priest on the tower of Babel, or by the ordinary man who superstitiously expects a month of bad luck if he sees it through glass, or a month of rain if the crescent is upside down—a position, by the way, that is astronomically impossible, even though cartoonists, with artistic license, often show it this way. (Artistically, 49 times out of 50, the crescent in a modern picture is wrong.) Religiously, for the fixing of time-factored celebrations, the priest-observer has the last word. In October, 1971, the Muslim community in cloudy Britain fixed the Eid festival which ends the Ramadan month of fasting by digital computer. The Royal Greenwich Observatory gave them a forecast of the date when the crescent would first be seen. Because of freak visibility and/or diligent observing in Mecca, the thinnest of crescents was sighted the evening before. The London *Times* reported "confusion," "frustration," and "disarray." The Muslim ulemas, orthodox priests, recommended in the future a return to naked-eye sighting, with telephone communication from widespread observing stations. The moon is more to civilization than a dusty pad for man's first footprints.

The rock painting at Canchal de Mahoma is a correct observational record. It was made no later than 7000 B.C., and is an end product of the art practiced through the Ice Age. The artist avoided representationalism of man, because of magic, taboo, or free choice, but he made a factual record of the moon. The month sequence starts at the lower left with the thin crescent, facing to the right, exactly as it shows in the sky at sunset. Then follows a count of six spots, one for each night. The eighth spot is large and separated, beginning a new sequence of four. This is the night of the first quarter; the sequence of four is the waxing phase to full. Three marks in a cluster show the nights of bright full moon. The waning sequence runs over the top of the god sign. Mark 21, accentuated, is for the queen of the dawn, last quarter moon, and the final 6 (counting the V sign as two) closes off the month with the crescent facing to the east (left) as it does in the sky.

The artist's diagram is truly remarkable. Unlike 98 percent of modern artists, he has painted the crescent correctly, and runs the sequence of illuminations counterclockwise, which is the correct orbital direction of the moon. Is this astronomy for astronomy's sake?

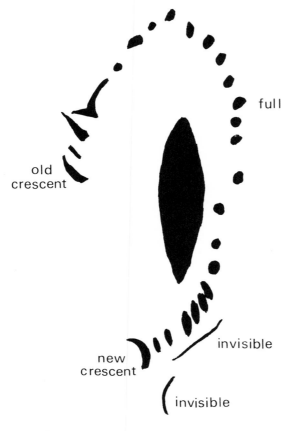

full

old
crescent

new
crescent

invisible

invisible

He leaves a big gap between old and new crescents, the day, or days, of invisibility—the moon has vanished and must be born again. For these moonless nights the artist added two thin notational lines at the bottom of the picture, two nights of bewilderment when the moon god was dead.

Plutarch, writing 5,000 years later in *Isis and Osiris,* said:

The Egyptians have a legend that the end of Osiris's life came on the 17th of the month, on which day it is quite evident to the eye that the period of the full moon is over. Because of this the Pythagoreans call this day the Barrier, and utterly abominate this number. For the number 17, coming in between the square 16 and the oblong rectangle 18, which as it happens are the only plane figures that have their perimeters equal to their areas, bars them off from each other and disjoins them, and breaks up the ratio of 16 and its eighth . . . the

231

numbers game: $16 = 4 + 4 + 4 + 4$ and $16 = 4 \times 4$;

$18 = 3 + 6 + 3 + 6$ and $18 = 3 \times 6$;

$16 + \frac{1}{8}(16) = 18$ (the epogdoon);

and 17 comes between 16 and its epogdoon 18, and moreover is an indivisible prime number, and the 17th is the awful night in the moon month when the moon begins to die.] The wood which they cut on the occasions called the Burials of Osiris they fashion into a crescent-shaped coffer because of the fact that the moon, when it comes near the sun, becomes crescent-shaped and disappears from our sight. The dismemberment of Osiris into 14 parts they [the Egyptians] refer allegorically to the days of the waning . . . from the time of full moon to the new moon. And the day on which she becomes visible after escaping the solar rays and passing by the sun they style "Incomplete Good"; for Osiris is beneficent. . . .

The Apis . . . comes into being when a fructifying light thrusts forth from the moon and falls upon a cow in her breeding season . . . they also call the moon the Mother of the world, and she has a nature both male and female, as she is made pregnant by the sun, but she herself in turn emits and disseminates into the air. . . .

Marshack claims there was a Plutarch-like legend behind the cave markings—not necessarily the Isis-Osiris myth, but a moon lore, a saga of the Ice Age, which stood at the roots of civilization. The run of dots are phrasings in the narrative; the breaks and turning points are vital events.

In Abris de las Viñas there is another wall painting. It is executed in red ocher. Apparently more sophisticated than the first example, it belongs to the same epoch—Azilian. Dating of the cave paintings is, of course, extremely difficult. There is no direct radiocarbon technique, and the artwork must be presumed to date to the charcoal and other artifacts buried in the floor of the cave. The Azilian culture, named after the first discoveries in Mas d'Azil, France, is assigned to the approximate time span 8000–6000 B.C. The cultural lens covered France and Spain.

The sign in the center of the Viñas pattern is clearly anthropomorphic, man or god. The moon story is shown by the 30 marks. It can be read from right to left, counterclockwise as at Mahoma, or from left to right. It reads the same numerically both ways. This is because of the symmetry of the moon's phases. The days of invisibility were included

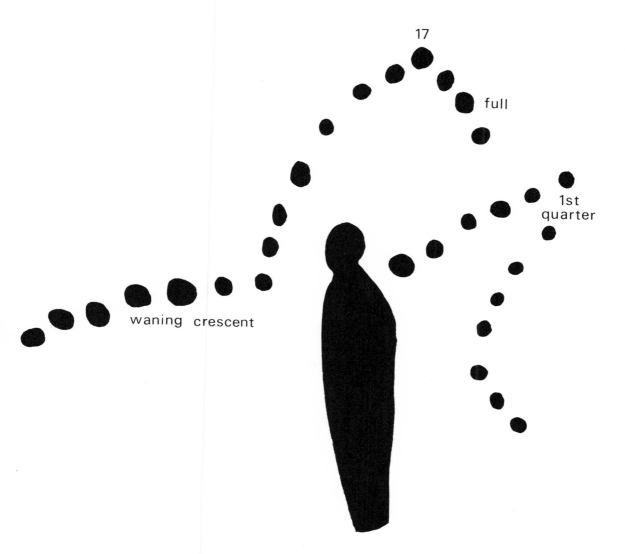

17

full

1st
quarter

waning crescent

FIG. 39. *Moon-god and the month marked at Abris de las Viñas, Spain.*

233

in the pattern to make up the total of 30 days. There are no crescents; it is entirely abstract. This is a confident, solid advance on the part of the artist. The sign can function as a perpetual calendar or moon computer. The panorama of the sky environment is captured on the rock wall for eternity.

I start at the lower left and read: "When the new-moon crescent appears there will be six more nights of crescent moon. Then on the eighth night the half-moon will show. It will be followed by five nights of the gibbous phase (almost a complete disk). The fourteenth night begins the illumination of the full moon. This will last for three successive nights. On the seventeenth night of the phases (shown by the spot at the top of the pattern) the moon begins to wane. It will decrease for a sequence of seven nights (seven declining dots), and then during a further seven nocturnal appearances it will become an early morning crescent and disappear at the change."

But this is a limited, factual interpretation by a twentieth-century scientist. It meant this to the artist as he watched and waited for the ever-changing moon, but in his culture it meant much more. The depths of his perception go beyond a limited scientific probing. With each step in technology man moves toward the moon, and away from the moon. It no longer plays a significant role in his culture. The moon is lost in the neon glare projected palely, synthetically, into the dome of the planetarium. Yet goddess Diana, virgin Artemis, "queen and huntress, chaste and fair," or Osiris, "kindly toward the young of animals and the burgeoning of plants . . . of reason and perfect wisdom," or Khonsu or whatever name the image held, the moon, the god-moon, lifted Ice Age man forward on his first giant step.

The Apollo capsule had a maintained, shirt-sleeve environment. The moon suits of the astronauts were air-conditioned. In one generation, Western civilization has moved into a constant temperature comfort, furnaced in winter, refrigerated in summer, humidified and dehumidified in antiphase with the seasons. The deep caves in Lascaux hold to a steady, year-round 50°F., which was the average habitation temperature of stately British homes in the Tom Jones era. Given a free choice of course, man will opt for 72° ±1, but with no free choice he adapts. Britishers used to label costly central heating as decadent, unhealthy. Now with a Common Market standard of living, "c.h.," as it is neatly abbreviated in the house ads, is a cultural necessity.

Paleolithic man lived at the edge of the ice barrier. He lived there by choice. The melting ice produced a lush fern vegetation. The greenery attracted the reindeer, and it was easy hunting in the scrub-tree tundra. The caves with fires at the entrance were a safe winter habitation for the family. Animal furs were sewn into suits. Man walked the earth carrying with him a layer of tropical comfort. Hunting in the Dordogne Valley was exciting, with no legal restrictions. A lookout posted on the high white cliffs of the canyon could see the herds far away on the velvet green floor, and signal tactics to his fellows below. Clear water ran at the mouth of the limestone grottoes. To Carleton Coon, writing in *The Story of Man,* it was a natural paradise: ''What more could a man want in those, or any other, days?''

Ice Age economy depended on flint stone, and on its manufactured derivative, the burin. Flint, sharp and shapable, was pulled from the walls of the caves. Nodules were mined and exported from places like Grimes Graves in north Norfolk, England. The burin was a narrow, sharp flint chisel. Thousands of them have been found in the cave layers from about 30,000 B.C. onward. The burin was made from a blade that was struck off with one blow from a core. Anthropologists see this as a forward step in productivity. Faced with a declining supply of raw material, and therefore an inflation in the value of flint, the workers mass-produced many blades from a single nodule.

The burin was designed to chisel bone and wood. It was the machine tool of the economy. A burin produced needles for winter-suit making, harpoons, spears, fishhooks, spear throwers, and hairpins. The burin was also an engraving tool. We can rationalize the making of hunting equipment as a necessity of survival, but not so the engravings. Ornamental spear throwers have been found carved with bird heads so delicate that the instrument could not be used in the hunt. There are beautiful but unnecessary decorations on harpoons and spears. There are notched ''batons'' which have no explanation except magic or ceremony. There are number patterns so finely engraved that a microscope is needed to reveal them. Ivory engraving with a burin chisel was a vital part of Ice Age culture. For 25,000 years, beginning with Cro-Magnon. Why?

It was an engraved mammoth tusk that broke the skeptics of Ice Age

235

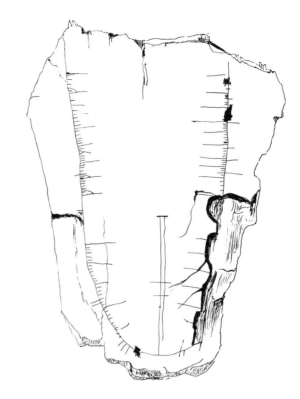

FIG. 40. *Engraved mammoth tusk from Gontzi, Ukraine, Russia.*

art. Edouard Lartet, a magistrate who gave up law for archaeology, found a fossilized tusk in the La Madeleine cave area in France in 1864. It was from the so-called reindeer layer. There was no doubt about its age or authenticity. The burin-scratched lines had clear-cut edges. Only natural ivory marks in this way; fossilized bone would flake along the line, producing a microscopically jagged edge. The engraving was made *before* the long process of fossilization. The figure of the ice elephant was depicted realistically in its fleshy, hairy shape. Only fossil rib-cage skeletons were known in 1864; the finding of whole quick-frozen mammoths in Siberia was to come later. The mammoth picture on the mammoth tusk had been drawn from life.

That shaggy ice elephant hugged the glacial wall from Britain, through France, Czechoslovakia, Poland, and Russia. The Magdalenian culture spread with it, and man deposited wonderful ivory engravings

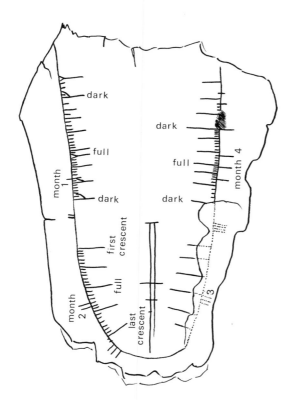

FIG. 41. *Lunar interpretation of the Gontzi ivory.*

across Europe. The beginning of this high culture was approximately 15,000 B.C. A man (or woman), as human as Thornton Wilder's Ice Man in *Skin of Our Teeth,* carved another of these tusks, found in the Ukraine, at Gontzi. It is not figurative, not decorative. The burin marks were placed on the mammoth ivory with watchmaker's precision. The markings are scientific, observational. The message is lunar.

A U-shaped line (the bone is drawn unrolled in Fig. 40) provides the time axis. The inward-facing marks are for illuminations, one for each nightly phase. The lines with V ends are for those special days when the moon is waning or "swallowed." Four complete months are recorded, with some extra days at the beginning and end. According to Marshack, there was a narrative, a moon lore with probably a different story for each month of the year.

The reading begins at the top right: there is a waning V sign, then 2 marks for the old crescent, then a "swallowed" day, the day of invisibility. Counting this day, the day of the change (death), as zero, and moving to the right we come to a long mark. Number 8. This signals the half-moon at first quarter phase. Three marks together show the three nights of the full moon—14 is extended, 15 is the exact "full," and 16 is a V sign to show the commencement of the waning of the moon. Number 25, just after last quarter, is a "swallowed" sign, and 30, another swallowed sign, ends the month with the second invisibility.

Between the first and second months are a pair of outward-pointing marks: "We have seen the moon die twice."

The second month is a simpler notation of 4 sets of 7. The changing moon was recorded in the preceding month in the swallowed sign, 30, so the series starts with the new crescent. Half-moon gets a special long mark, and so do full, last quarter, and last crescent. The two small marks at the end of the month are for the days of the death of the moon.

Note how there is an outward-pointing (/) mark for month 1, and a pair (//) for month 2. Month 3 is damaged, but there are 4 wide-spaced, outward-pointing marks for the fourth month. The central lines can also be interpreted as a summary notation.

There is a set of 3 outward-pointing marks between the second and third months; "We have seen the moon die thrice."

The tusk is damaged at the third month, but long marks still show.

The fourth month contains 30 marks, representing an interval of 29 complete, elapsed days. There are no swallowing marks for the waning or death of the moon in this month, but the sequence probably starts and/or ends on a day of moon change. The moon narrative is split up into 5 segments of 5 days, and 1 of 4. The full moon would fall on the long line, 15. The notation beyond the end of month 4 is either a summary of prior events or a commencement of new month 5. The tusk is damaged at this place, but we would expect to see 5 close-spaced, outward-pointing lines between month 4 and 5 to tell of the 5 previous moon deaths.

We do not know the full richness of the moon story, or the beliefs or environmental cognizance of the artist. We are stunned to realize how ivory scratches might be numbers, observations of the orbital movement of the moon. *Homo modernus* falls back on the computer-produced, unfailing ephemeris; newspaper predictions, calls to the observatory.

From ivory tusk to ivory tower, the ice man's notation compares with what college students do in a general science course when assigned the term project: "Observe, measure, and mark out in your own way without instruments the pattern of the phases of the earth's natural satellite."

There is no other interpretation of the Gontzi bone—unless it is called "ceremonial," which, as Movius says, begs the issue.

The Gontzi bone, 10,000–15,000 B.C., cave art, 35,000 B.C., this is the depth of penetration of Jung's archaic horizons in the subconscious mind. Those meager carved items, those occult symbols of the cave paintings, astro-archaeology cannot take us beyond. Voices and thoughts have escaped into the wider atmosphere. Perishable software.

I purchased a ticket from British Rail—Glasgow to Stornoway, "with connections." I was making a field trip to the Tursachan (stone mourners) of Callanish, on windswept Lewis, 80 miles north of "tight little island" Barra. My published calculations had been based on paper data, and a site inspection was called for.

It was a pleasant, eventful journey: slow steam train through the beauty of the Scottish Highlands, past Fort William and Loch Eil to Mallaig. Then by boat, across the Sound of Sleat, to Skye; minibus along the winding, heather-fringed roads of the island, past cairn and standing stone to Uig in Loch Snizort. From there the connecting ferry went to Port Tarbert, on Harris, but "not till the morrow," said the ticket collector, who waved me toward the scattered, white crofters' cottages between the shore and the steep hill. At Tarbert, the next day, the boat docked on schedule, but the much-punched ticket expired.

"But I was told it takes me to Stornoway."

"Och, no! What would they know about things up here, down in Glasgi?"

I reached Stornoway, by private arrangements, on the Sabbath. Callanish was a further 16 miles of open peat-and-heather prairie to the west. Nothing moved on the Sabbath, not a taxi nor an astronomer. (Remember the fertilizer salesman who lost a big order to his highland farmer client when he mentioned on a Monday something he read in yesterday's paper: "And have ye no better to read on the Sabbath?") My time was limited; I took a chance with the open road.

239

Three miles out, a car stopped. Two dark-suited gentlemen were going to a funeral on the west side of the island. Generously, the mourners took me to the Tursachan. We talked about the life of the highlanders, ancient (the lost-in-prehistory builders of the rings and cairns) and modern (hardy, warm-hearted, ingenuous people who live a life envied by smog-soaked city dwellers; if one joins the crofters' union, so I was told, one can rent a two-room, thatched-roof croft, with a panoramic mountain and loch view included, for 12 pounds sterling per year, and one can have unlimited peat-cutting rights, for fuel and roof repairs, for an additional 2 shillings and 6 pence p.a.). They left me, heading north on the winding road, and I turned to check the menhirs with the published charts.

On paper, the avenue of stones pointed to distant Mount Clisham, and to the position of moonset at the 19-year extreme, declination $-29°$. At the site I saw a complication. There was a slight, southward-increasing slope in the ground, and a low rocky outcrop obscured distant Mount Clisham. The moon, of course, could still have been seen in 1500–2000 B.C. if one walked up the avenue to the outcrop. Perhaps the site was chosen deliberately to make the moon appear to enter into the rock. I walked around the loch to the other stone circles. One, at least, was obscured to the south by a nearby hummock. ". . . the moon, as viewed from this island, appears to be but a little distance from the earth . . . the god visited the island every 19 years. . . ." Did the builders choose a site which made the moon appear to touch the earth? The idea, passingly intriguing, was unfortunately unprovable. It was sufficient to note that the various sight lines to the sun and moon, marked by rows and pairs of stones, gave a clear view out over the houseless miles of heather, hill, and loch. Callanish was corroboration. I completed the site inspection as a black squall came in from the Atlantic, ruffling the waters of the loch and sweeping horizontal rain against the stones.

On the mainland I met with Professor Alexander Thom. I found a tall, wiry, energetic, dolichocephalic Scotsman. I had previously described his work in *Stonehenge Decoded,* his discovery of the megalithic yard, 2.72 feet, the corresponding megalithic fathom, 5.44 feet, and the intricate geometry of those builders who measured and pegged out the ground a thousand years before Euclid.

The 2.72 feet (2 feet 8⅔ inches) is a gross average of circle diameters, distances to outlying stones and between centers. The stones in the circles are 1, 2, or more feet across, and there are errors (displacement of stones from the arc) of the same magnitude. Thom believes the megalithic yard was a standard unit, akin to the meter bar in the Paris vault. Special smooth-ended rods, accurate to three one-hundredths of an inch, were carried from location to location. Thom denies the alternative—that there might be slight differences in the unit across Britain, differences which are smoothed out by the gross averaging. Either way, the ancient British geometers were working with integral units. This means an underlying numerical system. Arithmetic before writing.

I haven't been able to decide for or against the claim of superprecision. It is strange how the megalithic yard is so close to the size of an average pace or stride. Also the megalithic fathom is the distance, more or less, between outstretched hands. Take a tape measure, hold one end in the outstretched hand, the other end on the tip of the nose. For an average person the distance comes out between 2 feet 6 inches and 2 feet 10 inches. There are differences of up to 8 percent in the length of the so-called standard in individual circles at the sites. And so the 2 feet 8⅔ inches as calculated could be the average of all the pacings in Britain lumped together. Then again people come long-armed and short-armed, but when a group clasps hands and makes a ring the differences average out. A group of "n" men (women?) clasping hands will make a ring with perimeter n units in length. A human linked surveyor's chain. The megalithic yard could be the average of a human chain.

From Land's End to John O' Groats they played the numbers game. When they scored a success they marked it out in permanent stone. Rules of the game: diameters must be in integral units, the perimeter must come out in even lengths of 2½ megalithic yards. Since many of the diameters are odd numbers, the geometers clearly accepted half-units in terms of radius. Each of the figures was measured out with rods, and scribed with a rope swiveled around with one end anchored. Or a human chain could be used instead of a rope in the style of the New England children's game "crack the whip" illustrated in the Winslow Homer painting.

Mathematically they were searching for a diameter with a whole number, d, which gave a perimeter 2.5p, where p is also a whole number. Now $p = \pi d / 2.5$, i.e., $p = 1.256 \ldots d$. The "$\ldots$" indicates an incommensurate number, where the decimals, like the figures for π (3.1415 . .), will never cut off. Because of the " . . . " there is no *exact* solution to the problem. The Stone Age geometers were tackling the impossible! But so are we, in our more advanced spheres.

They did not know π decimally, nor the equation constant, 1.256 . . If a group of circle designers settled for the first approximation, 1.25, the circle diameters would come out 4, 8, 12, etc. These diameters do occur frequently at megalithic sites. *They* found the solution by trial and error.

Dinnever Hill, Cornwall, is an example of a flattened circle, type A. The perimeter is divided into 3 equal arcs, spaced at 120°. The circle is perfect for the lower two-thirds. The upper one-third is composite, made up of a flat arc centered on the lower edge of the circle, and 2 small sharp curves with centers halfway out on the 120° lines. There are more than 30 examples of flattened circles on the moors of Britain. Thom identifies at least 6 constructs, including types A, B, ellipses, and egg-shaped figures.

The flattened circle was a bold attack on irrational π. By using two anchor stakes, a pseudo-circle was generated which made the perimeter/diameter ratio close to a whole number, 3. This strange construct is uniquely megalithic. Euclid missed; so did we. Was there a powerful magic for megalithic man in the flattened circle?

Thaddeus Cowan, professor of psychology at Oklahoma State, calls the ancient Britons an "inquisitive lot," "obsessed with a concern for perfection," and quite possibly frustrated by the irrationality of π. When one ceases to worry about Vietnam, inflation, and whether the cat has been put out for the night, there are other things.

Cowan suggests a scribing method for making the special flattened circles. Take a rope, fix it to an anchor post, and place two pivot posts on the 120° lines. Then scribe. The end makes a long, circular sweep for two-thirds of the circle, and two sweeps of shorter radius at the top when the midpoint of the rope hits the pivot stakes. Now take a longer rope, anchor it at the bottom of the circle, and scribe the flat arc to close off the figure at the top. Result: shape type A.

The ellipse, first discovered at Tormore, Scotland, by Archie Roy et al., was probably scribed by walking a loop of rope around two spaced stakes.

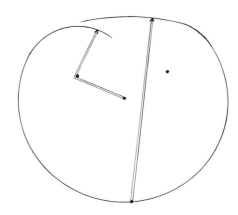

FIG. 42. (right) *Method of scribing, according to Thaddeus Cowan, using two anchor points and two pivot stakes.*

FIG. 43. (below) *Flattened circle marked with stones circa 2000* B.C., *Dinnever Hill, Cornwall, England.*

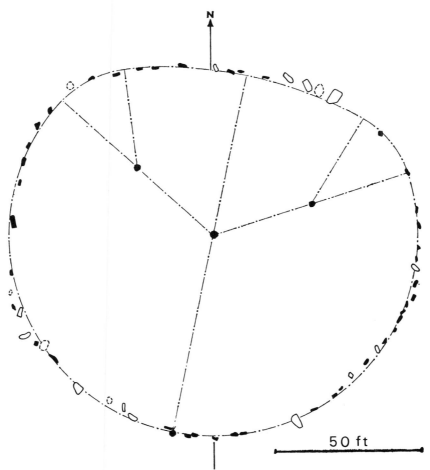

50 ft

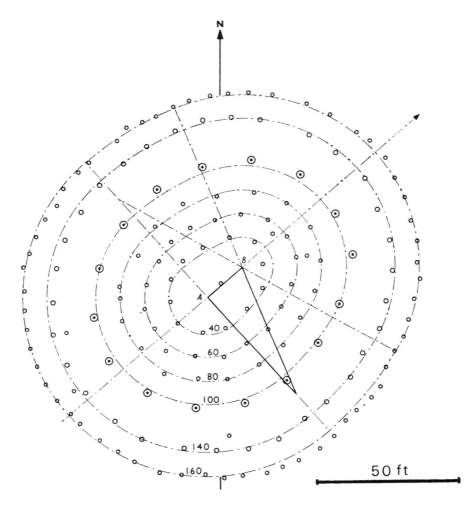

FIG. 44. *The geometry behind megalithic Woodhenge, Wiltshire, England.*

Stonehenge fits into the numbers game: diameter of Aubrey circle, 105 megalithic yards; perimeter, 330 megalithic yards (divisible by 2.5); diameter of inner faces of sarsen circle, 36 megalithic yards; perimeter 112½ megalithic yards (divisible by 2.5).

Woodhenge, on the sunrise line from Stonehenge, continued the fetish. The post holes, shown by the recently inserted concrete stumps, mark out 6 concentric egg shapes. The pivot points for the original rope

PLATE 58. *Cement blocks mark the excavated holes at Woodhenge. The axis of the elongated circles is directed toward the midsummer sunrise.* (*See Fig. 44.*)

scribing were placed exactly 6 megalithic yards apart. The perimeters of the eggs measured round numbers of megalithic yards—40, 60, 80, 100, 140, and 160. Integers, each divisible by 2, 2.5, 5, 10, and 20. A clever achievement. Was it number magic? Before this discovery the holes were no more than "post" holes, and Woodhenge was a roofed, communal hall. Now the holes speak numbers.

Between manuscript and galley proofs the B.B.C. put the theory to the test. A moment of truth in front of 2.5 million viewers. Do twenty people make 40 megalithic yards, thirty make 60, and so forth? The producer called in seniors from the nearby Amesbury School. Twenty linked hands, stretched tight, and matched the egg-shaped, concrete-posted perimeter precisely. A chain of thirty filled out the next, and forty the next. Patrick Moore turned to the camera and said: "an experiment, a magic ritual never done before in this ancient place; a human chain makes the pattern for the first time in history—or is it the *first time since four thousand years?*" I turned to measuring the young men and women—heights and vital statistics. Representatives of the modern race maybe, but how did they compare with neolithic man? And the further questions that always come from an experiment—why would they count in chains of ten? Was it a ceremony, a dance macabre (reference the child burial at the center), was it mathematical with axioms that we cannot now see?

The elongated axis of Woodhenge points to azimuth 49.2° east of north, the direction none other than midsummer sunrise. The structure is mathematical, counting by 2.5 and 10, geometrical, scribed with two pivots spaced 6 whole units apart, *and* it is astronomical. Recognition of this ancient brain power almost slipped through the fingers; despite the best intentions, destruction of megalithic sites goes on apace.

Numbers and the sky. More often than not the pattern in stone points to one or more of the Stonehenge horizon events—the rising or setting of sun or moon at the extrema. Stars also have been identified as targets, though I challenge these alignments on the grounds of practicability. A star, even brightest-in-the-sky Sirius, is a feeble object on the horizon, difficult to see, much of the time invisible in deep scintillations. The stones on the ground (remember the lines at Nasca) cannot be seen when there is no moon up; and the rising of the stars cannot be seen when the moon is up. Then, again, a star rises in the same position night after night. There is no need of marking the place. It can, with practice, be estimated from those stars in the constellation pattern which have already risen. But with or without the stars, there is now in the published literature a convincing array of evidence for megalithic astronomy. The "astro" culture lens covered the British Isles and western Europe. There was in 2000 B.C. a dedicated, life-consuming preoccupation with the sky.

The builders had an eye for beauty. Scotland provides the world with calendar pictures of sweeping glens, heaths and forest fir, ruined castle, loch and rocky beach. Scottish rings are in the most beautiful spots in the highlands—the Maxwellton Braes and Allan Waters of Robert Burns, and royal Scone. Was the poet descended from the geometers? He was bent on mathematics, as he put it, until "the sun entered Virgo [and] a charming *fillette* overset my trigonometry, and set me off on a tangent from the scene of my studies!" It was very similar in megalithic times (the scenery, that is); no castles, of course, but a better climate with more sun, warmer and with more trees. Despite what Caledoniaphobe Samuel Johnson said,* Scotland has noble prospects. The population density is less than 1 per square mile, with small scattered hamlets and single crofts. That is excluding the firths (Clyde, Forth, Tay) which had an upsurge during the period, brief in historical perspective, when coal and iron ore were ripped from the hills. In the eighteenth century, Edinburgh had a population of 40,000, and Glasgow was a quaint township of broad, neat streets, noted for its fresh country air. From the hills above Robbie Burns's birthplace in Ayrshire one can see across the waters of the firth the mountains of Arran Isle, place of the first-discovered stone ellipse. Beyond Arran, across blue Kilbrennan Sound, run the long, north–south purple hills of the Kintyre peninsula, and beyond that the isles of Islay and Jura, where "the wan moon is setting beyond the white wave."

Haggstone Moor, on the coast of Wigtownshire, is south of the poet's birthplace, but it shares the same vista over the Firth of Clyde. There is a menhir, "Long Tom," on the moor, a broken stone cairn, and several other large stones. The end of the Mull of Kintyre is marked by the cairn seen from "Long Tom." At the low extreme of its northerly setting (dec. $+18°.7$), the "wan moon" sets over the distant promontory of the Mull. The upper rim of the moon showed momentarily in the small notch, circa 1800 B.C., as it dipped behind the mountains in its slanting path. In Robbie Burns's time it went down just over one diameter to the left. The notch now carries the modern road which leads to the lighthouse at the end of the Mull.

There is a site at Ballochroy, at the north end of Kintyre. Three

* "The noblest prospect a Scotsman sees is the highroad leading to England."

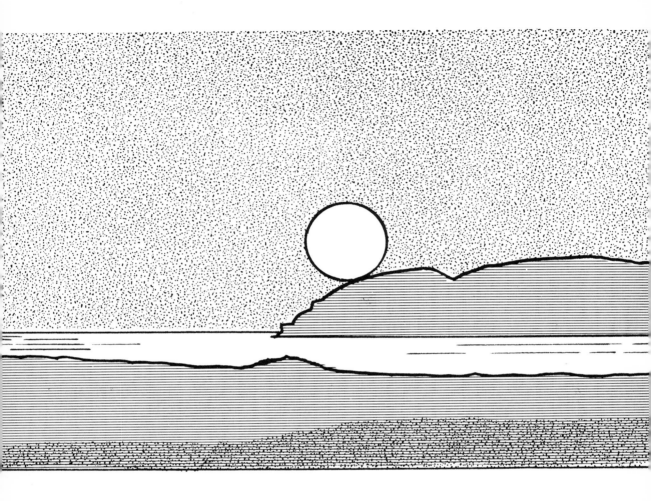

FIG. 45. (above) *Moonset over the Mull of Kintyre as seen from Long Tom, Hagg-stone Moor, Wigtownshire, Scotland.*

FIG. 46. (right) *Sun and moon observations at Ballochroy, Kintyre, Scotland.*

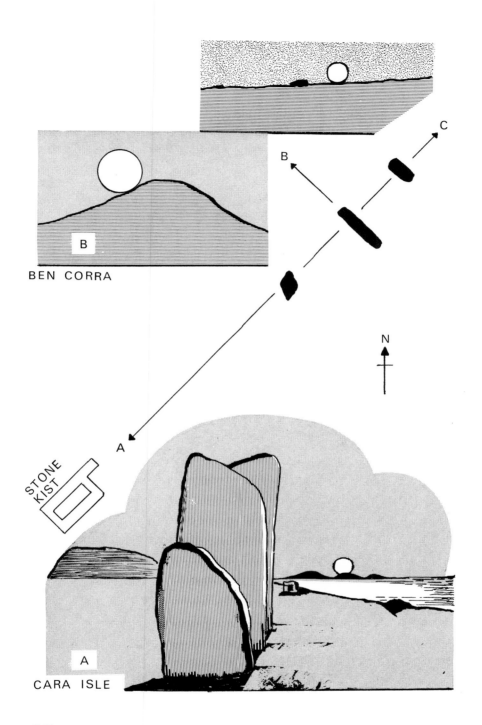

B

BEN CORRA

C

N

A

STONE
KIST

A

CARA ISLE

249

menhirs stand in line with a kist (rectangular stone-slabbed, lidded box). The azimuth is 226°, the direction of the sun, tangent on the horizon, at midwinter. Seven miles away on the sea horizon there is a tiny island, Cara, right on the line. Thom suggests that the ancient observers took advantage of distant natural markers to improve the accuracy. By carefully watching the last gleam of the sun as it slipped behind the edge of Cara, the observing error was reduced to a few seconds of arc. This is a dangerous assumption, difficult to prove as a generality (how many other islands are visible in the sound, and these with small protuberances, and if there happens to be a more impressive peak to the left or right of Cara, why did they not relocate the observing site and choose that?), but in the case of the Ballochroy sunset we have a definite astro-line to depend on, with or without Cara, because of the menhirs and kist.

Now Ballochroy is at 55°.7, the latitude where the midwinter and midsummer sunsets are 90° apart. The middle menhir is a slab placed edgewise across the line, roughly pointing to the summer sunset. Did it? Was this intended? There is a mountain peak, Corra Bheinn, on the distant island of Jura, which makes a more exact sunset marker. Did the builders draw attention to this natural far-sight with the thin, edgewise monolith? My working assumption in *Stonehenge Decoded* was that anything which shows today as clearly astronomical was known in antiquity to the builders. Unless proved otherwise, we give them the benefit of the doubt. In that case, there is another surprise at Ballochroy. The line in reverse points along an elevated horizon to the extreme northerly position of the moon. An ingeniously neat combination of site selection and astronomical knowledge!

With stone and mountains, Thom claims to have unraveled a megalithic calendar. The year was measured off by solar declinations at equal time intervals from the solstice or equinox. There were 16 intervals ("months") made by time-bisection of the year: 1/2, 1/4, 1/8, and 1/16. The year dividers were signaled by observation. Four of these hinge around Boreray, that precipitous island, avoided by present-day yachtsmen, in the stormy Atlantic near St. Kilda (not to be confused with a same-name island in the equally stormy Sound of Harris). The actual observing sites are: (1) a menhir at An Carra, South Uist; (2) a pointing slab on Benbecula; (3) a pointing slab at Clach ant Sagairt, North Uist; (4) a pointing slab at Clach Mhic Leoid, Harris. These places are scattered over a 50-mile arc of the Hebrides; the sun-marking object is 60 miles out in the Atlantic. Could they mark and observe so fastidiously, so precisely (from An Carra, Boreray is a fly-speck horizon bump, 4 minutes of arc high)? Did the astronomer-priests sail forth on a calendar circuit as did the pharaohs with the Nile-placed temples?

These things are amazing, startling. Yet there is an even greater acceptance gap to be bridged. If the notches and peaks on the horizon were used, then the accuracy was minutes of arc or better. The geometers could have seen a wobble in the extremes of the moon, ±9 minutes. And they could have used it for eclipse predictions. There are small horizon markings in the required positions. The period of wobble is 173 days, one-half the eclipse year (time taken for one revolution of the sun starting and finishing at the node, which is that place where the moon's orbit crosses the ecliptic). When the wobble reaches maximum amplitude, 9′, it signals the danger of an equinox eclipse. This vernier observation could give backup to the eclipse warning system at Stonehenge. It could not be used as an independent predictor, because it would entail observation of moon rise or set in the late morning or early afternoon daylight, which is impossible without optical equipment. Did they go this far? This is being debated and investigated as I write.

Whatever the outcome of the details, early man must be credited with an awareness and a depth of intellect hardly imaginable when Don Marcelino's daughter ran inside Altamira, or Lartet dug up the mammoth tusk. Prehistoric man had a fascination for numbers—magical, cabalistic, scientific.

A scientist once said: "If I can't attach a number to it, it doesn't exist!" (He had yet to invent a love meter, or a yardstick for the human urges.)

Stone Age numbers do not directly concern us in the twentieth century. The leap-year-averaged calendar is correct to within 26 seconds; we leave the following of the digital movement of the sun and moon to the computer machine.

Our twentieth-century numbers are supposedly aloof from those of

251

the Stone Age—body counts, the Dow Jones industrial average, the dollar figure attached to not-for-sale gold in Fort Knox. Britain joins the EEC by dropping the 36-inch unit of length in favor of the meter, flight bookings drop by an unprofitable 30 percent on Friday the thirteenths.

Western civilization is a giant leap away from the slow homogenesis of the caves. There is no turning back. It is a new, dynamic, ongoing system, self-controlling in its destiny, all-powerful, indestructible. The cultural lens is thick, growing fast, and secure.

Or is it?

13 CIVILIZATION NOW

How much longer do we have?

Barry Commoner, the Paul Revere of ecology according to some, the voice of doom according to others, expects a major ecological disaster in the next ten years. A whole species will be wiped out by a man-made poisonous change in the environment. It will be caused by a scientific, technical blunder, maybe the "ultimate" blunder. Will it be species *sapiens,* the single, unique species of the genus *Homo?*

Thirty-three scientists have banded together into a Movement for Survival. The movement intends to run political candidates on an ecology platform. This group, which includes biologist Sir Julian Huxley, believes the dangers to be so great as to threaten the civilizations of the entire world: ". . . if current trends are allowed to persist, the breakdown of society and the *irreversible* disruption of the life-support systems on this *planet* will occur, possibly by the end of the century, *certainly* within the lifetimes of our children." The italics are mine. "Irreversible" and "certainly" are strong words for eminent scientists to use in a public statement. No corner of the earth will be safe, they believe. The Survival Movement expects a future, fateful, deadly shock by about A.D. 2000. A lifeless world, quite different from the cinematic *2001: A Space Odyssey,* more like the climax of *War of the Worlds* dramatized by Orson Welles on the 1938 radio, causing national panic.

C. P. Snow, speaking at Ithaca College, and supported by Harvey Brooks, dean of Engineering and Applied Physics at Harvard University, rues a society where science is no longer viable. We will sow the seeds of decay, death, and social disintegration. *"It is a mere detail* whether this will come about first through some ecological disaster, through the decay and demoralization of the technical structure, or through a military holocaust." The italics are again my own.

These views are pessimistic. The sands of time are running out, they say. The future is bleak.

253

Science magazine *Nature* attacks the Movement for Survival as "reprehensible," "half-baked," and "mere speculation." The British editor wrote optimistically: "Who will say that the forces which have in the past 2,000 years helped to make civilized communities more humane can now be dismissed from the calculation simply because a new generation of seers sees catastrophe in the tea leaves?"

Scientist-philosopher H. G. Wells, writing his last revision of *A Short History of the World* during the carnage and devastation of World War II and a few years before his own death, saw the world picture as jaded and devoid of recuperative powers. "Man must go up or down, and the odds seem to be all in favor of him going down and out." He saw the writing on the wall: Adapt or perish! We "may not be as readily accessible to fresh ideas as the . . . minds of earlier generations." We may not, confessed this imaginative thinker, be able to "keep pace with the expansion and complication of human societies and organizations. That is the darkest shadow upon the hopes of mankind." But his very last words burst through with indomitable optimism. Whatever the size reduction of the population required by nature, whatever the challenge, his inner temperament leads him to believe that *Homo sapiens* will survive until the end of time.

We have two viewpoints, optimistic and pessimistic. This dualism is a source of power, a self-challenging of the mind, a creative tension, a cross-fertilization.

Spengler and Toynbee are in a sense a duality—civilization is doomed to collapse because it has reached its materialistic climax (Spengler), *or* it has the chance to survive through the power of creative leadership (Toynbee). Both sides, both viewpoints, recognize our future problem as environmental, a problem that has occurred before in lesser measure with previous species who for their brief hour strutted on the stage before ecology drew the curtain. It is the problem of the emergence in nature of a nature-dominating species. That we are aware of future disaster is something setting us apart from other species. Man's self-awareness gives him a favorable handicap in the survival game.

Civilization is a cloud-nine concept, difficult to explain or define, and distorted by the fact that we're in it. Some of the hardware artifacts which define civilization for archaeologists are touched on in Chapter

5—a coined currency, pottery, textiles, a written record, art. Sometime budget director Lewis Douglas squarely hinged the concept on a single magic number. When the dollar price of gold was changed in the Roosevelt New Deal he declared: "This is the end of Western civilization."

Robert Heizer, anthropologist at the University of California, uses desire as a hallmark: "With civilization comes a desire, as well as a means, of leaving a record for the future." Megalithic structures are, for him, civilization indicators. The erection and moving of large stones required social organization, planning, political maneuvering, and creative leadership. Neolithic man used his primary raw material, stone, recognizing in it long-lasting qualities. He moved immovable stones so that they would never move again. He sent astronomical and geometrical messages 4,000 years into the future. His megalithic constructions are forward-traveling time machines for his thoughts.

Perhaps the heart of a civilization is not to be found in the soil, perhaps it is in its thinking, the software which does not show with the spade. To make it tick, a civilization needs a set of ideas. It might be a set of attitudes, religion, or high-minded, philosophical goals. But not esoteric philosophic systems. These, as Grahame Clark points out, are comprehensible only to a few. This set must be shared by the members consciously, or at the upper levels of the collective subconscious. The ideas will evolve as the culture develops, and for survival, the set must always be in harmony with the environment. When the idea fades, the civilization collapses.

This is nothing more than a speculation, of course, and in its testing generalizations must be made. But I do not see how a culture group can hold together without a sharing of ideas, a common cause, a conceptual matrix. Ice Age man shared his ideas with his fellows even though he did not write. The cave art shows a common interest in animals, plants, the sky, the environment. Communicating was by word, deed, and art. No doubt the cave artist believed in magic and the occult—we can only guess darkly—but his set of ideas stayed in harmony with nature for millennia, and the culture survived. Judging from the uniformity of art and notations, the thinking, the conceptual matrix, did not change for thousands of generations, a time span fully a hundred times longer than the United States has so far existed.

Neolithic man broke away from Paleolithic. His idea was to develop agriculture and cattle farming, assist nature in her two kingdoms of plant and animal. In ancient Britain the set of ideas contained an esoteric component—the probing of numbers—that we cannot comprehend. There was an obsession with a very specialized geometry, and that number pattern contained in the round of events in the sky. The ruined stone circles and monolithic slabs convey to us some of this information. There must have been a deep system of thought beyond the bare geometry and numbers. It would be interesting to know if these ideas, whatever they were, spilled over in the flow of time into succeeding cultures. The astro-work at Stonehenge, as evidenced here, was picked up as a driving motive in turn by the Secondary Neolithic, Beaker, and Wessex culture. This astro-civilization ended before the Roman invasion. Did they give up, lose the package of ideas, the religious zeal, the magical drive, or whatever we might call it?

This happened in Yucatan. The system of building temple cities was in regenerative harmony with the environment: nature reclaimed an abandoned area and replenished the soil after a hundred years or so, and the population could continue to migrate rotationally and indefinitely without ecological risk. But this powerful system came to an end. By the time of the conquest the Mayan population was living in the jungle in disorganized, decadent units. The collapse might have been aggravated to some extent by intercity warfare, but more likely the population gave up belief in the system. The conceptual matrix collapsed.

There were, as Glyn Daniel put it in *The Idea of Prehistory*, "the obvious facts of Egyptian decay." After 30 dynasties, pharaonic Egypt was a shadow of her former splendor. "She poreth not upon the heavens, astronomy is died unto her, and knowledge maketh other cycles" (Thomas Browne, seventeenth century). Though for someone who knows modern Egypt, "decay" is not the right word, and the land of the Nile is indeed drawing on its great heritage.

The reason widely accepted for the spread of civilization across post-Roman Europe involved a new belief. The old Teutonic idea of the power of the tribe, the supremacy of blood-related bands, could have lasted indefinitely, a powerful application of modern group dynamics. But Christian ideas had entered the Roman Empire a few centuries before the Roman decline. Missionaries offered the tribes something not obtainable by the sword—a conditioned guarantee of life after death. This had been, and was, a gnawing anxiety of the Teutonic chiefs, and Anglo-Saxons, an anxiety not taken care of in the group infrastructure. Rome had failed to civilize Europe with its legions, but that process was achieved by Christianity. In essence a religion is a set of ideas. The gospel word took hold of men where force had failed; the new belief controlled individual lives and gave the cohesiveness needed in territorial space for Western civilization.

Ideas are dangerous. Fred Hoyle once said in a lecture that the spreading of one idea, the wrong idea, could destroy the world. When asked for one, he was glad he could not think of an example on the spur of the moment! But, he said, the course of world history would be radically different now if, in 1932, Adolf Hitler and the Japanese war lords had been given 30 pages of an idea—the theory and know-how of the atom bomb. And if those pages contained the blueprint for the thus-far unused radioactively lethal cobalt bomb, mankind might now be reduced to a few scattered families living in the caves.

The scientific revolution has lifted man in his quest for material progress and the understanding of nature. Scientific thinking has added a youthful second dimension to the mature humanities. The plethora of new ideas is startling—we must now contend with the thought that there are upwards of 1 billion inhabitable planets in our galaxy; that earthlike planets have an organic, souplike primeval ooze from which life develops; that intelligent species are an expected natural consequence of evolution; that there is a cosmic quarantine because of the immense distance between habitable planets, and if one system destroys itself the other systems are safe; that civilizations may attempt to communicate with us via radio signals; that intelligent life, whatever the form, will understand science and have a technology; that these exobiological systems may be more advanced—they may inject astro-ideas into earthbound thinking.

Beyond the boundary of present-day science we have the misty areas of clairvoyance, occultism, telepathy, Velikovskyism. A new idea from the misty area has it that UFO's are machines visiting us from the future—time machines carrying earth-born humanoids, genetically descendant (futuristically speaking) from *Homo sapiens*. The occupants, interested in history, are dialing back to what they think are some of the critical dates in our civilization to do some ''I was there'' investigation. (If I were given one wish by a genie I would ask for a time machine to go back to dates like 1776, 1066, and 2000 B.C., just to see for myself, to compare the standard textbooks with what I actually saw. Scientifically, a backward-traveling time machine is at odds with the theory of relativity. It would require, among other things, a negative sign in the square root of the time dilation equation.)

Personally I have seen no convincing evidence for the existence of UFO's. To me they are a non-idea. Those few that I have investigated personally have turned out to be explainable natural phenomena. But free speculation beyond the boundary of science is a right and a privilege for those who wish to go.

Ideas of twentieth-century man swell the printed literature, magnetize the strip on video tapes, and since Marconi, move out spaceward from the earth on speed-of-light radio beams. Ideas which will affect the future.

Take the growth concept. This idea of growth and expansion comes out of the old Puritan, *Mayflower*-carried work ethic. It is built into modern business as ''forward planning,'' and the economic system requires it as an essential for profitable survival. This is one element in American civilization that will, in the very long run, disappear. It has to. Unending expansion with limited resources is impossible. One cannot get a quart out of a pint jar. The law of supply and demand, relied on in the past as a stability factor, produces not a healthy balance but inflation. The economic factors must be gradually adapted to a stabilized system with no upward pointing curves—flat profits, flat inventory, flat consumption.

Paul Ehrlich recommended that Britain reduce her population to 30 million, curb the use of energy, abolish the internal combustion engine of the car (a disastrous resource sink), and plan for a stabilized environment with zero growth rate. Barry Commoner believes that man must quickly get back into the ecological circle and cause minimum disturbance in the doing of it. There is a swing away from the mechanicalism of Newtonian science in present-day thinking. There is the realization that man, despite his growing knowledge, despite his high-powered technology, may not be in full control of the situation. Nature may be stronger than man. At the beginning of the era of modern science three centuries ago Francis Bacon said: "Nor can nature be commanded except by being obeyed, and so those twin objects, human knowledge and human power, do really meet in one. . . ."

Today we live in a world of complexity. Half a million man-made chemicals now flood the eco-system, according to the Movement for Survival, giving shocks to the rivers and air. The behavior of these in the ecological cycle cannot be predicted. Even a trace chemical has the power to upset the balance. Fertilizers, insecticides, food additives, aerosols. Mercury, cause of the canned tuna fish scare, comes from the atmosphere. It is released from the soils with each new groundbreaking, and with increased road building, foundation digging, and bomb cratering the atmospheric mercury content has doubled in the last 50 years. Mercury causes mental derangement. Used without controls in the hat business last century it turned exposed felt workers "mad as a hatter." The combined effects of pollution and habitat destruction now threaten the extinction of 280 mammals, 350 birds, and 20,000 plant species. Combustion of fossil fuels is injecting carbon dioxide into the atmosphere which acts as a trap for solar radiation—net result, an inexorable climatic warming over the earth and a city-swamping rise in sea level as the polar caps melt. Reserves of metals, continues the MFS, will be exhausted in 50 years as consumption continues to rise. Copper will be more valuable than gold. Socially the gap between the industrial and developing nations will widen, the standard of living of the "haves" will increase relative to the "have-nots," and Africa, India, and China will never reach the material luxury enjoyed by the United States in the seventies. Socially and politically this will aggravate world tensions.

The prestigious Club of Rome, a gathering of 70 international scientists and businessmen headed by Aurelio Peccei, former chief of Olivetti (business machines), used a digital computer to predict pollution, population, and provisioning in the years ahead. A brainchild of technology asked to look into the technology of disaster! It found it, the same black clouds in the crystal ball as seen by the MFS. The computed curves have maximum slope, maximum ecological change, in the year A.D. 2020, "possibly by the end of the century, certainly within the life-

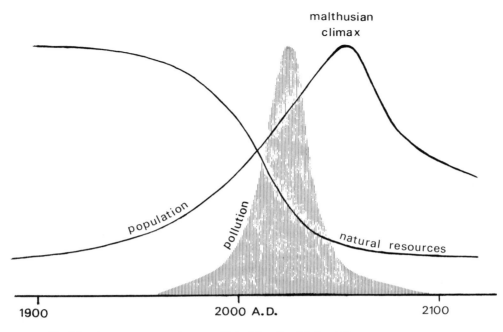

malthusian
climax

population

pollution

natural resources

| 1900 | 2000 A.D. | 2100 |

FIG. 47. *The future, computer-predicted by the Club of Rome.*

times of our children.'' The Malthusian Climax takes place in A.D. 2050. Thomas Malthus, English economist and friend of poet Coleridge, showed how the breeding of a species tended to outstrip resources. Population levels oscillated. Rabbits bred more rabbits and the food supply was used up. Starvation reduced their numbers; the green food grew again. Rabbits bred more rabbits.

For man the Malthusian Climax is a one-shot phenomenon. He is using up natural resources, minerals, etc., which will not grow again. The declining population post-2050 A.D. will be miserably short of everything. Dennis Meadows, who led the M.I.T. computer team, tried thousands of different working models. All the computed futures ended in disaster when a growth factor was included. There was one curve that worked: zero growth rate and reuse of all materials.

It does not take a computer to show the pollution changes during the last ten years. Airline pilots now see a haze stretching up to 5,000 feet which was not there before. Old photographic plates used esoterically by astronomers to study rare elements in the distant stars are now coming out of the plate stacks to be inspected for spectral lines caused by earth-atmosphere contaminants. A New Englander when he returned from a trip to Los Angeles said, ''I have seen the future and I don't like it!''

Science and technology, mostly the latter, are singled out as the root cause of the problem. But, of course, it is the mind of man that spawned them. Many of the danger signals are invisible and can be detected only by technological instruments: Strontium-90 in the glass of milk, saccharin, cyclamates, Iodine-131 on the green pasture, mercury and carbon dioxide in the air, DDT in the birds. These things are not as obvious as detergents frothing in the urine, LSD tearing at the brain. The ordinary man is baffled; he has to rely on technological science as prehistoric man relied on magic. There is mistrust and suspicion—is there collusion between the scientists and technologists, is the computer the sorcerer and are they the apprentices?

The future predictions are based on reason and logic. If the starting assumptions are the same, the logic, whether it is processed in the mind or in the computer, will predict the same end result. The scientists and businessmen were assuming a continuation of the trends of the last few generations. They built into the program no changes in these trends because they could not foresee any. They proposed external controls through the dollar and the pound. A person would be taxed at a higher rate if he had children (a *negative* child allowance); a proportionately higher rate would be charged for fuel if consumption exceeded proscribed limits; a heavy tax would be placed on equipment depending on its amortization period, the tax decreasing with increasing design age until the tax was zero on those items built to function for a hundred years or more.

But, of course, the calculations can be thrown off by an unexpected change. Suppose a powerful new idea took hold: suppose it was the fashion to have a family of one, the rationale being that it gave a better standard of living for the family unit, the best educational prospects for the child, and (admittedly in reverse of ancient and modern child psychology assessment) the optimum family environment. Birth control, including vasectomy, now makes this an attainable goal if it is the social will. A spread of this idea would send the computer tape reels spinning. By the year 2000 the population of the United States would

261

have dropped to 100 million; by 2020, the expected year of disaster, the figure would be 50 million—hardly sufficient to maintain a viable civilization in the 50 states. Eisenhower, in the 1957 recession, called on people to "get out and spend!" A future president might address the nation on 3-D, holographic, enhanced-color TV: "For the sake of our country, stay home and breed!" With the population halving each generation, he would be speaking in 2020 to a population top-heavy with the aged. Less than one-quarter of his listeners would be potent. His urge for population increase, like Pilgrim father John Alden's twinkle when he "spoke for himself," would take years to fully implement as the population curve moved on the low-slope portion of the exponential.

Ralph Waldo Emerson was an ardent, high-minded naturalist. An optimist, he saw the power of God in nature and the power of ideas in man: "Beware when the great God lets loose a thinker in this planet," he said. Beware of Emerson! It was he who injected the idea of unlimited growth into the flagging Puritanism of last century, at a period when America wished to build a culture superior to Europe: "Man is nurtured by unfailing fountains, and draws at his need inexhaustible power." "Who can set the bounds to the possibilities of man?" His idea as it stands is totally out of harmony. It is nature that sets the bounds. A century later, in our time, he would probably be the first to modify this self-reliant growth philosophy and frame his hopes within the limits of the eco-system. His Harvard College colleague and fellow Concordian, Henry Thoreau, was more practical. He stressed the balance of nature. He was an ecologist before the word was coined, before eco-thoughts echoed round the world!

Thoreau borrowed an ax and built a hut at Walden Pond, Massachusetts, where, according to a report in the Concord town newspaper, he aligned the foundation diagonal with a calendric sunrise direction (the equinoxes, March 21, September 22). He lived for two years as independent of society as a nest-building bird and wrote his inspired naturalist *Journal*. Birds came to his call, and fish swam through his fingers. Thoreau's aim was to reverse the Puritan order for the week—six days for the expansion of mind and spirit, one day for labor. He lived contentedly at subsistence level with minimal demands on the eco-system.

If the Paul Reveres of ecology are correct, then citizens of the industrial (*over*developed?) nations have a considerable adjustment ahead

FIG. 48. *Symbolic drawing by Allen Ginsberg.*

of them. Adjustments in material standards, and psychological. We may have to get used to the idea of a no-car family, a power level restricted to the heat budget of a seventeenth-century farm house, and smaller cities built closer together to minimize travel. (No jet-setting permitted!)

Student groups were among the first to voice concern over the threatened cataclysm. I attended a series of meetings, with my wife, during "Earth Week," 1970. New-style poet Allen Ginsberg (Ommmmmmm . . .) was there. He drew for us the classic picture of the three fish sharing a single eye inside a circle, which for him symbolized the interrelatedness of everything. Unofficial clubs and societies sprang up to discuss, plan, lobby, and take measurements of deteriorative changes—the pulse of pollution. They are the "our children" of the

263

MFS, the generation in which the problems must be faced—depletion of fuel resources, minerals, pollution from seabed to stratosphere, chemical derangements, noise levels, radioactivity levels, psychological strain in the pace of modern living, the unnaturalness in man's step from a stable environment to one that is exploding and where most things within reach of the fingertips are a technological product, unknown, unmade a generation ago.

These are the greater complexities. The eco-system on Salisbury Plain and in the Nile Valley was simpler and easier to manage. The ecology was balanced, the demands on natural resources minimal. There was an awareness, an awe and respect for the environment, and in those prehistoric times there was no doubt a sufficiently satisfying account of the place of man in the universe. In that ancient stable framework, man had achieved the essence of those goals that are now being set for civilization today.

14 LAST THOUGHTS

Again I sat at my desk, this time working on the problems of ionization in the high atmosphere produced by meteor particles. If Segal's *Love Story* was real, the first chapters were being enacted in the apartment buildings and streets of Cambridge beyond the tennis courts below.

The large frame of Immanuel Velikovsky came through the doorway. He was charming in disposition, firm in the handshake, scholastically gray in the hair, soft-spoken but powerful in the voice. He was accompanied by a friend from an educational institution in the Boston area, and wished to discuss *Stonehenge Decoded*. He sat down in front of the bookcase on the other side of my desk calculator. His companion closed the office door leading to the corridor and then joined him.

Dr. Velikovsky made a pleasantry about his being in the environs of Harvard College Observatory. HCO had figured in the heated controversy of the fifties and sixties later reported on as the "Velikovsky Affair." I had a first-edition copy of his *Worlds in Collision,* and he had written in the front flap: "Inscribed to Prof. Gerald S. Hawkins, Of Stones And Stars." He added two quotations from Isaiah 24 and Psalm 96.

Velikovsky had probably read my article, just out, in *Physics Today* which said:

My fellow astronomers have checked over the calculations and have remained relatively unexcited about the findings. A scientist who is primarily concerned with the solar system and beyond (with preference to the beyond) accepts without question that living beings will show some natural empathy with the sun and the moon whether they are ancient Britons, migrating birds, or soft-shelled crabs. [A reference to the clustering of laboratory crabs at the end of the tank under the tidal influence of the moon.] Similarly the values found from Stonehenge for the obliquity of the earth's axis and the inclination of the lunar orbit at about 2000 B.C. are not very exciting to an astonomer because they agree with modern extrapolations. These Stonehenge values are perhaps the best rebuttal of Velikovsky's thesis of cataclysmic shifts in the axis of the earth in the

265

first millennium B.C., but then Velikovsky's thesis has not been warmly accepted for other reasons.

Specifically, as far as I could determine, Dr. Velikovsky proposed two major cataclysms, one taking place at approximately 1500 B.C. to synchronize with the supposed date of Moses' exodus from Egypt, and another in 687 B.C., the time of Sennacherib's second campaign against Palestine. The first was caused by Venus passing close to the earth to take up, after several hundred perturbation orbits, the near-circular orbit of the present day. The second was caused by a close approach of Mars. In the first cataclysm the earth reversed its direction of axial spin. In both cataclysms the tilt of the earth's axis, obliquity, changed considerably. The hypothesis was based mainly on Biblical extracts, legends, and an unorthodox interpretation of modern scientific data.

I am not in any way opposed to new ideas—in fact I recognize them as an essential part of the search for knowledge—but ideas must be fostered, probed, developed, and presented to scientists within the framework of a scientific formulation. Each of Velikovsky's hypotheses would require of a scientist years of rewriting, checking, equal to the production of a full treatise or higher-degree thesis—much work. As it stands no one, and that includes Velikovsky, has sat down and produced the mathematical underpinning which could support the occurrence of these celestial mechanical cataclysms with or without nongravitational fields. In fact, scientific research has produced, as an offshoot, quantitative evidence against these hypotheses. One example is the new field of astro-archaeology alluded to in the *Physics Today* quote. Another is computer-reversed motion. Orbits can be projected forward in time (the future positions of the sun, moon, and planets are found in this way in the calculation of an ephemeris) and backward (the secret launching place of the Russian satellites was deduced by running the orbital motion in reverse). The solar system, with its nine planets, has been computed in reverse time for a period of thousands of years. Within slight cyclic variations the orbits are stable. Venus and Mars came nowhere near the earth in 688 or 1500 B.C.

I did not wish to get involved in the "affair." A thorough scientific response would require time off for the writing of a full-length book, maybe more, and the developing story, even so, would be well anticipated by my colleagues in the discipline before they turned the page. Dr. Velikovsky was a powerful debater, but he operated at a wavelength different from that of physical science, not within its quantitative limits. Continuing on that basis, his theory will never be proved, nor will it be authoritatively accepted.

Velikovsky realized that Stonehenge worked today as it did when it was built—sunrises, moonrises, and the cycles of 56, 30, etc. If it was built in 2000–1700 B.C., there could have been no cataclysmic axial or orbital change for the earth. As I understood his argument in the office, he was assigning Stonehenge to a later date, specifically one later than 687 B.C., arguing that the archaeological date was wrong, radiocarbon dating was unreliable, an old bone relic could have been dropped into holes dug during construction at a later period. Moving Stonehenge up to 600 B.C. would, of course, place it in the present earth-axis era, after the last great cataclysm. I pointed out that the change of obliquity was slow, that the archways would be as tolerable a fit in 600 B.C. as they were in 2000 B.C. or even the present era. But, I also pointed out, the fitting of Stonehenge into the prehistoric chronology of western Europe was a specialized and difficult task, and in my own research I left it to the archaeo-experts. If he wished to take up his arguments with them. . . .

Later, a Stonehenge-theory critic was to come out with "slipshod" and "unconvincing." Apparently Velikovsky picked up this review and went one further, denying the reality of the alignments.

The work in Peru and Egypt came after Velikovsky's visit. As it so happens, the time of rebuilding of the temple of Amon-Ra is close to or slightly preceding the first supposed cataclysm. I have not spoken with Velikovsky on this matter (the full account is currently in preparation), but he might well argue that the temple was rebuilt to point to the winter sunrise at that epoch because there was a need, because the earth's axis had tipped to a new position. I would disagree. The Amon-Ra alignment, like Stonehenge, works today with the small half-degree shift predicted by astronomical theory, which would not be possible if there had been another axial shift in 687 B.C. Also the temples prior to Hatshepsut's and Thutmose III's rebuilding are thought to have been along the present azimuth. Then there is the Gontzi bone, Woodhenge, Ballachroy, the dozens of other astro-structures, and the Gizeh Pyramids, built squarely to face the four cardinal points, which went up long before 1500 B.C.

Halfway around the world from Egypt, on the western shores of the Pacific, the influence of the sun-god is well known. The "land of the rising sun" was motivated in World War II by a solar-derived religion, Shintoism. In the "eight hundred myriads of deities" of old Shinto, starting 2,000 years ago, or maybe earlier, Amaterasu-Omikami, the sun-goddess, was dominant. The "myriads" in the pantheon included spirits of mountains, streams, trees, somewhat in the vein of the wacas of ancient Peru. I came across an old print showing the sunrise to the left of a sacred mountain viewed from a temple on Futamigaura. The alignment is marked by two natural rock pinnacles and a wooden gateway (trilithon).

As a comment on the power of a set of ideas, Shintoism in prewar Japan maintained: the sun-goddess is the founder of the state; the emperor is descended from the sun; he and his issue will rule Japan eternally; by divine relation with the forces of the sky and nature the Japanese race is more courageous, more virtuous, more intelligent than

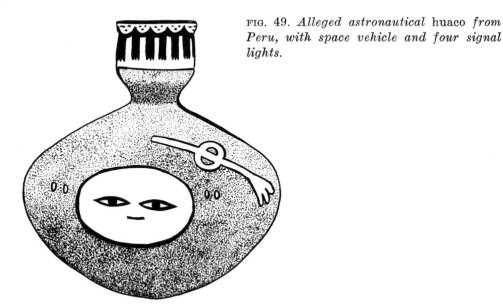

FIG. 49. *Alleged astronautical* huaco *from Peru, with space vehicle and four signal lights.*

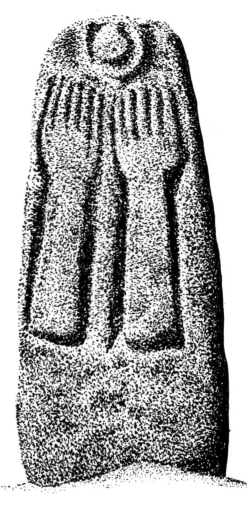

PLATE 59. *Hands reaching for the moon-god at Hazor temple, Sea of Galilee.*

other races; their morality is self-decided and unchallengeable; the emperor is ordained by the will of the gods to extend his sway over the entire earth.

From the Orient, back to the holy land of Western religions, we find gold-capped obelisks in Byblos, Lebanon, dedicated to the sun, and the hawk design of the sun-god was found in beaten gold in a second-century Byblos tomb. By the shores of the Sea of Galilee, at Hazor, a moon-god stone was found. A stele in a Canaanite shrine dating to the thirteenth century B.C. had outstretched hands reaching up to the crescent. Astronomically the disk in the crescent could be the "old moon in the new moon's arms," when earthlight faintly illuminates the full disk, and sunlight the crescent. Canaanite influence is in the Old Testament, Job, the Psalms, and Canaanite thinking influenced Israel. The Hazor temple is the closest yet discovered to the plan of Solomon's temple in Jerusalem, which was solar-oriented.

The response to and interest in astro-archaeology continued; the research and correspondence now filled five file-cabinet drawers. It was a pleasant afterhours chore to read and reply to letters. One American lady tourist sent a postscripted card from Salisbury. "I know where the missing stones are," she announced: "in the 17th century graveyard at Avebury." To her the crude pyramidal slabs on the tombs were the missing lintels: "Your mysterious Johannes Ludovicus DeFrerre was the stonemason; the letters on the tomb stones are in the same style!" Interesting detective work, but probably not substantiable. J. L. De-Frerre did carve his name at Stonehenge—trilithon stone 53, but my information has him as an "antiquarian," not a stonemason.

A person reported a bluestonelike object in a garden at the village of Wroughton, and Swindon Museum had investigated. Inquiries led nowhere; there was no record.

A gentleman from Sittingbourne, Kent, recorded a local legend that "might" relate to the heel stone at Stonehenge, sometimes called the "friar's heel." The devil was in the act of stealing the church bells when he was surprised by the priest. The devil fell, and his boot made an impression "visible today" on the stone at the churchyard gate.

The devil, a woman, and a number game figure in John Smith's "Inoculator of the Small-Pox" folktale:

The Devil . . . dressing himself like a gentleman, and taking a large bag of money in his hand, presented himself before the good woman as she was sitting at her table, and acquainted her of the purchase he was about to make; the fiend, at the same time, pouring out his money on the board before her, and offering her as much for the stones as she could reckon, while he should be taking them away.

The money was in odd sorts of coins, such as four-penny half-penny pieces, nine-penny pieces, thirteen-penny half-penny pieces, and the like; but nevertheless the Devil's proposal seemed so very advantageous, that, notwithstanding

FIG. 50. *Sunrise through the gateway of a Shinto temple.*

271

the difficulty there would be in reckoning the money, the woman could not avoid complying with it . . . she had no sooner laid her hands on a four-penny half-penny coin, than the Devil, with an audible voice, cried out, hold, and said, the stones were gone. The woman, disregarding what he had said, however peeped out into her backside, and to her great amazement it was even so, as Satan had spoken; for the common deceiver of mankind in an instant took down the stones, bound them up in a wyth, and conveyed them to Salisbury Plain. . . .

Dr. Smith favored the other legend, that Stonehenge was built by a race of giants. He quotes Thomas Elliot: "I myself . . . three or four miles from Stonage, beheld the bones of a dead man, found deep in the ground; which being joyned together, was in length 13 feet and 10 inches; whereof one of the teeth my father had, which was of the quantity of a great wallnut. This I have written because some men will believe nothing that is out of the compass of their knowledge."

Transcendentalist Emerson was "ready to maintain that some cleverer elephants or mylodonta had borne off and laid these rocks one on another. Only the good beasts must have known how to cut a well-wrought tenon and mortise, and to smooth the surface of some of the stones."

I received a clipping from Ica, Peru, to which there was "no comment." It was another Nascan puzzle pot with what was purported to be the face of an extraterrestrial visitor (Martian?), a spaceship, and four interplanetary navigational markers. Personally, all I could see was a late-type Nascan face, an arrow, and four spots.

An ex-meteorological officer reported factually on dawn visibility conditions. In routine work, cloud cover, temperature, and fog visibility measurements are made at fixed clock hours, and so sunrises are not normally reported on. This letter, therefore, was particularly interesting and valuable. Living within 20 miles of Stonehenge, he had observed solstice and equinoctial sunrises for 48 years—quite a record when one notes that the midsummer sun rises by the clock at 4:30 A.M. His father, also a meteorologist, made similar observations before him, and father and son together logged 281 dawns at the "henge" over a period of more than 80 years. The combined tally was:

Sunrise at:
Midsummer   15 Perfect; clear cloudless sky.

	26	Partial; broken cloud, high nimbus.
	14	Poor; thick haze, faintly seen.
	27	Nil; rain, low cumulus.
Midwinter	26	Perfect; clear, striated alto-cumulus.
	9	Partial; broken cloud, fine.
	18	Poor; mist, or seen after rising.
	20	Nil; cloud, rain, fog, snow, mist.
Spring equinox	36	Perfect; brilliant sky, high alto-cumulus.
	15	Poor, mist, squalls.
	8	Nil; rain, mist, low cloud.
Fall equinox	48	Perfect; high pressure clarity.
	11	Poor, partial, in cloud or haze.
	8	Nil; thick cloud, mist.

From this it can be deduced that the sun was visible on 78 percent of the occasions—a surprisingly high batting average—and on 125 dawns (45 percent) the visibility was perfect. My correspondent pointed out another surprising fact: the chance of seeing a sunrise was 20 percent greater at the equinox than at the solstice; the least perfect conditions were at midsummer! To him Stonehenge was a weather observation station. Predictions for the coming winter were made at the fall equinox, for summer at the spring. St. Swithin, he said, martyred by drunken Danes near Winchester, was born and brought up within 5 miles of the monument, and "it is not insignificant" that St. Swithin's Day is a weather forecast day—if it rains in England on St. Swithin's Day it will, supposedly, rain for 40 days after!

On the basis of these 281 dawns it would appear that the odds today for a successful sighting are better than even. In the Stonehenge era, climatological data indicate that the sky might have had greater clarity, approaching Mediterranean conditions, but it is difficult to tell whether the actual cloud cover was less.

For comparison I made a similar set of observations in the winter of 1966/67 during a sabbatical leave in Spain. It was, ostensibly, the place of best visibility on the southern shore, the Costa del Sol, looking out over a clear horizon. I observed the rising of the sun, the moon, and the brightest star in the sky, Sirius. The result:

Sunrise	15	Perfect; clear, complete sunrise seen from first gleam to disk standing tangent on the horizon. (4 occasions showed the "green flash" referred to in Chapter 3.)
	7	Poor; broken cloud.
	1	Nil; overcast.
Sirius rise	1	perfect; on horizon, apparent magnitude 4.
	13	Poor; not seen until about 1° above horizon, then scintillating to invisibility.
	6	Nil.

These observations were made in the months of November and December, probably the worst months on the Costa del Sol. It can be figured that the chances of seeing some portion of the sunrise are 95 percent, a factor of 2 better than Salisbury Plain.

What surprised me was the poor showing of the rising stars. Sirius, the best prospect, was seen rising on the horizon on only 1 occasion out of 20. The chance of seeing anything of the rising star within a degree or so of the horizon was 25 percent less than for the sun. Even when seen, the star was a disappointing object, scintillating from magnitude +4 to fainter than +5, that is to say from a condition like the faintest stars to being totally invisible. This threw further doubts into my mind concerning star-horizon observations by early man, either in the British stone circles or on the Peruvian desert. It was not an impressive or easy-to-see phenomenon.

The moonrises were clearly seen, similar in visibility to the sun, but these have not been included in the tabulation because in December the moon in its swing had moved from over the Mediterranean to the distant outline of the Sierra Nevada, a mountain range with apparent elevation between 1° and 1½°. I was interested to find that on the day before full, and on the evening of the full, the lunar disk was visible as it rose over the sea horizon. This visibility would be a critical factor at Stonehenge if, as I have suggested, the time of the rising of the moon was used to give final warning of the imminence of an eclipse. The moonrise was clearly observable, even though it came up more than an hour before sunset.

One of the Sirius risings, feeble though it was, was witnessed by two *guardia civil*. Circumstantially there is very little difference between a star-gazing astronomer and a smuggler. I explained and pointed to where the star would rise. My black-hatted khaki-caped guards were skeptical. To my relief Sirius came up with stopwatch precision. But it was scintillating—flashing! It is to the credit of the officers that they stood there a full five minutes to watch the star (contraband signal?) rise from the sea with the constellation.

An ex-sea captain questioned whether Stonehenge could be used for tidal predictions. Yes. The tides are controlled by the gravitational pull of the moon and sun, and are, allowing for the particular "tidal constant" of a port, locked in phase with the rising and setting of the nearest body, the moon. Neap tides, occurring at the quarter phase, and so-called spring tides occurring at the new and full, could be predicted by counting around the 30-stone sarsen ring or, more satisfactorily, the 29 and 30 Y and Z holes. Especially high tides occur when the sun and moon are in line and on a certain longitude on the ecliptic. These latter tides follow the 18.61-year cycle and are, in principle, predictable by use of the 56 Aubrey holes. Personally I do not see sufficient evidence to carry through with this suggestion. Alexander Thom believes it to have been a factor in the Scottish lunar circles where tidal conditions between the islands were a life-and-death matter.

A literary lady drew my attention to a passage from none other than Voltaire. In *Zadig,* that passingly unreal acme of heroes became prime minister and with characteristic diplomacy settled an important issue:

> He ended just as happily the great lawsuit between the white magi and the black magi. The whites maintained that it was an impiety, when praying to God, to turn toward where the sun rises in the winter; the blacks asserted that God abhorred the prayers of men who turned toward where the sun set in summer. Zadig ordained that people should turn whichever way they wanted.

The Beltane Fires were mentioned many times in that question period that follows at the end of a lecture. Huge bonfires were lighted in Scotland, Ireland, and other parts of the British Isles at astronomical dates during the year—time-factored punctuation marks, dependent on the declination of the sun. The ritual continued up until the mid-nineteenth century. The written evidence is somewhat confused because Christian missionaries attempted to stop the ritual, to shift the date to an ecclesiastical calendar, or, when this failed, to unobtrusively merge the new religion with the old custom. Ethnologists linked the ceremonies with the Druids, and the Beltane Fire was taken to be a representation of the druidic Celtic sun-god. Usually there was a pair of fires, and people (and animals) passed between. Fires were lighted across the country on the night of midsummer's eve, midwinter, and at the spring and fall equinox. At Norwich, England, a fiery wheel was rolled, each midsummer, down a hill to represent the solar orb on the decline.

Fires were lighted on four other dates when the sun's declination was $16°.3$, north or south. This declination fixed calendar dates which were one-eighth of a year after the solstices and equinoxes, approximately February 4, May 6, August 8, and November 8 on the present Gregorian calendar. The year was therefore divided into eight approximately equal portions. These divisions are very close to the solar alignment dates found in the megalithic structures by Thom, and by Lockyer before him. Since the megaliths predate the Celtic Druids, the Beltane Fires might be something handed down from the darkness of prehistory.

The candles (electric) on the Christmas tree now replace the midwinter Beltane Fires. Perhaps Hanukkah candles are similarly calendric. The February blaze was absorbed by a great church festival, Candlemas, with the lighting of more candles. May 6 has become blurred with the Maypole, Morris dancing, and international May Day labor celebrations. November festivities have been taken over by the church celebration of Allhallows Eve. In the United States, instead of Druids, we have little pumpkin-carrying trick-or-treaters. This is "instant tradition" as far as I am aware—no similar Halloween ritual exists outside America. In the United Kingdom it is the custom to light bonfires and fireworks on the night of November 5, the excuse being to burn Mr. Guy Fawkes in effigy for his fiendish plot (stacking 1.2 tons of gunpowder in 32 barrels in the basement of the House of Parliament for the purpose of blowing up the full assembly, including James I, on November 5, 1605). But in all probability this ritual picks up in the collective subconscious that druidic fire date, solar declination $-16°.3$, that heralds the onset of winter.

Trees, bushes, and fertility figured in the calendar celebrations. Rowan, the mountain ash, was used on May Day, and the sacred mistletoe at midwinter and midsummer. Is the kiss under the mistletoe a leftover fertility rite? And what of the notorious rites of spring?

PLATE 60. *At Carnac, Brittany, France, rows of stones and isolated menhirs mark the extremes of the sun and moon on the horizon.*

Wells and springs, supposedly sacred and druidic, have been found near stone circles. Folklore has these places bewitched and magical, like the Peruvian waca. At the well of St. Aelian, Denbighshire, Wales, a "priestess" would, upon request, place a curse on whomsoever one wanted, dropping a pin into the well as she named the victim. Nowadays the folklore has modified positively. Cursing wells have become wishing wells; coins replace pins.

Legends and myths are intriguing software; the rational roots, if there have been any, are gone. But they rise to the conscious stratum and weave into the literature—like the legend of Atlantis and its King Coelus, used by Inigo Jones to support his theory that Stonehenge was dedicated to the sky-gods. Jones quotes from Diodorus of Sicily:

They write (Diodorus himself was quoting other legendizers), he which first reigned over the Atlantides was Coelus, and that he invited men, living dispersedly before throughout the fields, to convene, and dwell in companies to-

277

gether, exhorting them to build towns, and reducing them from wild and savage to the conservation of civil life . . . was a diligent observer of the stars, and foretold men divers things to come: the year, before confused, bringing into order, according to the course of the sun, reducing it also into months after the moon's course, and appointing likewise the several seasons of the year. Whereby many, ignorant of the perpetual course of the stars, and amazed at his future predictions, did verily believe he participated of Divine Nature. . . .

Nancy G. Westerfield captures the modern mood in her poem "At Stonehenge":

> Romula Bett of Beaver Falls, unaccompanied,
> Confronts the Heel Stone, and finds,
> From the National Monuments guidebook,
> That the Druids had nothing to do with it.
> How to untell the fifth grade at Beaver Falls?
>
> The catter of foreign tongues confounds Miss Bett:
> (Bank-Holiday English sit ferries for France;
> The French come to Stonehenge).
> The rattle of foreign coins confounds Miss Bett:
> She counts her shillings.
> The shatter of foreign planes confounds Miss Bett:
> American planes from the aerodrome towards Old Sarum
> Blast the sky,
> Dictate the terms of compromise to the Mother Country.
> Magna Mater! When did the Druids die?
>
> Time was.
> The fractured instant claps, closes the past.
> (Where did the processional Avenue wend?
> Where did the Western Avon Flow?)
> Time is.
> These figures in modern dress
> Rampant, with runic signs, describe a ring—
> Ring within ring to the monuments outermost barbed-wire ring—
> And Tess-like, Miss Bett stands ringed as one stoned.

278

Time will be.
Will be mandatory for Miss Bett;
Will be: England sinks;
Will be: home;
Will be: unaccompanied old age.
Sun on the altar at Stonehenge
Strikes the chambered heart to death.
Miss Bett in a lunar mood must meet the Salisbury bus.
Shutting at seven, the broken astronomical time-wheel
Marks time yet.*

Thomas Hardy had Stonehenge in his mind again in "Channel Firing," April, 1914, four months before the guns of August:

That night your great guns, unawares,
Shook all our coffins as we lay,
And broke the chancel window-squaɪ
We thought it was the Judgement-Day

And sat upright. While drearisome
Arose the howl of wakened hounds
The mouse let fall the altar crumb,
The worm drew back into the mounds,

The glebe cow drooled. Till God called, "No;
It's gunnery practice out at sea
Just as before you went below;
The world is as it used to be . . ."

Again the guns disturbed the hour,
Roaring their readiness to avenge,
As far inland as Stourton Tower,
And Camelot, and starlit Stonehenge.

The British literary monolith Thomas Carlyle invited Emerson to join with him to take a look at "the uncanny stones." They went to the Plain, via the George Inn, Amesbury, on Friday, July 7, 1847, a New

---

* Copyright 1966 by the Reporter Magazine Company.

279

World and an Old World philosopher in a preworld setting. Carlyle made some biting comment about "travelling Americans," and Emerson let off a salvo* in praise of the United States:

I surely know, that, as soon as I return to Massachusetts, I shall lapse at once into the feeling, which the geography of America inevitably inspires, that we play the game with immense advantage; that there and not here is the seat and center of the British race; and that no skill or activity can long compete with the prodigious advantages of that country, in the hands of the same race; and that England, an old, an exhausted island, must one day be contented, like other parents, to be strong only in her children.

Carlyle looked back to that golden age of intellect, claiming that the men who had once lived in preliterate England were greater than any of her writers.

Emerson, in *English Traits*, continues with his nineteenth-century impressions: "After dinner we walked to Salisbury Plain. On the broad downs, under the gray sky, not a house was visible, nothing but Stonehenge, which looked like a group of brown dwarfs in the wide expanse,—Stonehenge and the barrows—which rose like green bosses about the Plain, and a few hayricks. On the top of a mountain, the old temple would not be more impressive. Far and wide a few shepherds with their flocks sprinkled the Plain, and a bagman drove along the road. . . ."

They tried out the taboo on numbering the stones: "We counted and measured by paces the biggest stones, and soon knew as much as any man can suddenly know of this inscrutable monument. There are 94 stones, and there were once probably 160." (Actually both numbers were incorrect.) They remarked on the folklore of the sunrise alignment: "In the silence of tradition, this one relation to science becomes an important clue; but we were content to leave the problem, with the rocks." (Actually, Carlyle could have taken the clue further. He could have calculated the alignments. Philosopher, historian, writer, he was also astronomer-mathematician, and had at one time applied for the post of astronomer at Edinburgh Observatory.)

Emerson chided British archaeologists for exploring the pyramids and tombs of Egypt while Stonehenge awaited the spade, but out there

* *English Traits,* lectures by Emerson delivered in 1848 and published in 1856.

PLATE 61. *"On the broad Downs, under the gray sky . . . nothing but Stonehenge . . . and, all round, wild thyme, daisy, meadowsweet . . . and the carpeting grass"* (*Ralph Waldo Emerson*).

on the plain with Carlyle, "The old sphinx put our petty differences of nationality out of sight." He left Stonehenge with a nostalgia: "Within the enclosure grow buttercups, nettles, and, all round, wild thyme, daisy, meadowsweet, goldenrod, thistle, and the carpeting grass. Over us larks were soaring and singing,—as my friend said, 'the larks which were hatched last year, and the wind which was hatched many thousand years ago.'"

It would be wrong to postulate that Stonehenge was once part of a worldwide astro-culture. It is limited to three Neolithic and Early Bronze Age "lenses" which cover Britain and possibly are related culturally to western Europe. There is no evidence for the Smith-Perry

281

Heliolithic race, spreading out as a semicircular wave from the Nile across Europe; in fact the contemporary archaeological data argue incontrovertibly against it. The Heyerdahl hypothesis of trans-Atlantic migration (Egypt, Morocco, South America) followed by trans-Pacific rafting (Peru, Easter Island, Indonesia) is no more than a suggestion at the present time, and a full evaluation has yet to come.

Astro-archaeology has revealed an idea, a driving force, an intense following of the sun and moon. The mind of man came under the influence of these space objects as early as 20,000 years ago, when he carved ivory mammoth tusks to encapture the lunar phases. He was interested in numbers from the bone-carving era, and in numbers and geometry from the megalithic builders to the classic Greek scholars. In each instance the work was probably overlaid with magic, mysticism, and the occult. He was aware of the complexities of the earth-sky environment. He had a time-factored consciousness. He punctuated the year of the seasons with sun- and moon-marked dates. He built structures beyond his immediate, earthly need, almost beyond his physical resources, to link by astro-alignment man on earth with the gods in the sky.

The American explorer Edward Thompson, treasure trover in the Sacred Well of Chichen Itza, may have echoed a part of this ancient empathy with the cosmos when he stood where the Maya had been:

I stood upon the roof of this temple one morning, just as the first rays of the sun reddened the distant horizon. The morning stillness was profound. The noises of the night had ceased, and those of the day were not yet begun. All the sky above and the earth below seemed to be breathlessly waiting for something. Then the great round sun came up, flaming splendidly, and instantly the whole world sang and hummed. . . . Nature herself taught primal man to be a sun-worshipper and man in his heart of hearts still follows the ancient teaching.

Perhaps we shall never know the true significance of the sky in the lives of ancient peoples. Did a gossamer idea spread outward, transferred by contact between cultures, and was this idea the critical step toward civilization, the emergence of man as that species with transcendental consciousness? Or was the awareness a natural response of different races, different cultures, to the unifying stimulus of the sky? We find evidence for this influence from before the time of writing, from deep prehistory, on the continents of Asia, Africa, the Americas, and on the Pacific Islands.

The wider response is here in the United States now with the turning to ecology; it was here when Henry Beston spent a full solar cycle living on the great surf beach of Cape Cod, testing his brain's response in the psychological experiment of breaking away from a technocentric world. He wrote, in *The Outermost House:*

A year indoors is a journey along a paper calendar; a year in outer nature is the accomplishment of a tremendous ritual. To share in it, one must have a knowledge of the pilgrimages of the sun, and something of that natural sense of him and feeling for him which made even the most primitive people mark the summer limits of his advance and the last December ebb of his decline. All these autumn weeks I have watched the great disk going south along the horizon or moorlands beyond the marsh, now sinking behind this field, now behind this leafless tree, now behind this sedgy hillock dappled with thin snow. We lose a great deal, I think, when we lose this sense and feeling for the sun. . . .

I fell asleep uneasily, and woke again as one wakes out-of-doors. The vague walls about me breathed a pleasant smell of sand, there was no sound, and the broken circle of grass above was as motionless as something in a house. . . . In the luminous east, two great stars aslant were rising clear of the exhalations of darkness gathered at the rim of night and ocean—Betelgeuse and Bellatrix, the shoulders of Orion. Autumn had come, and the Giant stood again at the horizon of day and the ebbing year, his belt still hidden in the bank of cloud, his feet in the deeps of space and the far surges of the sea.

My year upon the beach had come full circle; it was time to close my door. Seeing the great suns, I thought of the last time I marked them in the spring, in the April west above the moors, dying into the light and sinking. I saw them of old above the iron waves of black December, sparkling afar. Now, once again, the Hunter rose to drive summer south before him, once again Autumn followed on his steps. I had seen the ritual of the sun; I had shared the elemental world. . . .

Perhaps the horizons of antiquity have carried through those long, eventful generations beyond Stonehenge and are a basic subliminal part of our civilization today.

283

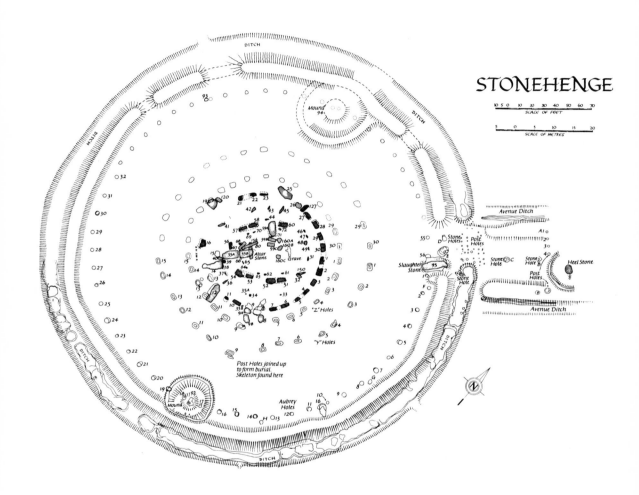

STONEHENGE

APPENDIX: ASTRO-ARCHAEOLOGY

INTRODUCTION

In recent years the archaeological knowledge concerning Stonehenge in Wiltshire, England, had reached a level of detail sufficient to encourage other disciplines to attempt to investigate the purpose of the structure. Radiocarbon dating and other archaeological evidence indicate that the work at Stonehenge began around 2000 B.C. with the digging of a ditch and holes. This date is uncertain by a century or so, and is based on the radiocarbon dating of a charcoal fragment using the revised half-life for C_{14}. The erection of the stone parts of Stonehenge, the trilithon archways, sarsen circle, etc., commenced about 1700 B.C. The details of the various structures will be described later in this article (Figs. A and B). It was possible to show (Hawkins, 1963) that even though building and rebuilding lasted at the site for several centuries, the post holes, stones, and archways continued to align with the rising and setting of the extreme positions of the sun and moon on the horizon. The sun, of course, would touch these extreme positions during one tropical year, but the moon would require 18.6 years to complete a cycle. Thus it seemed evident that Stonehenge, built and rebuilt by different cultural groups, had a consistent astronomical building plan throughout the period.

Archaeological excavations established the number of holes in the various circles that had been dug and subsequently refilled, either by natural causes or by man. The numbers in the circles were very significant from the astronomical point of view. A circle of 29 holes and a circle of 30 holes seemed to represent the long and short synodic months of ancient calendars. The 56 Aubrey holes could well represent a seasonal eclipse cycle. It was therefore suggested that the circles at Stonehenge were used for computing the phases of the moon and also for predicting the month of the year in which eclipses would take place (Hawkins, 1964).

The determination that Stonehenge was an elaborate astronomical observatory and the suggestion that it was also a computer resulted from a direct interaction of the two disciplines of astronomy and archaeology, and the resultant merging

Reprinted, with minor revisions, from *Vistas in Astronomy* (1968), ed. Arthur Beer, Vol. 10, pp. 45–88 (Oxford and New York: Pergamon Press).

was called "astro-archaeology." The field of research fits well within the topic of the history of science in general, or the history of astronomy in particular—that is, if one is willing to overlook the rigorous definition of history as resulting from the written word. Stonehenge is wordless and correctly belongs to prehistoric times, but perhaps the reading of information from alignments of stones and the number of holes in various circles can be regarded as information retrieval analogous to reading. It is the unwritten evidence, the *pre*history of science.

The notion that early man made astronomical observations was quite prevalent in early folklore, though unproved. Stukeley (1740) remarks on the fact that the principal line of the whole Stonehenge work points to the northeast, "whereabouts the Sun rises, when the days are longest." From the context of this sentence it appears that Stukeley, even in 1740, was claiming no originality for this suggestion. The Gaelic people of Scotland seem always to have referred to the fact that the many stone circles in that part of the world pointed in some way to the sun. In 1893 Magnus Spence suggested sun and moon alignments

FIG. A. *Stonehenge. Aerial view from 500 feet, showing the approach path, Aubrey holes, and south. The slaughter stone is on the extreme left.*

FIG. B. *Stonehenge. Aerial view from the west. The large trilithons 51–52 and 53–54 are in the center; the Aubrey holes, enclosing ditch and south mound, are seen beyond the standing stones.*

for the stones and burial chambers near Maeshowe in the Orkneys, and detailed calculations have later shown that some of his suggestions were correct. Sir Norman Lockyer demonstrated that the axis of Stonehenge points to the midsummer sunrise and used this fact to establish an archaeological date (Lockyer and Penrose, 1901). Lockyer suggested several alignments for other megalithic structures in the British Isles, and also alignments with certain stars. According to him, most of the temples in Egypt and Greece were aligned to point to the rising or setting of certain stars—a suggestion that will be discussed in this article. Recently Thom (1965) has discussed the intricate geometrical basis for the megalithic structures in the British Isles and suggested solar, lunar, and stellar alignments among the stones and stone circles.

Certain aspects of previous work in astro-archaeology have been justifiably criticized. Lockyer, for example, attempted to estimate the construction date of Stonehenge from the alignment of sunrise in the avenue, whereas the chosen instant of sunrise was not known (any point within the 1° arc between the first

287

flash and disk tangent on the horizon could have been used), and exact dating was therefore invalid. The alignment of Egyptian temples with stars was computed on the basis of construction dates that have since been shown to be erroneous.*

1. Construction Dates Should Not Be Determined from Astronomical Alignments

The science of archaeology has now advanced to the stage where fairly accurate dates can be given for most prehistoric structures. The relative chronological sequences established around the world have been powerfully augmented by the absolute chronology of radioactivity. Any astronomical dates based on positions of the sun, moon, or planets will be less accurate because of the extreme slowness of the changes in the obliquity of the earth's axis and the orbits of the bodies in question. Also, without written documentation, it cannot be established whether ancient observers marked the first gleam of sunrise, the time when the disk was bisected by the horizon, or the final instant when the sun left the horizon. Occasionally further uncertainties arise when it cannot be established whether or not trees or other vegetation was growing on the horizon at the time of erection of the structure. These ambiguities when combined with the relatively slow changes in the tilt of the earth's axis can produce an uncertainty in an astronomical date of several thousand years.

Star alignments might intrinsically be capable of a more accurate dating, but the uncertainty of the particular star that was used together with the unavoidable placement errors made when the structure was erected will invalidate the astronomical dating technique. Over any particular thousand-year period there is a possibility of finding more than one star at a particular declination at different times. Each star that passes through such a declination "window" gives a different possible date of construction, and in the absence of a written record there is no way of determining which star, if any, is appropriate to the monument. For example, Capella was at declination 38.85° in 510 B.C., and Arcturus was at the same declination in 1350 B.C.

---

* Outside the realm of physical science are the many varied suggestions that have become loosely connected together under the title "pyramidology." Significance is looked for in the ratios between the lengths and heights of various ancient structures; meaning is derived by attaching numbers or the letters of the alphabet and summing the numbers in particular words; suggestions are made concerning prehistoric superraces and superknowledge. Archaeologist F. Petrie is said to have remarked that he once caught a pyramidiot in the act of chipping a stone in the pyramids to make its dimension come more into agreement with a particular crank theory.

2. Alignments Should Be Restricted to Man-made Markers

Whereas it is logical to suppose that a row of stones or a pair of archways was designed to point to some celestial object at its rising or setting, it is unjustifiable at the present time to assume that natural objects were so used. It may indeed be true that from a given location the moon at a particular point in its cycle rises over a prominent hill on the horizon, and the site may have been chosen on the basis of this fact. However, the single act of the selecting of the site is not sufficient evidence that the builders were aiming at the moonrise. There are many natural points of interest in the average horizon: other hills, valley clefts between hills, isolated boulders and islands. Any of these could reasonably be included as markers following criterion (5) below.

If, on the other hand, a distant hill is marked by the pointing of a row of stones or by other obvious artifacts then, of course, the alignment may validly be used. The man-made alignment in itself establishes the astronomical significance, and the distant hill then provides interesting but redundant information.

3. Alignments Should Be Postulated Only for a Homogeneous Group of Markers

Logically one must investigate all the possible alignments that can be presumed from a set of markers (see criterion 5). For n objects there are $n(n-1)$ permutations. This represents the maximum number of alignments that can be obtained from the set of markers. This number increases rapidly as n increases and ultimately reaches a stage where an alignment can be found for every celestial object on the horizon, and any inferences are meaningless.

Let us, for the sake of argument, concede that the builders of a certain monument were attempting to mark certain points on the horizon. It is much more difficult for us retroactively to prove their intentions than it was for them to make the original alignments. For example, let us suppose that two directions are to be marked using two stones for each alignment. In the act of setting four stones in place the builders have already generated 4×3 possible directions which they may, or may not, need or use. Looking back on such a work, the prehistorian must at the outset recognize the possibility of a dozen assumed deliberate alignments whereas only two were intended. As the number of markers increases, the problem rapidly degenerates to the insoluble level.

This problem of recognition of markers is discussed more fully under criterion (5). The problem is greatly alleviated by rejecting markers that are distinctly nonhomogeneous, such as a burial tumulus viewed from a stone circle, or the center of a circular ditch viewed from the entrance to a long barrow grave. To be consistent, all man-made objects of the same chronological epoch must be

289

considered if inhomogeneous markers are to be used, and then the number of possible interrelations will usually be found to be prohibitive.

4. All Related Celestial Positions Should Be Included in the Analysis

If an alignment with midsummer sunrise is postulated at a particular site, then the total group of four risings and settings of the sun at midsummer and midwinter must be considered in the analysis. Similarly, an alignment to a solstice extreme of the full moon implies a pattern of seven other solstice points of rising and setting. If only one alignment out of a group is marked, then the significance of the alignment is less sure.

If it is postulated that an alignment points to a star of a certain magnitude, then all stars of equal or greater brightness should be included as possible targets for that site. There are 39 stars of first magnitude or brighter and 145 stars of second magnitude or brighter. Thus the significance of a star alignment is very small for stars of faint magnitude.

5. All Possible Alignments at a Site Must Be Considered

As stated in criterion (3), the number of permutations in a group of objects is $n(n-1)$. This, however, is the absolute maximum of possible alignments, and many of these possibilities can be eliminated by inspection of the site or plans.

As an illustration, take the example of two stones to which two more are added, thus making a row of four. The two extra stones produce ten extra permutations, all of which repeat the directions marked by the original pair. No superfluous directions are produced. This redundancy is well worthwhile from the point of view of present-day mathematicians, but for the person who erected the extra stones it was a different matter.

Within a group of markers there are other directions that can be excluded from the point of view of practicality. Certain stones in a group may be too close to consider as alignments, and other stones may be set in patterns that seem to be architectural rather than astronomical. Also, with archways it is usually possible to see only in a very limited number of directions, and other possibilities are excluded because one cannot see through the archways at a slanting angle.

The above criteria are set up so as to prudently limit the theories and conclusions to those that have the greatest chance of being correct. Evidence may then be sought that can further support or refute these theories. It is very difficult to calculate the mathematical significance of a group of alignments, and therefore the criteria adopted here may indeed be overstringent. Normal probability theory implies a random process, but this does not exist at an astro-archaeological site, because there is usually some sort of pattern in the arrangement of the structure. One cannot assume, for the probability calculation, that the builders were operating at random, and the statistics of the blindfold marksman shooting at a target do not rigorously apply.

Ideally, all of the above criteria should be followed. The conclusions from a given site become progressively less reliable when one or more of these criteria are not fully met. Briefly, the principle may be summarized: adopt homogeneity of markers and of targets, and avoid proliferation.

METHOD OF ANALYSIS

It is presumed that an accurate site plan is available and that the altitude of the apparent horizon, or skyline, is known in all directions around the site.

Rectangular coordinates (x, y) are chosen with the y-axis in a northerly direction and the direction of the x-axis A_0 degrees east of north as shown in Fig. C. Two selected points, i and j, can be joined by a line and the angle between this line and the x-axis is θ where

$$\tan \theta = \frac{(y_j - y_i)}{(x_j - x_i)} \tag{1}$$

The azimuthal direction, A, of j as seen from i is given by the relation

$$A = A_0 - \theta \tag{2}$$

Consider a point with declination δ on the celestial sphere. The geometric altitude h of this point above the astronomical horizon in the direction A is found by solving the spherical triangle ZPS, Fig. D. The triangle is marked by the zenith of the observer Z, the north celestial pole P, and S, which is the point with declination δ on the vertical circle of azimuth A. The angle between Z and P is $90° - \lambda$, where λ is the latitude of the observer.

FIG. C. *Coordinate system for a site plan.*

FIG. D. *Celestial sphere showing the astronomical triangle.*

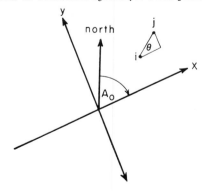

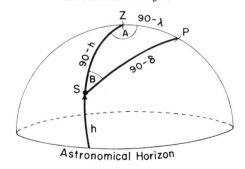

291

Thus

$$\sin B = \frac{\cos \lambda \sin A}{\cos \delta} \qquad (3)$$

and

$$\sin h = \frac{\sin \delta \sin \lambda - \cos \delta \cos \lambda \cos A \cos B}{1 - \cos^2 \lambda \sin^2 A} \qquad (4)$$

The angle h is not the apparent altitude that would be observed by looking from point i to point j at the *site* in question. Additional small corrections have to be made for atmospheric refraction, parallax, and the altitude of the skyline above the astronomical horizon. These effects are shown in Fig. E, which is a schematic representation of the disk of the sun or moon intersected by the skyline.

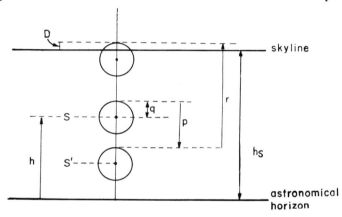

FIG. E. *The position of the sun or moon for various observers.*

An observer at the center of the earth would see the sun in the direction S. This corresponds to the point S in Figs. D and E. The upper limb is raised by the semidiameter q. An observer on the surface of the earth sees the sun in position S', where p is the parallax angle. Finally, atmospheric refraction bends the ray of light so that the sun appears to be raised by the angle r.

In Fig. E the sun is shown with its upper limb a distance D above the skyline, which itself is an altitude h_s above the astronomical horizon. Thus, if the alignment were intended to mark the first gleam of the sun, the error, i.e., the angular distance between the upper limb and skyline, is given by the relation

$$D = h + q - p + r - h_s \qquad (5)$$

The refraction, r, is a function of geometric altitude, $h + q - p$, and is given in Table 1 from the average values of Bessel. Because of this dependence on alti-

TABLE 1

ATMOSPHERIC REFRACTION AS A FUNCTION OF GEOMETRIC ALTITUDE

Geometric altitude (deg)	Refraction r (deg)
−0.58	0.58
−0.46	0.56
−0.34	0.54
−0.23	0.53
−0.11	0.51
+0.01	0.49
+0.13	0.47
+0.25	0.45
+0.36	0.44
+0.47	0.43
+0.59	0.41
+1.15	0.35
+1.70	0.30
+2.24	0.26
+2.76	0.24

tude, the upper limb of the sun is refracted less than the lower limb, and the disk of the sun appears to have an elliptical distortion. However, this differential refraction is taken into account by equation (5) if the tabular value of r is read for the appropriate value of geometric altitude. For example, the geometric altitude of the upper limb is $h + q - p$, and the lower limb $h - q - p$. The mean values for the sun, moon, and star are given for various conditions in Table 2.

Because of the elliptical shape of the earth's orbit, the distance of the sun from the earth varies by ± 1.7 percent. There is therefore a small variation for the sun in the value of q ($\pm 0.005°$). The variations in p are negligible.

The ellipticity of the moon's orbit causes a $\pm 0.014°$ variation in the value of q and $\pm 0.052°$ in p. For both parameters the $+$ sign is taken when the moon is at perigee, which occurs with a period of 27.554551 days.

When the sun or moon is bisected by the horizon, these variations in q do not apply, but those in parallax do.

Table 1 is for a station at sea level when the surface pressure, P_o, is 1,002 millibars, and the surface temperature, T_0, is 10°C. At different surface conditions (T, P) the value of r must be multiplied by a factor f_1 where

$$f_1 = 1 - 0.0036 \ (T - T_0) \ 0.0010 \ (P - P_0) \qquad (6)$$

293

TABLE 2
SEMIDIAMETER AND PARALLAX OF THE SUN AND MOON

Sun	Position	q (deg)	p (deg)
Object	Tangent on skyline	−0.267	0.002
	Bisected	0	0.002
	First gleam	+0.267	0.002
Moon	Tangent on skyline	−0.259	0.951
	Bisected	0	0.951
	First gleam	+0.259	0.951
Star	Bisected	0	0

At a height H meters above sea level the values of r should be multiplied by a factor f_2 where

$$f_2 = e^{-H/8400} \qquad (7)$$

It is convenient to represent the vertical error in an alignment, D, by the corresponding horizontal error, E. Except at the terrestrial poles and equator, all celestial objects rise or set obliquely, Fig. F. Thus to a first approximation, a plane projection of the sky as shown in Fig. F gives

$$\frac{D}{E} = \tan B \qquad (8)$$

The angle B is equal to the angle ZSP in the spherical triangle of Fig. D, and the value is therefore given in equation (3).

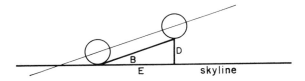

FIG. F. *The oblique angle of rising of a celestial object.*

The declination of the sun at any epoch changes from a maximum of $+\varepsilon$ at midsummer to $-\varepsilon$ at midwinter where ε is the obliquity of the ecliptic and is given in Table 3.

The maximum declination of the moon at any epoch changes from $+(\varepsilon + i)$ to $+(\varepsilon - i)$ with a period of 9.305 years, where i is the average inclination of the orbit of the moon. The minimum declinations change from $-(\varepsilon + i)$ to

$-(\varepsilon - i)$ with the same period. The inclination of the moon's orbit may be represented simply by the equation

$$i° = 5.15° \pm 0.15° \qquad (9)$$

where the small variation of ± 0.15 is in phase with the eclipse year. The $+$ sign applies during the two eclipse seasons, for example June and December, 1964, and the $-$ sign applies in the months between, i.e., March and September, 1964.

The average values of the extremes of the moon $[\pm(\varepsilon \pm i)]$ are given in Table 3. For eclipse months the values of $\varepsilon + i$ will be numerically greater by $0.15°$, and the values of $\varepsilon - i$ will be smaller by the same amount.

Declinations for stars are given in the 5,000-year catalog of the Smithsonian Astrophysical Observatory (Hawkins and Rosenthal, 1967).

If the object, and hence declination, is known, the equations can be solved for D. If the object is not known then the equations can be solved by iteration, putting $D = 0$.

TABLE 3

EXTREME DECLINATIONS OF THE SUN AND MOON FOR 3,500 YEARS

Year B.C.	Sun $\varepsilon°$	Moon $\varepsilon° + i°$	Moon $\varepsilon° - i°$
4000	24.112	29.262	18.962
3500	24.072	29.222	18.922
3000	24.027	29.177	18.877
2500	23.979	29.129	18.829
2000	23.928	29.078	18.778
1500	23.873	29.023	18.723
1000	23.816	28.966	18.666
500	23.757	28.907	18.607

ASTRONOMICAL RESULTS AT STONEHENGE

As an example of the calculation of astronomical alignments, let us consider Stonehenge, longitude 1.83 W., latitude 51.17 N. Plate 15 (see page 59) shows the results of a stereoscopic aerial survey carried out in June, 1965. The plan, which shows contours and heights of stones above mean sea level, was made by Hunting Surveys for the Smithsonian Astrophysical Observatory with the support of the National Geographic Society. The post holes labeled "A" near the heel stone have been located through the darkening of the grass in that area. The station holes 92 and 94 have been located with reference to their ditches, using the official plan (Newall, 1959). There are many other features beneath the turf that cannot be indicated by this air survey.

Archaeologists have divided the building of Stonehenge into three main stages with further subdivisions covering the period from 2000 B.C. to 1500 B.C. approximately. The stone circles, trilithon archways, and horseshoe array constitute the main portion of Stonehenge III. This is shown schematically in Fig. G. The outer ring of Y and Z holes was added at the final phase of Stonehenge III. The date of a deer antler has been determined as 1700 B.C. by the British Museum (1960). The antler was found buried at the base of the ramp leading to the stone hole of the great trilithon and may be taken to indicate the com-

FIG. G. *Reconstructed plan of Stonehenge III.*

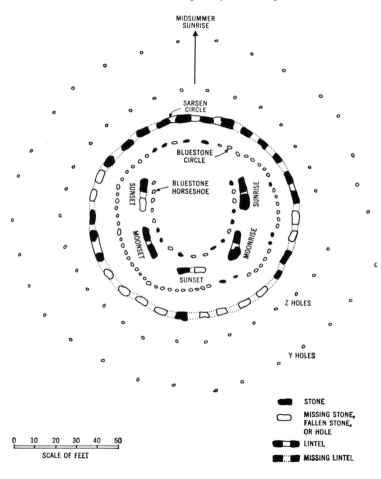

MIDSUMMER
SUNRISE

296

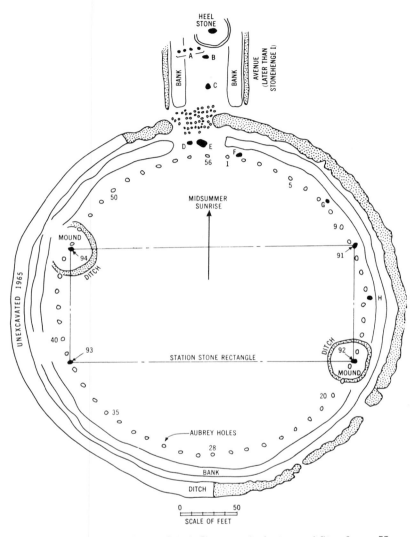

FIG. H. *Plan of Stonehenge I including certain features of Stonehenge II.*

mencement date of the building of Stonehenge III. The date of completion is uncertain; it appears that the Y and Z holes were left open to fill with wind-blown soil.

Stonehenge II preceded III and was a set of concentric stones erected within the boundaries of the later structure but never taken to completion.

Stonehenge I consisted of the ditch, bank, heel stone, and set of 56 Aubrey holes as shown in Fig. H. Carbon dating of a charcoal fragment gives 1850 B.C.

297

for the Aubrey holes. The avenue and parallel ditch were thought to have been made at the time of Stonehenge II. The four station stones, 91, 92, 93, and 94, are considered to have been erected after the placing of the Aubrey holes because the ditch around 92 cuts through an Aubrey hole (though there is a possibility that it could have been vice versa). No other chronological facts are available, however, for these stones; for convenience they have been indicated in the diagram for Stonehenge I.

By following the procedure outlined in the section on analysis, certain astronomical alignments can be deduced as given in Table 4. It is assumed that the disk stands tangent on the horizon. An error of $-0.53°$ indicates that the upper limb lined up, $-0.27°$ that the disk was bisected, and so forth. Measurements of the altitude of the horizon have been kindly supplied by Mr. C. A. Newham, the value of obliquity has been taken for the mean date of the various structures, 1800 B.C., and a mean value, 5.15°, for the inclination of the moon's orbit has been assumed. These more accurate data may be compared with previously published values (Hawkins, 1963), and it can be seen that the astronomical fit is slightly improved.

Archaeologically we must regard Stonehenge I and III as entirely separate structures unless evidence appears to the contrary. It is interesting to examine these results with regard to the criteria that I have laid down. The archaeological date has been assumed for the calculation in conformity with criterion (1), although, in fact, the exact date would make very little difference to the results because the azimuths of the sun and moon are unaffected by precession. These celestial bodies do not change by more than one degree over a period of 4,000 years, and the alignments recur with tolerable precision even today.

Stonehenge I obeys fairly well the principle of homogeneity. Alignments are made between stones or holes that were presumed to contain stones in most cases. A few of the holes, notably the "A" holes, are thought to have originally contained posts, but these are reasonable substitutes for stones. Stonehenge III uses homogeneous markers in that alignments are from one archway to another. The view of the heel stone through archway 30–1 is a minor exception to this. To make this solution homogeneous, one would have to include the view of all the stones of Stonehenge I through the archways of Stonehenge III, but a visit to the site encourages one to single out the heel stone from all the other stones because of the dramatic vista that it provides.

The astronomical targets are the extreme positions of the sun and moon on the horizon. All of these twelve points are considered in the analysis, and only two do not appear to be marked. There is some inhomogeneity in postulating both the sun and moon as targets, although of all the celestial bodies these two form a unique and complementary pair.

TABLE 4

ASTRONOMICAL ALIGNMENTS AT STONEHENGE DETERMINED FROM AN AIR SURVEY

Point j	Point i	Azimuth E. of N.	Object	Horizon	Error D
Heel	Center	51.222	Sun +23.906	0.60	+0.47
91	92	49.759	Sun +23.906	0.60	−0.44
Heel	30–1	51.601	Sun +23.906	0.60	+0.71
94	93	50.633	Sun +23.906	0.60	+0.10
23–24	59–60	307.267	Sun +23.906	0.37	+1.69
92	91	229.759	Sun −23.906	0.53	−0.40
93	94	230.633	Sun −23.906	0.53	−0.94
6–7	51–52	131.766	Sun −23.906	0.30	+0.79
15–16	55–56	230.193	Sun −23.906	0.53	−0.66
A1	Center	43.645	Moon +29.056	0.60	+0.98
93	92	320.193	Moon +29.056	0.37	−0.85
94	91	319.825	Moon +29.056	0.37	−0.66
21–22	57–88	316.560	Moon +29.056	0.37	+1.12
92	93	140.193	Moon −29.056	0.35	−1.41
9–10	53–54	142.011	Moon −29.056	0.35	−0.50
93	91	297.294	Moon +18.756	0.37	+1.38
8–9	53–54	122.746	Moon −18.756	0.33	+0.19

Thus, independently, the results of examination of Stonehenge I and Stonehenge III give strong indications of astronomical alignments. The fact that the astronomical pattern of azimuths is the same even though at first sight the two structures are so dissimilar gives further confirmation that there was some unity of purpose in all the work at this site. Hitherto the construction was regarded as separate units built by different invading cultures. The astronomical result indicates some continuity of purpose either by cultural mixing or by transference.

On the basis of this fairly sure result one is encouraged to look further. Near the Aubrey holes are holes F, G, and H. There are not true stone holes and may represent the disturbances caused by tree roots in the past. Atkinson (1960) was disposed to regard them as unnatural because of their placement close to the outer bank, although later he has expressed doubts (private communication). Certainly they have in the past been considered important enough to designate by letter, and there are no other depressions that have been found by excavation in the area. Viewed from 93, H marks the winter sunrise, and F marks the equinox sunrise. From the practical point of view it would be simple to mark spring and fall by bisecting the angle H-93-94. The midsummer sunset is marked by 94 as seen from G.

There is an additional set of large holes at the entrance, Fig. H, which presumably belong to either Stonehenge I or II. In conjunction with 94 these holes mark the equinoctial sun and moon. It is difficult to believe that these alignments could have been set up to mark the full moon, because the chance of the full phase occurring on the exact day of the equinox is small. However, if the moon was observed at the equinox regardless of its phase, then these lines could be significant. Whether or not these holes mark the equinoxes, they do fit into the well-established solstice pattern. Holes *B*, *C*, and *E* are close to the midsummer sun line, and *D* lines up with the midwinter moon as seen from the center. Approximately one-half of Stonehenge has been excavated to date, and there may be additional holes awaiting discovery. Everything found so far fits the astronomical theory, and it will be interesting to test any holes discovered in the future.

A reasonable case for astronomical alignments having been established, it is interesting to look for other possible corroboration. The circles of stones and filled-in holes yield numbers that are related to the movement of the moon and sun around the zodiac. I have suggested that these circles were used as a comput-

FIG. I. *Midsummer sunrise at Stonehenge (wide-angle photograph, 1964).*

ing device to determine the phase of the moon and to predict eclipses. The 30 sarsen archways give the greatest integer to the mean length of the synodic month, 29.53 days. Thus the phases of the moon could be followed by marking off one archway each day, even during cloudy spells and the short period of invisibility near the new moon. The 30 Y and 29 Z holes were an improvement in the counting device. Alternate months could use the short 29-day interval, giving a mean month of 29.5 days—a counting system that was known to exist in later eras elsewhere in the world. There is not space here in this statement of the computer hypothesis to discuss exactly how these rings might have been used, although several possible procedures and modes come to mind. It is sufficient to point out that the rings contain numerical information that corroborates the possible connection with the moon.

The numbers associated with the bluestone circle and the rings of Stonehenge II have not been definitely established by archaeologists at the present time. The current estimates for the stones in the bluestone circle are 59, 60, and 61. The first figure, of course, would give the best fit to the lunar month.

The nodes of the moon's orbit regress around the ecliptic with a period of 18.61 tropical years. This is the time interval required by the moon to return to the extreme azimuths at the winter and summer solstices. For example, the full moon that occurs within a period of 15 days on either side of the winter solstice rises over hole A1 as seen from the center of the monument in 1587 B.C. It does not return to that position until the year 1568 B.C. Sometimes this cycle is completed in 18 years, so that the overall average for the period maintains the value 18.61. This slow return of the moon to its extreme azimuthal position is a phenomenon that takes place in the other siting lines—along the rectangle of the station stones and in the archways of Stonehenge III. A search, in ascending order, for integers to describe this cycle (Hawkins, 1965a) shows that 56 is the best fit. This is the number in the circular array of Aubrey holes.

I have suggested that the Aubrey circle is a computing device for predicting the year in which the moon will reach its extreme azimuth. It could be operated by moving a group of 6, 3, or 1 stones around the circle—it is not pertinent here to discuss at length the exact mode that the Stonehengers might have chosen.* In Fig. J, I illustrate the single-zone method in which a marker is

---

* A variation of my original method has been suggested by Hoyle (1966) in which two stones are used for the nodes and one each for the sun and moon. All the various methods are essentially equivalent, predicting the swing of the moon and the day of an eclipse. The six-stone method (Hawkins, 1964) and the four-stone method (Hoyle, 1966) predict the day of an eclipse for all months of the year. The node-stone method of Fig. J will also perform for the other months of the year by subdividing the two semicircles between the solstice markers. However, in my opinion, the system at Stonehenge points to an interest primarily in eclipses at the solstices.

301

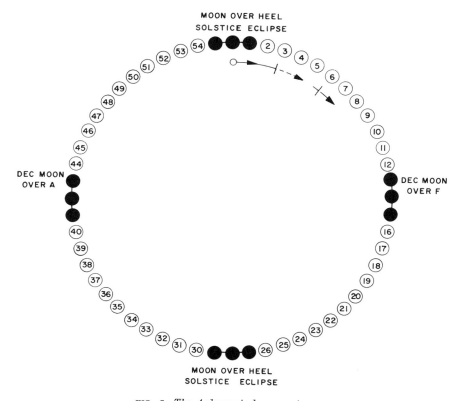

FIG. J. *The Aubrey circle computer.*

moved three holes each year. Nor is it pertinent to discuss the exact method which could have been used to mark the hole. It would doubtless have been a method permanent enough to last for a full year. It is sufficient to note that the circle contains numerical information concerning the period of regression of the nodes of the lunar orbit.

If one stands at Stonehenge at the time of an eclipse of the moon, it becomes obvious that eclipse predictions can also be made at Stonehenge. Apart from the effects of refraction and parallax the moon is seen exactly opposite to the sun at the time of an eclipse. Suppose that an eclipse is to take place during the evening of the winter solstice. As the sun sets in the great trilithon, the moon rises over the heel stone. If it rises exactly at sunset, it will, of course, rise in the earth's shadow and will move out of the shadow during the next hour or so. If the moon rises a few minutes before sunset, then the eclipse will take place during that night, and the time of occurrence can be estimated (Hawkins,

302

1965a). Similar eclipse conditions at different seasons of the year are governed by the other alignments.

As one might expect, the rising of the moon over the heel stone at any particular season is governed by the regression of the nodes and hence by the 56-year cycle. For example, for every rising of the winter moon over hole A1 as seen from the center there will be two moonrises over the heel stone. This condition takes place at periods that average 9, 9, and 10 years, successively. Thus, if we restrict ourselves to a certain calendar month, say the 15-day interval before and after the winter solstice, eclipses of the moon and/or sun can be predicted by the Aubrey hole computer. The method has been indicated for the single-stone mode in Fig. J.

Now although the azimuthal swing of the moon and eclipses are related phenomena, they can be considered separately. We can suggest that the Stonehengers were aware of one or the other, or both. But we cannot suggest that they were aware of neither without removing the only practical suggestion that has so far been put forward for the reason for and possible use of the 56 Aubrey holes.

By all standards, such astronomical knowledge and sophistication seem to be well in advance of the capabilities attributed to the various "barbaric" cultures of ancient Britain. To improve the credibility, one will find it helpful to break down the suggestions into the simplest possible terms. The azimuthal alignments could have been marked first by posts and then by stones. The accuracies are no better than one would expect from primitive methods. The azimuthal changes over several years could be transmitted orally and posts could be left *in situ* to help the memory. If one was willing to go on for one or two generations, but no more, then "56" would be the end result of the experiment.

It seems that the Stonehengers were grappling with some aspects of the no-

FIG. K. *The saros, lunar calendar, and the Stonehenge cycle.*

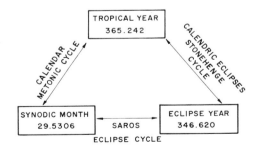

303

torious trio of numbers represented in Fig. K, the length of the lunar month M, the tropical year T, and the eclipse year E. Man has sought for ages for a commensurability between these incommensurable numbers. On the left-hand side is the problem of the lunar-solar calendar. Meton, about 432 B.C., was supposed to have offered the solution $19T = 235M$. The base of the triangle governs the repetition of eclipses during a certain number of eclipse years. In the eighteenth century Halley suggested the solution $223M = 19E$, and the solution became known as the saros cycle. It is a very good cycle for predicting eclipses, but there is no evidence to show that it was definitely known in antiquity. At least one out of every three eclipses in a particular saros cycle is not observable at a given location because of the rotation of the earth. Furthermore, it requires the counting off of 235 lunations, or 18 years 11 days. Thus it is doubtful whether the cycle would ever have been used in antiquity.

The Stonehenge cycle concerns itself with the third side of the triangle, and has more practical value than saros. I suggest that the Stonehengers had found the commensurable solution $56T = 59E$. This relation predicts eclipses of the sun and moon at the solstices every nine or ten years as shown in Fig. L. At least one-half of the lunar eclipses and one-third of the solar eclipses will be visible at Stonehenge either totally or partially. There is a danger period that extends a year before or a year after the critical year, and the likelihood of having a "dud" year with no eclipses taking place is quite small. From the practical point of view the cycle is locked in phase with the tropical year, and one simply has to follow a year count such as 9, 9, 10, or 19, 19, 18. Interestingly enough, the cycle of 19 years after which the winter full moon will reappear over A1 is also the Metonic cycle of the lunar-solar calendar.

If this knowledge existed in prehistory in Britain, has any of it been transferred into the written record? R. S. Newall (1959) has pointed out the reference in Diodorus to the Hyperborean temple which could possibly be Stonehenge. G. de Santillana has drawn my attention to the quotation from *Isis and Osiris* by Plutarch concerning Typhon, the demon of eclipses. Plutarch quotes Eudoxus as stating that Typhon is associated with the figure of 56 angles. There may be other similar references in the classics.

FIG. L. *Solstice eclipses from 1600 B.C. to 1480 B.C.*

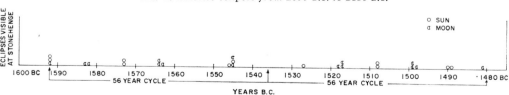

These statements can be regarded as secondhand evidence as to what was going on at Stonehenge. Elsewhere in antiquity the nodes of the lunar orbit were treated as a sort of celestial body. Typhon would indeed take up 56 equally spaced positions around the ecliptic during one Stonehenge cycle. Aaboe (1964), from a study of Babylonian tablets of the last three centuries B.C., has suggested that their arithmetic scheme was based on the notion of a division of the ecliptic into π equal parts that were to be taken in steps of Z at a time, so that π phenomena corresponded to Z complete revolutions in the ecliptic. Actually, as suggested by Aaboe, the π interval represents successive synodic phenomena, but the interval can also be based on the tropical year. For "Typhon" the geometrical basis of the Babylonian method would be the one shown in Fig. J. The Stonehenge computer in this mode is behaving almost as an analog computer. The marker is moving around the Aubrey circle so as to keep in step with the movement of the nodes of the moon's orbit around the ecliptic.

Neugebauer (1964) has shown that observations of the azimuth of the moon on the horizon were probably carried out in antiquity in a manner similar to the alignments at Stonehenge. He has shown that the "gates" described so clearly in the astronomical section of the Book of Enoch are fixed azimuths on either side of due east and due west, rather than the signs of the zodiac as hitherto supposed. The moon rises for several nights in the first gate, then moves to the second gate, and then retraces its path through the gates as the month progresses. Parts of the text of Enoch are dated around 200 B.C., but it is a composite of many authors and the astronomical chapters may perhaps carry a trace of information from prehistory.

OTHER SITES

I have shown (1965b) that the rows of stones at Callanish in the Outer Hebrides are aligned on the extreme declinations of the moon and sun. The number of alignments is fewer than at Stonehenge, there are no imposing archways with restricted vistas, there are no circles which can be used to compute the motion of the moon, and therefore the astronomical results are not as impressive as those at Stonehenge. The long avenue at Callanish does, however, point with remarkable accuracy to the azimuth of the moon at its lowest declination. At this period of the lunar cycle the full moon is so low that it skims the southern horizon. This may have been noticed by the ancient Scots and been the inspiration for the structure at Callanish. Thom (1965) has confirmed the lunar and solar alignments for that site. Thom has also computed sun and moon alignments for more than one hundred other stone circles and stone alignments in England, Scotland, and Wales. There thus seems to be an astronomical culture associated with most of the megalithic sites in Great Britain. To illustrate this culture it is sufficient to concentrate on the best-preserved structures and most reliable fixes. In Scotland a row of at least 18 stones marks the equinox sunrise at the "Eleven Shearers"; the axis at Loanhead marks the solstice sun; the line of seven stones at Dervaig points to an extreme of the solstice moon.

Thom has extended correlations to certain stars and also to the declination of the sun at 16 equally spaced intervals through the tropical year. These extensions may require some further justification, based perhaps on the criteria listed in this article, to establish their validity. For example, Thom uses the star alignments to date the structures to a precision of 10 years, he uses stars down to magnitude 1.8 which proliferates the targets, and he sometimes uses inhomogeneous markers.

J. Dow (1965) has investigated Teotihuacan near Mexico City for possible alignments with the Pleiades and/or the sun.

In connection with the implications of astro-archaeology for the history of science, it is interesting to note the suggestion of mathematical capabilities within nonliterate cultures. Thom (1955, 1961, 1962, and 1964) has demonstrated that the layout of the stone circles and other megalithic formations in the British Isles implies considerable knowledge involving the use of the equivalent of a straight edge and a compass, and, possibly, the numerical relations of the Pythagoras theorem. Roy, McGrail, and Carmichael (1963) have published an example of a stone ellipse on Machrie Moore, Arran. Alexander Marshack (1964) has produced evidence to show that an engraved mammoth tusk from the Upper Magdalenian culture probably represents a tally of three or four lunations. Cave paintings from Canchal de Mahoma and Abri de las Viñas in Spain can be interpreted as anthropomorphic signs surrounded by notations for the days of the synodic month.

Sir Norman Lockyer published a series of articles under the title "Notes on Stonehenge" that covered many megalithic sites from the Orkneys to Cornwall (1901, 1902, 1905, 1906). He suggested alignments to the sun and to particular stars. His calculation of the midsummer alignment at Stonehenge has been confirmed by the writer, and several other sites have been confirmed by Thom. Other sites in Great Britain mentioned in these articles by Lockyer might well repay further investigation.

It is generally agreed that Lockyer overstepped the hyphen in astro-archaeology, making comments that most regrettably outraged the archaeological experts. His article "Some Questions for Archaeologists" (1905) should never have been permitted into print by the editor of *Nature*, who at that time was Sir Norman himself. In *The Dawn of Astronomy* (1894) Lockyer devotes several hundred pages to a discussion of Egyptian chronology, mythology, religion, and calendric system, from the point of view of an astronomer. Such an extensive effort was premature, and he did not proceed at an appropriate scholastic pace by publishing step by step in the scientific journals and thus benefiting from the appraisal and criticism of other scholars. Despite the unfortunate context in which they are found, several of the suggestions in *The Dawn of Astronomy* seem to be valid when judged in terms of the criteria of this paper. The measurements of the great temple of Amon-Ra at Karnak are sufficiently accurate to establish that this mammoth temple is aligned to the midwinter sunrise. The temple of Isis at Denderah seems to be aligned to the rising of Sirius, and the alignment is confirmed by the inscriptions at the temple.

It would be of great interest to examine the Egyptian temples with regard to lunar alignments. The sun and stars do not vary greatly in azimuth from year to year and present a fairly simple observational challenge. The moon, on the other hand, as marked in the British Isles, presents a much more challenging problem.

REFERENCES

AABOE, A. (1964), "On Period Relations in Babylonian Astronomy, *Centaurus,* Vol. 10, pp. 213–31. Also: *Vistas in Astronomy,* ed. by A. Beer, Vol. 9 (Oxford: Pergamon Press, 1967).

ATKINSON, R. J. C. (1960), *Stonehenge* (London: Pelican Books).

BRITISH MUSEUM (1960), "British Museum Natural Radiocarbon Measurements II. BM-46. Stonehenge, Wiltshire," *American Journal of Science Radiocarbon Supplement,* Vol. 2, p. 27.

DOW, J., "Astronomical Orientation at Teotihuacan," Paper read at Society for American Archaeology, Urbana, Ill., May 8, 1965.

HAWKINS, G. S. (1963), "Stonehenge Decoded," *Nature,* Vol. 200, pp. 306–8.

———— (1964), "Stonehenge: A Neolithic Computer," *Nature,* Vol. 202, pp. 1258–61.

———— (1965a), "Sun, Moon, Men, and Stones," *American Scientist,* Vol. 53, pp. 391–408.

———— (1965b), "Callanish, a Scottish Stonehenge," *Science,* Vol. 147, pp. 127–30.

———— and ROSENTHAL, S. (1967), "5000-Year Star Catalog," *Smithsonian Contr. Astrophysics.*

HOYLE, F. (1966), "Stonehenge—An Eclipse Predictor," *Nature,* Vol. 211, pp. 454–56.

LOCKYER, J. N., and PENROSE, F. C. (1901), "An Attempt to Ascertain the Date of the Original Construction of Stonehenge from Its Orientation," *Proceedings of the Royal Society of London,* Vol. 69, pp. 137–47.

LOCKYER, J. N. (1901), "An Attempt to Ascertain the Date of the Original Construction of Stonehenge from Its Orientation," *Nature,* Vol. 65, pp. 55–57.

———— (1902), "The Farmers' Years," *Nature,* Vol. 65, pp. 248–49.

———— (1905), "Notes on Stonehenge," *Nature,* Vol. 71, pp. 297–300, 345–48, 367–68, 391–93, 535–38; Vol. 73, pp. 153–55.

———— (1906), "Some Questions for Archaeologists," *Nature,* Vol. 73, pp. 280–82.

———— (1906), "Notes on Some Cornish Circles," *Nature,* Vol. 73, pp. 366–68, 561–63.

———— (1965), *Dawn of Astronomy,* reprint (Cambridge: M.I.T. Press).

MARSHACK, A. (1964), "Lunar Notation on Upper Paleolithic Remains," *Science,* Vol. 146, pp. 743–45.

NEWALL, R. S. (1959), *Stonehenge, Official Guide-Book* (London: Her Majesty's Stationery Office).

NEUGEBAUER, O. (1964), "Notes on Ethiopic Astronomy," *Orientalia,* Vol. 33, pp. 49–71.

ROY, A. E., McGRAIL, N., and CARMICHAEL, R. (1963), "A New Survey of the Tormore Circles," Transactions of the *Glasgow Archaeological Society,* New Series, Vol. 15, Pt. 2, pp. 59–67.

SPENCE, M. (1893), *Standing Stones and Maeshowe of Stenness* (Carluke: T. Spence).

STUKELEY, W. (1740), *Stonehenge, a Temple Restored to the British Druids.*

THOM, A. (1955), "A Statistical Examination of the Megalithic Sites in Britain," *Journal of the Royal Statistics Society,* A, Vol. 118, Pt. 3, pp. 275–95.

———— (1961), "The Geometry of Megalithic Man," *Mathematics Gazette,* Vol. 45, pp. 83–92.

———— (1962), "The Megalithic Unit of Length," *Journal of the Royal Statistics Society,* A, Vol. 125, Pt. 2, pp. 243–51.

———— (1964), "The Larger Units of Length of Megalithic Man," *Journal of the Royal Statistics Society,* Vol. 127, Pt. 4, pp. 527–33.

———— (1965), "Megalithic Astronomy: Indications in Standing Stones," *Vistas in Astronomy,* ed. by A. Beer, Vol. 7 (Oxford: Pergamon Press). See also: Vol. 11 (1967).

BIBLIOGRAPHY

AUBREY, JOHN, manuscript on Stonehenge, reprinted by William Long in *Wiltshire Archaeological Magazine,* Vol. 16, 1876.

BARCLAY, EDGAR, Stonehenge and Its Earthworks, D. Nutt, 1895.

BARGUET, PAUL, *Le Temple d'Amon-Rê à Karnak,* Cairo, 1962.

BERNARDIN DE SAINT-PIERRE, J. H., *Paul and Virginia,* Harper and Row, 1968.

BESTON, HENRY, *The Outermost House,* Viking Press, 1964.

BREASTED, JAMES H., *The Conquest of Civilization,* Harper, 1938.

BREUIL H., and OBERMAIER, H., *La Pileta,* Monaco, 1915.

BUSHNELL, G. H. S., *Ancient Arts of the Americas,* Praeger, 1965.

CERAM, C. W., *Gods, Graves and Scholars,* Alfred A. Knopf, 1958.

———, *Hands on the Past,* Alfred A. Knopf, 1966.

CHARLETON, WALTER, *Chorea Gigantum,* reprinted by D. Browne, Jr., 1725.

CIEZA DE LEON, PEDRO DE, *Crónica del Perú,* 1554.

CLARK, GRAHAME, *Aspects of Prehistory,* Univ. California Press, 1970.

———, *Prehistoric England,* Batsford, 1962.

COMMONER, BARRY, *Science and Survival,* Viking Press, 1966.

COON, CARLETON, *The Story of Man,* Alfred A. Knopf, 1965.

DANIEL, GLYN, *The Idea of Prehistory,* Pelican, 1964.

EMERSON, RALPH WALDO, *English Traits,* Phillips Samson and Co., Boston, 1857.

GARCILASO DE LA VEGA, *Historia General del Perú,* Madrid, 1722.

GRAZIOSI, PAOLO, *Palaeolithic Art,* McGraw-Hill, 1960.

HAMMERTON, J. A., *Wonders of the Past,* Fleetwood House, London, 1925.

HARDY, THOMAS, *Selected Poems,* Macmillan, 1961.

HEMINGWAY, ERNEST, *Short Stories,* Charles Scribner's Sons, 1938.

HEYERDAHL, THOR, *The Kon Tiki Expedition,* Allen and Unwin, 1950.

———, *The Ra Expeditions,* Allen and Unwin, 1971.

HOYLE, FRED, *Of Men and Galaxies,* Univ. Washington Press, 1964.

ISKANDER, ZAKY, and BADAWY, ALEXANDER, *Brief History of Ancient Egypt,* Madkour Press, Cairo, 1965.

JONES, INIGO, *Stone-Heng,* reprinted by D. Browne, Jr., 1725.

LOCKYER, J. NORMAN, *The Dawn of Astronomy,* M.I.T. Press, 1964.

———, *Stonehenge and Other British Stone Monuments,* Macmillan, 1909.

MASON, J. ALDEN, *The Ancient Civilizations of Peru,* Pelican, 1964.

MARSHACK, ALEXANDER, *Science,* Vol. 146 (1964), p. 146.

———, *The Roots of Civilization,* McGraw-Hill, 1972.

Montesinos, Fernando, *Memorias Antiguas Historiales y Políticas del Perú,* Madrid, 1882.

Morley, S. G., *The Ancient Maya,* 3rd ed., Stanford, Ca., 1956.

Mystery of Stonehenge, C.B.S.-TV News, documentary film, McGraw-Hill film texts, 1965.

Osborne, Harold, *South American Mythology,* Paul Hamlyn, 1968.

Pizarro, Pedro, *Relation of the Discovery and Conquest of the Kingdoms of Peru,* Cortes Society, New York, 1921.

Poma de Ayala, F. Guaman, *Nueva Corónica y buen gobierno,* Inst. d'Ethnologie, Paris, Vol. 23, 1936.

Prescott, William H., *History of the Conquest of Peru,* 1847.

Reiche, Maria, *Secreto de la Pampa, Nazca, Perú,* Stuttgart-Vaihingen, Lutzweg 9, 1968.

Sawyer, Alan R., *Ancient Peruvian Ceramics,* Metropolitan Museum of Art, 1966.

Ščerbakiwskyj, V., *Eiszeit* (1926–27), p. 115.

Smith, John, *Choir Gaur,* Salisbury, 1771.

Stone, E. Herbert, *Stonehenge,* Robert Scott, London, 1924.

Stukeley, William, *Stonehenge,* Innys and Manby, at the West End of St. Paul's, London, 1740.

Thom, Alexander, *Megalithic Lunar Observatories,* Oxford Univ. Press, 1971.

————, *Megalithic Sites in Britain,* Oxford Univ. Press, 1967.

Thompson, Edward, *People of the Serpent,* Houghton Mifflin, 1932.

Velikovsky, Immanuel, *Worlds in Collision,* Macmillan, 1950.

Voltaire, *Zadig,* New American Library Inc., 1961.

von Kliest, Heinrich, "Michael Kohlhass," trans. by Charles Passage, *Nineteenth Century German Tales,* in *Great European Short Novels,* Harper & Row, 1968.

Webb, John, *Vindication of Stone-Heng Restored,* reprinted by D. Browne, Jr., 1725.

Wells, H. G., *A Short History of the World,* Pelican, 1945.

Wilder, Thornton, *Bridge of San Luis Rey,* Albert and Charles Boni, 1928.

Williams, Jay, *Uniad,* Charles Scribner's Sons, 1968.

INDEX

Page numbers in *italics* denote illustrations.

315

ILLUSTRATION CREDITS

319

73 74 75 76 77 10 9 8 7 6 5 4 3 2

DATE DUE
